The Life and Death of
Andy Ducat

The Life and Death of
Andy Ducat

Jonathan Northall
Foreword by Clare Taylor MBE

First published by Pitch Publishing, 2022

Pitch Publishing
9 Donnington Park,
85 Birdham Road,
Chichester,
West Sussex,
PO20 7AJ
www.pitchpublishing.co.uk
info@pitchpublishing.co.uk

© 2022, Jonathan Northall

Every effort has been made to trace the copyright.
Any oversight will be rectified in future editions at the
earliest opportunity by the publisher.

All rights reserved. No part of this book may be reproduced,
sold or utilised in any form or transmitted in any form or by
any means, electronic or mechanical, including photocopying,
recording or by any information storage and retrieval system,
without prior permission in writing from the Publisher.

A CIP catalogue record is available for this book
from the British Library.

ISBN 978 1 78531 853 5

Typesetting and origination by Pitch Publishing
Printed and bound in Great Britain by TJ Books, Padstow

Contents

Acknowledgements 9
Foreword 11
Introduction 13
  1. The Early Years 15
  2. Up the Arsenal and Down the Oval 22
  3. Finding His Feet 34
  4. On the International Stage 49
  5. Aches and Pains 65
  6. Sold and Broken 82
  7. For King and Country 101
  8. One Cup … 113
  9. … One Cap 130
10. Fulham Bound 151
11. Into Management 172
12. Time at the Crease 185
13. Season in the Sun 201
14. Stumps 220
Postscript: 'Nothing showy, insincere or envious …' 238
Bibliography 243
Timeline 247
Cricket Statistics 248
Index 250

Football positions

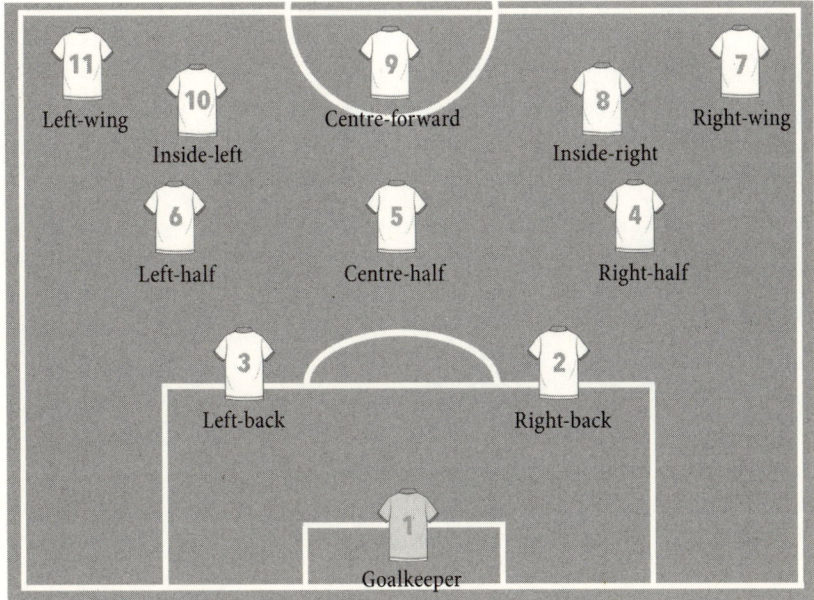

Cricket positions

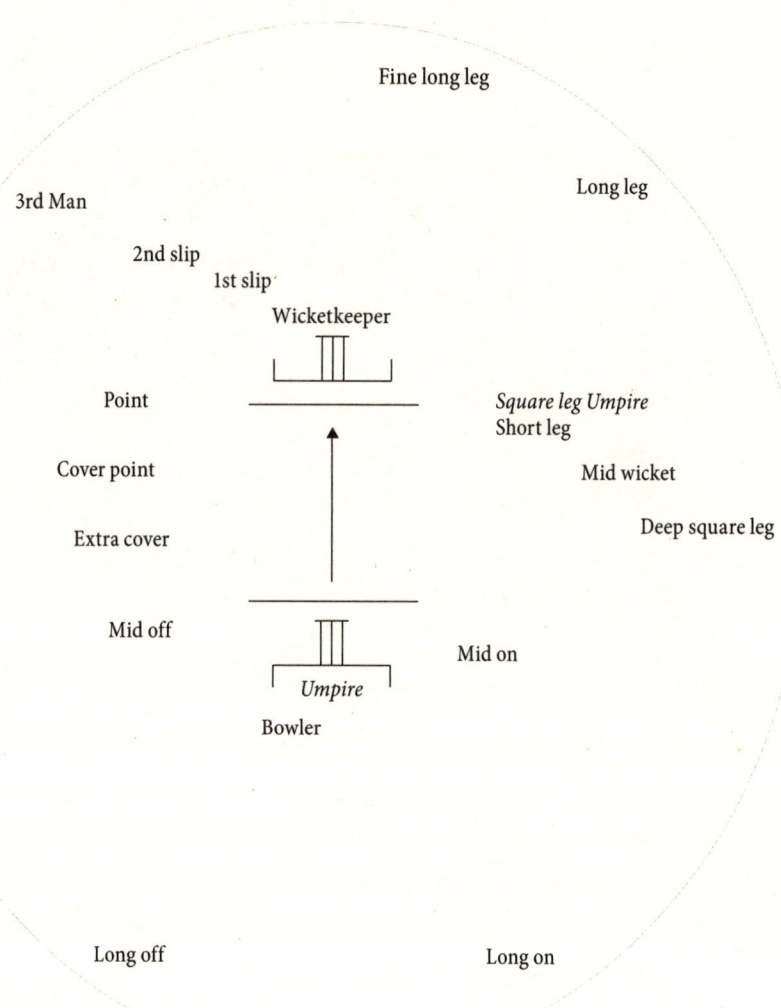

Acknowledgements

THERE ARE many people to thank for assisting in pulling together so much information about the different aspects of Andy's life. First, I would like to thank Peter Miles for his assistance with Andy's time in Southend. Peter has proved that there is at least one other person who thinks that Andy has been neglected by history.

For Andy's cricketing exploits, the following have been most helpful: John Broom, Grace Bottomley at Eton College, Stephen Chalke, Martin Chandler, Steven Lynch at *Wisden Cricketers' Almanack*, and Richard Whitehead.

For the footballing element, I would like to thank several people. For Woolwich Arsenal material, Andy Kelly was so helpful. Rob Bishop, Simon Inglis, and John Lerwill all helped with Aston Villa-related material. With my Fulham questions, club historian Alex White pointed me in the right direction, and Dave Wilson assisted. Clive Nicholson shared his knowledge of Fred Spiksley which was helpful and fascinating. Other footballing material was added by Paul Reed (Footballers' Battalion) and Sven Vantomme with his excellent research on the Front Wanderers.

Others I would like to thank include William Bynum for his expert medical advice, Linda Fox, a distant relative of Andy who provided family information, and Alan Finch for his assistance with obtaining Home Guard records.

Many thanks to the team at Pitch Publishing, including Graham Hales, Dean Rockett and Duncan Olner, for allowing Andy's story to be told in print.

Finally, a massive thank you to my family who, once again, have endured my obsession to unspeakable lengths at times.

Foreword

AS A member of the same 'elite club' as Andy Ducat, it is an immense honour to write the foreword to this book celebrating his life and achievements.

Much like Andy, I played most of my careers in an 'amateur' era. My letter to say I had been selected for the Women's Cricket World Cup in Australia, in 1988, asked for £729 airfare and £50 for a blazer!

On one of my first trips away with the England football team, to Russia, we had to take our own kit to train in as there was none available from the Women's Football Association.

Obviously, both organisations wanted commitment, and at times it was difficult to juggle both, and I attempted to finish one season before I started the next. The task became harder once out-of-season tours for both sports became commonplace, and I feel that is why now it just wouldn't be possible. I am so glad I had the opportunity to be able to play both sports at the highest level.

In the book, Andy comes across as a very unassuming, humble man whose achievements were recorded in a very different time to mine. He was a trailblazer in both sports, scoring 300 in a day for Surrey and playing in the 1920 FA Cup Final, the first to be settled using extra-time, although I'm not too happy about him captaining Villa to victory against my hometown team, Huddersfield Town!

I suppose the clearly defined seasons allowed him the opportunity to play at the highest level. However, it still required skill, ability, and a dedication to practise for which he must be admired.

I love the stories of getting married in the morning and playing for Surrey in the afternoon, albeit with a confetti welcome on to the pitch, and Villa donating to the hospital he was in when he broke his leg so he was treated on a private ward. And he was still in hospital six weeks later ... how times have changed! Even his transfer fee of £1,000 to Villa in 1912 brought a smile.

A tragic heart attack at the crease at Lord's denied many future players the wealth of his knowledge and experience, but Andy's is a heart-warming story which made me smile and laugh out loud. It deserves, and needs, to be told.

Clare Taylor, MBE

Introduction

HE WAS looking gaunt. Definitely not his usual self. However, he was as trim as the day he first stepped on to a cricket field as a professional back in 1906. The cricket whites were as crisp as ever too; though perhaps hanging a little on a 56-year-old frame. After more than 23,000 first-class runs and an England cap, the brain was still as keen, and sharp, even if the body was not as it once was.

After packing his bag for the day, he left the house at Great Enton and travelled towards London and a venue he knew well. He had played at Lord's on many occasions, usually in Surrey's colours, but today was a different kind of match. The annual game between his Home Guard battalion and their Sussex counterparts was being held, again, at the 'home of cricket'. It would be good to see fellow volunteers as well as NCOs outside of the more serious setting of defending king and country. Even the battalion commander was making an appearance.

The journey to Lord's had been eventful. A car accident no less. However, there was still a game to be played and everything would be OK once the pads were strapped on and a few hits out of the middle of the bat had been achieved. Last year's game had been unfortunate, but he was no stranger to getting out for a duck. It was part and parcel of the game. He told his pupils at Eton College that. He was no stranger to getting runs either. Those same charges had witnessed that recently too.

THE LIFE AND DEATH OF ANDY DUCAT

There was life in the old dog yet. Only the day before, the doctor performing a check-up for insurance purposes had stated that he was good for at least another 20 years …

CHAPTER ONE

The Early Years
1886–1905

BRIXTON WAS a vibrant place in the 1880s. Trains and trams had made Brixton accessible to central London and it was growing rapidly. The construction of Electric Avenue in 1888, named after the new form of lighting used to illuminate the ornate canopies enveloping the streets, epitomised the development of the area. Long before Eddy Grant sung about violence on the streets of Brixton, it was a place of prosperity rather than unemployment and racial tension.

Andy Ducat was born on 15 February 1886 at 4 Rattray Road, Brixton. Andy's parents, Andrew and Florence, were both over 30 and had been married for less than two years. Andrew was a Scotsman, born in Arbroath in 1853, but had moved to London where he met Florence. The pair married in Wandsworth in the summer of 1884 and set up home at Rattray Road.

Andrew was the third-born child of James and Louisa. Most of Andrew's siblings, of which there were nine, stayed in Scotland. Florence came from a smaller family with four siblings, all of whom stayed in the London area. Florence was closest to elder sister Gertrude, who would live with the Ducats for many years after Andy's birth. Not long after Andy was born, Florence's father James died. Two months later, her sister Eleanor died at the age of 43.

Although Brixton was vibrant, it was not immune from violence and the shadow of London's most famous serial killer, Jack the Ripper, was cast there for a short while. Edwin Colocitt was arrested in 1891 for several stabbings of women in Lambeth and Brixton. Although some newspapers speculated that Colocitt might be the famous murderer, The Macnaghten Memoranda, penned by leading investigator Sir Melville Macnaghten, ruled him out as a credible suspect. Colocitt lived in Ducie Street, less than a mile from where the Ducats were living when he was arrested.

Much of the housing catered for the middle classes, but a continuous influx of working-class people started to change the dynamic of Brixton. At some point after 1891, the Ducats decided that they were going to move to Southend. We know from the 1891 Census that they were in Brixton but had moved to Southend by the 1901 Census, although we cannot be exact as to when the move took place. What we do know is that Andrew started a building company in Southend and that Andy's schooling commenced at Brewery Road School in Southend.

The school was opened in 1892, therefore it was still relatively new when Andy joined, and is still around today. It is now called Porters Grange Primary School & Nursery, but many of the original buildings are still in use. According to the Southend-on-Sea School Board in 1901, Brewery Road 'maintains its reputation for very good order, with thoroughness and intelligence in the instruction'. The school was the first real outlet for Andy's sporting talents, and it was football where we first see him excelling.

In an interview with *Illustrated Police News* in 1913, Andy looked back fondly on his days at Brewery Road. 'As far as I can remember, football was my first love in the way of games, and I was about ten years of age when I became a full-fledged member of my school team at Brewery Road.'

By 1900, he was captaining Brewery Road's football team and he led them to the schools' championship. Needing to avoid defeat in their final game against rivals Technical School, Andy marshalled the defence to keep out the opposition and secured a draw to win the shield. The *Southend Standard and Essex Weekly Advertiser* reported that Andy's play 'was uniformly good'.

* * *

The Ducat family suffered an awful tragedy at Christmas time in 1900. Andrew's brother James was a lighthouse keeper for the Northern Lighthouse Board (NLB) and was posted at Eilean Mòr, one of the Flannan Isles off the coast of western Scotland. The isles are a desolate archipelago, 20 miles west of the Isle of Lewis and subject to harsh weather and heavy sea swells of the North Atlantic Ocean.

James Ducat, Thomas Marshall, and Donald McArthur were stationed at Eilean Mòr with another keeper rotating, so three men were always stationed to operate the lighthouse. On 15 December, a ship passed the lighthouse in poor conditions, but the light was not in operation. On reaching Leith, the port area of Edinburgh, three days later they reported the occurrence. A relief ship, the *Hesperus*, was unable to sail due to poor weather until 20 December.

Hesperus reached Eilean Mòr by Boxing Day and signalled to the island, but no one responded. The relief keeper went ashore and discovered that beds were unmade, clocks had stopped working (due to not being wound) and the fire was long burned out. He returned to the ship to get help and the island was searched thoroughly, but all three men had vanished.

An investigation was undertaken, and it was explained that two keepers had gone to secure a box containing ropes and a wild sea had swept them away. The third keeper had gone to try and help them, breaching NLB protocol by leaving the lighthouse unattended, and had also been swept out to sea.

The Flannan Isles mystery, as this tragic event has come to be known, has been told many times in popular culture. It featured most recently in a 2018 film, starring Hollywood actor Gerard Butler playing James, called *The Vanishing*. Much supposition as to what happened has been made over the years but it fails to capture the human cost of the three lost lives.

***

Andy's schooling was finished at Crompton House School which would later become Southend Grammar School. Crompton House was situated at Warrior Square in Southend and was styled as 'a high class school for the sons of gentlemen'. It was run by the Rev. George Henley Manbey M.A. Oxon. It would be the influence of Manbey, arguably, that impacted on Andy throughout the rest of his life, including his attitude to sport.

Manbey was a graduate from Oxford University, and had spent time as the vicar of St Alban's Church in Acton Green before moving to Southend. Manbey's family motto was 'Ne tentes aut perfice', meaning roughly 'All or nothing', 'do not attempt, or carry it out thoroughly', a concept we see time and time again in Andy's life. Manbey was also a huge believer in abstinence from alcohol and was president of the Southend Temperance League. One can imagine the headmaster epitomising Victorian values, almost scolding his charges about what they put into their bodies. We will see later how, as a professional sportsman, Andy was fastidious in his approach to diet.

Although Manbey had interests in chess and horticulture, he was clearly a fan of sport. Football featured prominently in his advertisements for the school. He was also a lover of cricket – how could a gentleman who had studied at Oxford not be? With Crompton House so positive about football and cricket, Andy had an outlet for his sporting prowess, and it would not take long for him to show how much talent he possessed. Fortunately, many of the scorecards from matches were published in the *Southend Standard and Essex Weekly Advertiser*.

In May 1901, Crompton House played Minima and Andy took five wickets in their first innings. He then followed up with 23 with the bat, not impressive until you see that the team were bowled out for 32, which was Bannerman-like[1] in its proportions. The following week, at Leigh Hall, Andy took another five wickets as the home team were dismissed for 32 in their second innings. Against Technical School, nine wickets in the match plus 28 runs in a team total of 64 secured a draw. Later in the season, Andy took another six wickets against Technical School.

In June, Rev. Manbey featured in a match against Leigh Hall and shared a small partnership with Andy as Crompton won: there was another six-wicket haul for Andy as well as top-scoring again. Against Lindisfarne, Andy batted and bowled superbly. In the first innings, Andy took nine wickets. He took two more in the second before Lindisfarne declared to leave Crompton House needing 73 to win in 35 minutes. Andy batted at No.3 and thrashed 35 not out to win the match.

The 1902 season for Crompton House started against a newly formed team from Westcliff, and Andy took eight wickets. The *Southend Standard and Essex Weekly Advertiser* commented that Andy had 'found his spot'. Against Technical School, he took another eight wickets for 16 runs. Later in the season, he took nine in an innings against the same opponents. Against Lindisfarne, he took another five-for as well as scoring 25 of the team's 51 runs. By the end of the season, Andy represented Prittlewell in the Southend and District League, despite being just 16. He top-scored with 23 and picked up two wickets to underline his ability. A week later, he represented the rest of the league against the champions, Benfleet, and made the second-highest score of the match.

In 1903, Andy's batting came to the fore. Representing Crompton House, he scored 96. A schoolmaster, Mr Whalley, had the next highest, as Crompton House posted 156. In response, Southend mustered just 32, with no batsman getting into double figures. Andy took three wickets while two of Manbey's sons, Bernard and Basil,

---

1 In the inaugural Australia–England Test match in 1877, Charles Bannerman scored 165 of Australia's first-innings 245. It remains the highest percentage of a team's total by one batsman in Test history.

were among the wickets. Andy hit a century for Crompton House, probably his first recorded one, against Hadleigh Wednesday.

It was not just cricket where Andy excelled for Crompton House. His football skills developed too. Having moved from being a fullback to a forward, Andy could not stop scoring. In 1901, he had a remarkable game. Against St Mark's, he scored a goal after ten minutes. The ball was returned to the centre spot for the game to restart. St Mark's kicked off, Andy gained possession of the ball and ran through the defence to score again. At the end of the match, he had six goals in an 11-1 thrashing. In the following season, Andy scored all six in a 6-2 win at St George's. The *Southend Standard and Essex Weekly Advertiser* commented that Andy had a 'magnificent game' and was 'easily the best forward on the field'.

* * *

His footballing exploits were not limited to school football, and he played for Westcliff Athletic. In the 1902/03 season, Andy won a runners-up medal with Westcliff in the Mara League, a junior competition.

Before long, Andy had moved to Southend Athletic where he was playing in a men's league rather than in junior football. He played in some friendly matches, getting goals as a forward, before being selected for the first team in the Southend and District League. Despite being just 17 in late 1903, Andy was excelling. He was scoring regularly for Southend Athletic and was getting noticed.

One of the misnomers about Andy's life is that he played for Southend United. Peter Miles has researched the early years of Southend United, and written books on the subject, and has provided clarity. Andy had already signed for Woolwich Arsenal, and played for them for a year, when Southend United were founded in 1906. However, there is a Ducat connection to the club because Andy's father was part of the group that decided to form a new football club at a meeting at the Blue Boar public house. Once Southend United had started playing, Andrew Ducat's building business constructed a 200-seat timber stand on the east side of their Roots Hall ground.

Just before Christmas 1904, Woolwich Arsenal manager Phil Kelso watched Andy play for Southend Athletic at South West Ham. At the end of the match, Kelso approached the Southend officials and notified them of his intention of speaking with Andy about signing for Woolwich Arsenal. Athletic were desperate to hold on to Andy, at least to see out the season, as he already had 12 goals in the South Essex League.

By the beginning of January, Andy had spoken with Kelso but had not signed for Woolwich Arsenal. However, that changed at the end of the FA Amateur Cup game at Cheshunt. The *Daily News (London)* confirmed that Andy had signed for Woolwich Arsenal as an amateur.

CHAPTER TWO

Up the Arsenal and Down the Oval
1905–1907

ANDY MADE his senior debut for Woolwich Arsenal on 11 February 1905, in a home match against Blackburn Rovers. Phil Kelso made the decision to replace Bill Gooing, the 30-year-old centre-forward, with Andy. Early in the match, Andy's nerves were on show when he bumped into a team-mate as he wandered back to the centre of the pitch. He gave a nervous smile before getting back into position.

During the match, Andy was more inclined to pass the ball rather than take a shot. In one particular passage of play he dribbled 'a dozen yards', according to the *Woolwich Gazette*, and played in Tom Fitchie rather than shoot.

With five minutes of the game remaining and a frustrating goalless draw looking likely, Andy was once again on the ball with an opportunity to shoot. Instead, he decided to pass to Tommy Briercliffe. The home crowd, who were constantly vocal in their criticism of their team, cried 'Oh Ducat' in frustration of another opportunity lost. However, Andy's pass was the right one, and Briercliffe joyously hit the back of the net. Another quick goal killed off Blackburn, and the match was won 2-0.

Andy's next outing was in a friendly against Corinthians, and he scored his first goal for Woolwich Arsenal. Once again, he was criticised for not being selfish enough in scoring positions. The following week it was back to league action, and despite an easy 3-0 victory over Sheffield United, a League goal was not forthcoming. Two days later, Andy did find the net twice in a friendly against Scottish club Queen's Park, although the opposition goalkeeper performed poorly.

Andy's first away game in the league was at Roker Park against Sunderland. Andy did not mark the occasion with a goal but was involved in an unsettling incident with Sunderland's centre-half, William Fullarton. In a clash to get the ball, Fullarton fell and landed awkwardly, breaking his collarbone. Not the kind of memory that a young footballer such as Andy would have wanted so early in his professional career.

In the games against Stoke and Derby County, the whole of the Woolwich Arsenal forward line, not just Andy, drew blanks. A friendly was arranged against Burnley because league opponents Everton were playing in the FA Cup semi-finals, and Andy found the net again. League goals were not forthcoming, but Phil Kelso still saw enough from his young centre-forward to persist in selecting him.

At the beginning of April 1905, Woolwich Arsenal faced Small Heath at Plumstead in a match where both teams had failed to score. With five minutes remaining, Andy picked up the ball and burst into the box. With just the goalkeeper Nat Robinson to beat, his shot was blocked, although John 'Sailor' Hunter was on hand to score. However, Billy Jones, who had the fantastic nickname of the 'Tipton Smasher' in honour of a boxer from the same town, equalised for Small Heath.

Andy's next opportunity was the rearranged game with Everton, but he failed to score again. He did clash with the opposition keeper, Welsh international Leigh Roose, as Arsenal lost 1-0. This would not be the last time that Andy and Roose would come together on a football pitch.

At Manchester City, Andy would be subjected to the physicality of 1 football. Andy was brought down by Sammy Frost. Undeterred by such tactics, Andy matched the intent. He could have won the match when put clean through but decided to shoot early rather than take on the goalkeeper. A late penalty by the great Billy Meredith meant the 500 travelling fans returned south defeated.

Another friendly, this time against his old club Southend Athletic, brought goals for Andy. He scored both in a comfortable 2-0 win. His first goal was outstanding, going in off the crossbar. The *Southend Standard and Essex Weekly Advertiser* were glowing in their match review; it noted how Andy had improved by being 'quicker in turning' and how accurate his passing had become.

After defeat against bottom-placed Notts County, he scored twice in a friendly against New Brompton, continuing the pattern of no league goals but plenty in friendlies. Andy's final chance to break his league goal drought came on the last day of the season against Everton.

Once again, Leigh Roose was standing in Andy's way, but this time the result was different. In the first half, Andy took Jim Bellamy's knee-high pass and placed it beyond Roose. Andy should have earned a penalty before scoring, but the referee, Mr Bye, did not award the foul. It was not the best of games for the referee, who made several poor decisions. Andy should have scored again in the second half but headed wide.

* * *

The 1905/06 season started inauspiciously for Andy, as he missed the first two games. The home match against Notts County in the middle of September saw Andy return to the team. He mustered a 'scorching shot' according to the *Athletic News* but could not hit the back of the net in a 1-1 draw.

In the next match, against Stoke, Andy picked up an injury that would see him ruled out of the Woolwich Arsenal line up for three-months. Stoke had signed Roose from Everton and he kept Andy and the Woolwich Arsenal frontline at bay. Andy appeared to strain himself in the game and left the pitch for a considerable amount of time before returning. A 2-1 win for table-topping Stoke continued their unbeaten start to the season.

Andy was out of action for about a month before reappearing for the reserves. A pair of braces against Chatham Athletic and Watford signalled that he was ready to compete for first-team action. It was also a continuation of his form from last season. Andy appeared to be too good for the lower levels of football, but top-flight action was still a step up.

It was two days before Christmas when Andy was recalled for an away game at Preston North End. Two days later, Woolwich Arsenal were in action again. A bumper Christmas Day crowd of 25,000 poured into a sunny Plumstead for the match against Newcastle United. Within two minutes of the start, the home team opened the scoring when the Newcastle goalkeeper failed to hold on to a shot.

Arsenal were buoyed by the fast start and attacked the Newcastle goal in search of more. Having scored again, they then conceded before Andy made his mark on the game. The ball came over from a corner, and Andy made no mistake to increase the lead to 3-1. Kelso was bellowing from the touchline as his team were in the ascendancy.

With Newcastle struggling, the home crowd were treated to what the *Woolwich Gazette* called 'the finest goal seen at Plumstead in a long time'. Andy received the ball about 30 yards out from goal and, despite pressure from Newcastle defenders, struck it magnificently for his second goal of the game.

Losses at Aston Villa and Liverpool dampened the excitement of the festive Newcastle victory. Andy missed an excellent opportunity on Merseyside and his place in the team was under pressure. A goal against Sheffield United in a one-sided 5-1 win helped matters before the distraction of an FA Cup fixture with West Ham United.

If Arsenal thought that a home cup tie with a non-league team would improve their fortunes, West Ham, of the Southern League, had other ideas. Goalkeeper George Kitchen, who also took penalties for the team and scored from the spot in this game, was in fabulous form. Making some great saves, including a stinging shot from Andy, he kept the score to 1-1 and earned his team a replay.

They succumbed in the replay at a muddy Upton Park, but not without a tremendous fight. West Ham took the lead within five minutes before Andy equalised. Woolwich Arsenal won the game 3-2 but it was not the springboard for recovery as expected.

Back in league action, their season got decidedly worse. A home defeat to Notts County, followed by Stoke's come-from-behind victory, saw the Plumstead team at the bottom of the league and looking favourites for relegation. Defeat on New Year's Day had seen them drop into the relegation zone, albeit briefly, but this looked terminal.

Not only were their problems on the pitch. The vitriol from the AGM had reappeared and rumours were circling about backroom unhappiness. So much so, that the players issued a formal denial of unrest on 1 February. An informal meeting took place about Woolwich Arsenal's current form and 'to refute that discontent and friction existed between the players, the trainer, and the manager Mr Kelso', said a letter reproduced in the *Woolwich Gazette*.

Andy spent the next two months out of the first team as Woolwich Arsenal put together an FA Cup run and strung some much-needed league victories together. Having reached the FA Cup semi-finals, it was Newcastle United who finally ended their progress.

On Andy's return to the first team, away at Manchester City, victory secured Arsenal's First Division status. Playing at inside-right, Andy had a poor game, but a 2-1 win was achieved. In the final home league game of the season, Andy scored against Bury in a 4-0 rout.

The season was not quite finished as the Southern Charity Cup was still to be completed. A 5-0 win in the semi-final against Tottenham Hotspur meant that victory in the final against Reading would give Andy his first professional honour. Although Andy could not get on the scoresheet as he had in the semi-final, a Percy Sands goal was enough to secure victory. The cup was presented by famous music-hall comedian George Robey, who had also acted as a linesman in the game. The *Woolwich Gazette* did not explain why.

***

News of Andy joining the groundstaff at Surrey County Cricket Club was first aired at the annual general meeting of Southend Tradesmen's Cricket Club in February 1906. He had played for the club and their chairman announced that they were losing his services to Surrey. Having been born in the county, Andy was fully eligible to play for Surrey. The chairman asked the rhetorical question as to why Essex, where Andy had spent most of his life, had not signed such a prospect.

As soon as the football season ended, Andy was at The Oval where he was soon on the pitch. He made several appearances for Surrey Club and Ground. Against Peckham and District, he starred with bat and ball: 46 runs and four wickets. Another four wickets against Battersea and 29 runs, and a catch, against Wanderers pushed Andy to the edge of selection of Surrey seconds in the Minor Counties Championship.

To further press his case, he pulled off a superb catch as a substitute fielder in Surrey's match against Oxford University on 22 June. Fielding for the Varsity team, Andy was at long-off when Ernie Hayes clubbed another ball down the ground as he had done for the last hour or so. Hayes was on 218 at the time and accelerating his innings. However, Andy pulled off a running catch to dismiss his prospective county team-mate.

With his stock rising, he was given his chance by Surrey in the seconds against Lancashire. With Lancashire bowled out for just 105 in their first innings, Andy batted at No.7 and produced the only half-century of the match before another Lancashire batting collapse gave Surrey an easy innings victory. Incidentally, a future fellow dual international appeared in the game; Harry Makepeace, who had won an FA Cup winners' medal with Everton earlier in the year, opened the batting for Lancashire.

In the next game, Surrey won again by an innings and this time it was Kent on the receiving end of a heavy loss. In a twist of fate, another future dual international was playing for the opposition. This time it was Wally Hardinge, then on the fringes at Newcastle United, and he top-scored in both innings for Kent.

Up next for Andy was a far sterner test. Surrey faced Staffordshire in back-to-back games and that meant one thing: facing S.F. Barnes. The mercurial bowler, who had four England caps, took wickets for fun, and did so against Surrey. In the first match at Stoke, Barnes took 6-47 and 6-63 in a comfortable win by six wickets. Andy contributed 14 and 24 in what would have been an excellent experience.

Just to prove that he was learning quickly, he scored 65 and 74 in the return fixture. Barnes was among the wickets in the first innings, with 7-71, but was less effective in the second. The match ended a draw, but Andy was the big winner with such fine performances.

As August rolled around, another excellent performance pushed Andy in line for a senior debut. Against Wiltshire, he scored an impressive 81 in a four-wicket win for Surrey. On 23 August, Andy's name appeared on the Surrey team sheet for the first time in the County Championship. Replacing the club captain, Lord Dalmeny, Andy batted at No.7 against Northamptonshire at the County Ground.

He had to wait until the second day of the match to bat and scored 18 before being run out. The match was a tight affair until Tom Rushby took 5-7 in 5.2 overs in Northamptonshire's second innings to help deliver an easy eight-wicket win for Surrey.

Although Andy did not feature in the last two County Championship games, he had broken through and made his debut. His name was on the same team sheet as Ernie Hayes, Tom Hayward, and a young Jack Hobbs. He could go back to Woolwich

Arsenal for the 1906/07 football season safe in the knowledge that his first cricket season at Surrey had been a successful one.

* * *

After joining up with Woolwich Arsenal, Andy's first task was to switch back into football mode. Although his fitness would have been no problem, his team-mates had been practising in pre-season so some games in the reserves were required.

During September, Andy and Woolwich Arsenal reserves were prolific. Against Leyton, Andy scored 'four or five' goals in a 7-0 thrashing. There were another seven against Norwich City with Andy bagging two.

While the reserves were in fine form, the first team also started their league campaign as if last season's dalliance with relegation had not happened. Four wins out of five saw Arsenal in second place. The form of the front five, Tim Coleman and Peter Kyle in particular, meant that Andy would have to be patient to get his chance. An injury to Percy Sands meant it looked like he would miss the Liverpool match and Andy would deputise at centre-half, but the captain recovered to lead his team to victory and to the top of the table.

Coleman's red-hot start to the season saw him selected for the English League versus Irish League match in Belfast, giving Andy the chance to replace him in the next match. Andy boarded the train at Paddington station with his team-mates for the following day's game at Bristol City with the knowledge that he was playing for the league leaders.

If he was overawed by the prospect, it did not show because he opened the scoring at Ashton Gate. A deft finish, with placement rather than power, set Woolwich Arsenal on the way to a 3-1 victory. Despite the performance, Andy found himself out of the team for the next match with the returning Coleman preferred.

Goals against Leyton and Oxford University made sure that Phil Kelso was reminded of his 21-year-old forward, but a bout of influenza would delay his chances of breaking back into the first team. On 1 December, Coleman was rested after being selected again for the English League, so Andy stepped back in. At home to Sunderland, Andy's touch was lacking and he struggled to control balls played in to him. Perhaps illness had dulled his footballing senses. Arsenal failed to score, and Sunderland became the first team to leave Plumstead with a win that season.

Unsurprisingly, Andy found himself out again and further opportunities became scarce. On Christmas Day, he was recalled for a friendly against Glasgow Celtic but he was as wasteful as his fellow forwards. More goals in reserve games against Sittingbourne and Cambridge University led to a recall in February, against Bristol City, to replace Coleman but he drew another blank in a 2-1 defeat.

Frustratingly, Andy would feature just once more in league action in the 1906/07 season: in a 1-0 home defeat to Sheffield United. Woolwich Arsenal finished seventh in the league and reached the FA Cup semi-finals for the second successive year, but Andy was mostly surplus to requirements.

As the season ended and Andy joined up with Surrey for the summer, there were rumours that he would not re-sign for Arsenal. The *Southend Standard and Essex Weekly Advertiser* suggested that he would concentrate on professional cricket. It is not hard to accept that this may well have been the thought process. The football season had not gone as well as he would have hoped. Opportunities were limited as well as having to cope with the physical strains of playing professional sport all year round. Whatever Andy had contemplated about his future at the football club, the *London Daily News* of 3 May confirmed that he would take his place for the Reds in 1907/08.

* * *

His cricket season started in earnest with a trial match; Surrey's first XI played against the 'Next Sixteen' of which Andy was one. Batting conditions were not ideal as the pitch was drying out after rain. A score of 4 before being clean bowled by 'Razor' Smith ensured Andy would not be making the first XI soon.

May started brightly for Andy with 91 for Surrey Club and Ground against Guy's Hospital. His first start for the second eleven was against Kent and he contributed 41 and 24 in a match that should have been a winning one. However, with ten runs to win and three wickets in hand, Surrey somehow found a way to lose by a solitary run.

Yorkshire were the next opponents, and the result was more emphatic. Robert Frank took the first five Surrey wickets, all with wicketkeeper Arthur Dolphin's assistance (three stumpings and two catches) which set the tone for an easy Yorkshire victory. It had not been a great start for Surrey seconds, who were about to begin their Minor Counties Championship campaign.

The tournament had been restructured on a geographical basis, and Surrey were placed in the Midlands division alongside Berkshire, Buckinghamshire, Wiltshire and Worcestershire seconds. There would be eight matches with the winner of each division meeting in the semi-finals.

At The Oval, Buckinghamshire were the first opponents, and rain affected the match. Surrey won via scoring more runs in the first innings, but it would not count as a full victory. In response to the visitors scoring 323, Surrey responded with 490 but Andy was run out for just 3. If Andy had found his football season frustrating, the cricket one was not being any kinder.

Things turned around in the next match. At Park Lane in Reigate, Surrey were playing Berkshire and bowled them out for 84. In reply, Surrey lost their first wicket with the score on 9, and Andy came in to bat. He stayed for 205 minutes and scored at a rate of more than a run a minute. Mainly supported by Amos Spring, who added a century to his 6-44, Andy registered his first double century with a marvellous 210. It passed Surrey's Minor Counties Championship record of 207, scored by Fred Holland two years previously and set up an innings-and-195-run victory.

Andy's reward was a recall to the first XI for Surrey's match against Oxford University. However, scores of 19 and 8 were not nearly good enough to break into the team where Hayes, Hayward and Hobbs were scoring with impunity. Having blown the opportunity, Andy would not make another appearance for the first XI in 1907.

Back in the Minor Counties Championship, the match against Worcestershire on 22 July was the first opportunity to score the runs he needed. Despite an easy victory by an innings and 221 runs, Andy was again found wanting. Surrey scored 241 in their first innings, but Andy contributed just 5. Overnight rain made day two's batting difficult. Bill Hitch's 11 wickets made sure that Andy would not bat again as Worcestershire were bowled out twice, for 53 and 108.

The day after the match, Andy turned out for his old club to gain some much-needed confidence. Southend Tradesmen were playing Wadham Lodge and Andy proved to be far too good with bat and ball. Wadham Lodge batted first, and Andy was soon among the wickets. When the final man fell, with the score on 87, he claimed his sixth wicket.

Strapping on his pads, Andy opened with George Molyneux, a fellow footballer who played for Southend United. Andy was finally out for 133 after scattering the ball to all parts of Southchurch Hall Park.

If Andy's innings had been recuperative, it was not immediately obvious. Scoring just 10 against Wiltshire at The Oval, in another one-sided victory, was not the improvement he required. However, Andy was among the runs against Berkshire. A Bank Holiday encounter at the County Ground in Reading saw Andy post scores of 50 and 40 as Berkshire were awarded the win on first innings. A heavy rainstorm made an afternoon run chase impossible, and the match ended early.

After that relative success, Andy's season ended badly with scores of 1, 1, 5, 0 and 9. Against Kent, slow left-armer George

Wingham took Andy's wicket for the third time that season. Buckinghamshire's fast bowler George Wilson bowled Andy twice in the match which Surrey won to qualify for the semi-finals of the Minor Counties Championship.

The venue for the semi-final was Cardiff Arms Park where Surrey's opponents were unbeaten Glamorgan. Harry Creber and Jack Nash led their bowling attack, and dominated the match. Surrey lost by four wickets to end their season. Andy's 0 and 9 were symptomatic of a batsman who was out of touch and struggling.

It was not quite the end of the cricket season as he featured in a charity match on 12 September. Andy played for a team of League Footballers against the Gentlemen and Players of Essex in aid of the West Ham Hospital which was funding an extension. Andy opened the batting for the footballers and the team score was on 42 when the Essex team brought on a pace bowler called Young, who ran through the line-up. Andy was one of his eight wickets for the miserly total of 15 as the footballers lost ten wickets for 40. Losing his wicket again to pace, bowled, was surely part and parcel of being out of touch and not a technical flaw. Surely?

CHAPTER THREE

Finding His Feet
1907–1909

THE 1907/08 football season would be when everything changed for Andy Ducat, but he would not have thought that when he joined up with Woolwich Arsenal's reserve team. A goal against Spurs reserves was a solid start before a poor outing in the Southern Charity Cup against Reading. Arsenal used three first-team players in a match which was lacking in quality. Andy played centre-forward and was inept; hardly getting a shot all match in a 1-0 home defeat.

A simple positional change was all that was needed for Andy. The move to half-back, predominantly right-half, saw his fortunes begin to turn around. With the benefit of hindsight, it is obvious that Andy's skill set lent itself to the change. In modern footballing terms, half-backs were midfielders who linked up play between defence and attack. Andy's obvious fitness, due to being an all-year-round professional sportsman, would have given him 'a good engine', i.e., being able to run long distances during the game.

Against Croydon Common, livewire centre-forward Ernie Colpus gave Andy and his colleagues plenty of trouble in his new position. However, a 'remarkably good game' against Crystal Palace, according to the *Kentish Independent*, highlighted Andy's promise in the new position. Also, scoring a goal in the 8-1 thrashing was morale-boosting.

More assured performances against Brentford and Fulham reserves in October 1907, along with another goal, this time from the penalty spot, brought Andy back into contention for the first team. In the following month, the opportunity came when he replaced John Dick at right-half against Nottingham Forest. *The Observer* noted that Andy had a 'strong game', and he made the critical pass to set Tim Coleman up for the second goal in a 3-1 win.

Despite impressing on his return to the first team, he was dropped the following week when John Dick was available. The *Woolwich Gazette*'s football writer was critical of the move and continued to criticise Phil Kelso and his 'foolish policy'. Kelso had recently announced that he would be leaving Woolwich Arsenal at the end of the season to run a hotel in Largs, 33 miles west of Glasgow. The constant pressure and criticism had clearly affected the manager. It was not only the local newspaper calling for Andy's inclusion, but the fans too. In the *Woolwich Gazette*, prior to Andy's recall, it was the 'public ... asking for the inclusion of Ducat'.

On 21 December, Andy was recalled to the first team at the expense of Dick for the match against Everton. His defensive capabilities were tested against Jimmy Settle. The Everton forward had been the league's top-scorer in the 1902/03 season and was an England international with six goals in six appearances. Andy put in a solid performance in a 1-1 draw.

In a 12-day spell over the Christmas and New Year period, Andy played six matches, an astonishing number in such a short time. Draws on Christmas Day (Newcastle United) and Boxing Day (Liverpool) were followed up with a thumping 4-0 win against Sunderland. It was the New Year's Eve match at Owlerton Stadium, which was renamed Hillsborough in 1914, where the fixture congestion started to tell. The ground was covered in snow and in the freezing cold The Wednesday were ruthless in a 6-0 rout. The following day, Arsenal were at Roker Park, where Sunderland exacted swift revenge with a 5-2 win.

If Woolwich Arsenal's form was poor, it was not because of Andy. While his team was losing their FA Cup first-round tie to Hull City after a replay, Andy was selected for the North versus South trial match to represent England in the forthcoming Home Internationals against Ireland, Scotland, and Wales.

The match took place two days after Arsenal's dour draw against Preston North End; *The Guardian* commented that Andy was the only Arsenal player who 'played first class football' against Preston. The trial took place at Manchester City's Hyde Road where a muddy pitch and windy conditions made it difficult to play. In a 4-4 draw, *The Times* thought Andy was a 'fully justified' selection. The *Woolwich Gazette* were soon to call for his selection to the England team against Ireland. It had been a phenomenal turnaround from a reserve-team player to being on the verge of an England cap.

When the team was announced for the match in Belfast, Andy was not named in the starting line-up. Ben Warren of Derby County was selected in the right-half position. It was not totally bad news because Andy would travel as a reserve. While on the journey to and from Ireland, he had plenty of time to come to terms with the departure of Phil Kelso as manager. Although it was supposed to happen at the end of the season, Kelso left after a home defeat to Aston Villa and was replaced by George Morrell. Like Kelso, Morrell was Scottish and had managed Greenock Morton before heading south to take the reins at Plumstead.

While Andy had been on international duty, Morrell's first game in charge was against Liverpool but defeat saw Woolwich Arsenal drop down to 18th in the First Division. On returning to the team against Middlesbrough, Andy's tussle with the 'prince of dribblers' Freddie Wilcox helped the home team to a timely 4-1 win. The next match, against Sheffield United, saw an old cricket adversary Wally Hardinge up front, with honours ending even.

Despite some indifferent team performances, and results, the visit of runaway leaders Manchester United saw Arsenal get their best win of the season. With seven minutes remaining, the home team benefited from defensive misfortune to steal the win 1-0. Andy put in another fantastic performance with the *London Daily News* declaring that he was 'the most brainy half on the field'.

With Arsenal needing cash, an offer for Peter Kyle proved too tempting and the forward was sold to Aston Villa. Several clubs had been after Kyle. As a result, Andy made a rare appearance at centre-forward at Blackburn Rovers, and netted the equaliser. He reverted to his usual position at right-half for his last two matches of the season. His final game was against Everton where he conceded a penalty with an accidental handball, before laying on the pass for Charlie Lewis to win the game in the last minute. The result ensured that Woolwich Arsenal would remain in the top flight.

The FA wanted Andy to go on an end of season tour to Austria-Hungary, but he was contracted to Surrey so could not travel for England's matches against Austria in Vienna, Hungary (in Budapest) and Bohemia (in Prague). International representation would have to wait, at least until next season.

* * *

Surrey's pre-season trial match had a kind of *Britain's Got Talent* vibe about it with batsmen getting 15 minutes at the crease to impress. If you were out then you were out, then those on the periphery had their chance. Andy's audition saw him last his allotted time before having to retire with 9 to his name.

Having not done enough to press a claim for first-team action, Andy started the 1908 season playing for Surrey Club and Ground. Ten runs, two wickets and a catch against Mitcham were a reasonable return, but Andy's batting caught fire and there may well have been a feeling of déjà vu from his football season.

On 21 May, Andy struck a fine century against Barnes at The Oval. Joining the fantastically named the Honourable Seton Robert de la Poer Horsley-Beresford at the crease, Andy and Horsley-Beresford helped Surrey Club and Ground to a total of more than 500. Beresford scored 152 while Andy was bowled for 105. Five days later, it was Andy who scored a 'Daddy ton' by plundering The Wanderers' bowlers for an unbeaten 179.

Unsurprisingly, the Surrey committee were impressed with Andy's form and selected him for the seconds against Yorkshire seconds. Surrey batted first and their openers, Philip Slater and Albert Baker, got the innings off to a magnificent start with a partnership of 209. Baker, who had represented Surrey in the County Championship since the start of the century, managed to kill a sparrow with a shot on the leg side which the *Yorkshire Evening Post* seemed only too happy to report on.

Andy came in after the first wicket fell and contributed 17 before being caught and bowled. The innings would have been quite forgettable had he not scored nine runs from a single ball. An all-run five was turned into nine with an inaccurate throw going to the boundary for four overthrows. The bowler was Major Booth, who would die in the arms of fellow cricketer Abe Waddington on the first day of the Battle of the Somme in 1916.

When Yorkshire batted, Andy had a particularly good day with the ball and claimed four wickets. Three of those mopped up the Yorkshire tail to give Surrey a 96-run lead. Also, two catches did his cause no harm at all. In the second innings, he scored a quick 63 as Surrey tried to force a win. Yorkshire easily held on for the draw, but Andy benefited most of all. He was given the news that Jack Hobbs was being rested for the next County Championship match, against Somerset at The Oval, and he was selected.

Winning the toss, Surrey batted first and got off to an indifferent start with Marshal losing his wicket for 9. Tom Hayward was next to fall, but not before completing 22,000 runs in County Championship matches when he reached 21, which brought Andy to the wicket. Immediately, he increased the pace of scoring and was particularly effective on the on side. Having scored 26, he was bowled by the former Surrey leg-break bowler Len Braund. Jack Crawford then took control for Surrey with a 'memorable innings' according to *The Guardian*. His 226 was his highest score in first-class cricket and drove Surrey to 507.

Somerset's reply was so inept that they were bowled out twice in less than a day to give Surrey the win and a day off. Crawford, to emphasise his man-of-the-match status, took four wickets in each innings while 'Razor' Smith helped himself to a ten-wicket match haul.

The return of Hobbs saw Andy miss the next three matches before being recalled to face Cambridge University in a much-changed line-up. In the unfamiliar position of opener, he scored 47 and 6 against a spirited team who reduced Surrey to 110/6 in their run chase but eventually lost by four wickets. Andy also played in the match against Oxford University, who were also brave after being forced to follow on, before he was given another chance in the County Championship.

Despite getting his highest Championship score of 29 in the second innings against Warwickshire, it was clear that it was not enough runs to stay in the team. With the likes of Hobbs, Hayward, Crawford, and the destructive abilities of Marshal, Andy's inconsistency was not enough to earn a regular place.

Before Surrey could drop Andy, an infected mosquito bite created an enforced absence. The bite was on Andy's left wrist and required, what the *Athletic News* called, a 'lancing operation' as well as some time for the wound to heal.

By the end of July, Andy was fit enough to return and was brought back in the match against the touring Gentlemen of Philadelphia. It was the third such tour undertaken by the Philadelphians, and they were led by John Lester while ably supported by John Barton King and Herbert 'Ranji' Hordern. King was a fine fast bowler and Hordern possessed a devilish googly in his bowling armoury.

Despite a strong start by Surrey, the Gentlemen fought back well; from 148/3, Surrey were bowled out for 210 in their first innings with King taking 6-47. Andy was one of King's victims, after scoring 16, as the American continued his fine bowling form on the tour. In the second innings, Andy batted much better, despite being troubled early on by King. Andy was 'deceived ... with six consecutive balls' from King, according to *The Times*, but contributed 41 before falling to Hordern. Marshal's quickfire hundred allowed Surrey to set a competitive total before they bowled out the Gentlemen in less than 40 overs.

Andy missed the next County Championship match, against Nottinghamshire, but was back in the team against Middlesex which began on the following day. Brought in for Jack Crawford, Andy took his opportunity to consolidate his place with a quality innings of 76. While Marshal was playing a Kevin Pietersen-like innings, described as 'club style' by *The Guardian*, Andy was scoring briskly with well-timed drives and cuts. It was all the more impressive when considering the Middlesex attack included Frank Tarrant, Albert Trott, and Jack Hearne. An innings victory for Surrey was all the sweeter for Andy.

Having locked in a place for the rest of his season, until he was required to pull on his football boots, Andy generally performed well. Scores of 34 against Sussex, the runs made predominantly on the leg side, as well as 26 in a low-scoring innings against Yorkshire justified Surrey's trust in their young batsman. Against Kent, Andy produced his highest score to date with 77 not out in another Marshal-inspired innings victory. His last two games, against Essex and Gloucestershire, were not overly successful but Andy was in a far better situation than at the start of the summer.

* * *

A combination of poor results and an injury meant that Andy's football season started badly. Woolwich Arsenal's opening match, at home to Everton, was a disaster, as they were soundly beaten 4-0. Another defeat, against Notts County, who had narrowly avoided relegation the previous season, left Arsenal at the bottom of the table.

A win at Everton, giving swift revenge over the opening-day defeat, brought some comfort before Andy was injured against Newcastle United. In the first half of the match, which Arsenal would go on to lose, Andy sprained his ankle and immediately left the field which left his team a man short. The away team fully capitalised.

As well as missing league matches, Andy was left out of the English League team to play in Belfast against their Irish counterparts. It gave others the opportunity to stake a claim for a position at right-half for the Home Internationals in early 1909. It could not have come at a worse time for Andy, who would have been in line for an international place.

Andy returned after a month on the sidelines to help his team come from 2-0 down at Anfield to secure a well-earned draw with Liverpool. Playing for the home side were Sam Hardy and Jimmy Harrop, who would later become colleagues at Aston Villa. A 4-0 win against Bury and a draw at Sheffield United, again featuring Hardinge, left Arsenal ninth in the table.

November saw Andy get into goalscoring positions, but not get on the scoresheet. At home to Aston Villa, a header from a corner was goalbound but was cleared off the line. It was a costly chance with Villa scoring, on the break, five minutes from time when Joe Bache netted the winner. In another home game against Sunderland, it was old adversary Leigh Roose who denied Andy. This was less costly, as Arsenal were thrashed 4-0.

It was not only bad luck in front of goal that made life difficult but playing conditions too. Bad light could be an issue but poor weather may have helped Arsenal get a last-minute winning goal at Chelsea. The following week Blackburn Rovers were helped at Plumstead by muddy, foggy conditions. With winter around the corner, pitches were cutting up which could make conditions difficult.

On Christmas Day and Boxing Day, Arsenal played Leicester Fosse away and at home. It does make one wonder if the fixtures secretary could have been more imaginative than having teams play each other twice on consecutive days. Woolwich Arsenal took three points out of four, with a 1-1 draw on Christmas Day before winning the return 2-1. In the home game, Andy gave away a penalty for handball, which Pollock scored for Leicester.

Andy missed the next game against Sheffield Wednesday. The result, a 6-2 loss, was disputed due to the terrible condition of the pitch. Arsenal protested to the League Management Committee that the ground, which was frostbound, was not playable and the result should be annulled.

Another defeat at Newcastle, who would be crowned champions, meant that the upcoming FA Cup first-round match against Croydon Common would be a welcome relief from the difficult league campaign. The non-leaguers had been drawn at home but were amenable to moving the game. There were rumours that Woolwich Arsenal would have paid to host the fixture, according to the *CroydonCommon.com* website, but the Crystal Palace was decided as the venue.

Croydon Common, who played in the Southern League Division One, had already played eight matches to get to the first round proper. John Lewis, who had won one cap for Wales, and Ernie Colpus had scored 23 times in qualifying for the Robins. They dominated from the start of the match and took a surprise lead around the 30-minute mark, but Arsenal equalised almost immediately. Throughout the match, Croydon Common had the better of the play but needed their goalkeeper Bob Evans, another Welsh international, to 'make some excellent saves from Fitchie' as reported by *The Referee*. It's an interesting comment as Evans had been suffering from flu prior to the game and, according to *CroydonCommon.com*, was given an injection of strychnine at half-time to get him through the second half. The alkaloid now used as a pesticide, which can be lethal to humans in doses as low as 5mg, was believed to be a performance enhancer in Victorian and early Edwardian times.

After holding their league opponents to a 1-1 draw, Croydon Common were beaten in the replay with Andy scoring in a 2-0 win. It would have been scant reward for Andy, who had been named reserve for the North versus South match and missed a chance for an international call-up.

Arsenal drew Millwall, another Southern League team, in the second round but were beaten in a replay to end their FA Cup campaign. The London Association Challenge Cup remained as the last chance for silverware but defeat in the twice-postponed semi-final by Leyton ended that possibility.

In the First Division, things were taking a turn for the better with a draw at Hyde Road against Manchester City. The home team started well and were already a goal up when they were awarded a penalty. Diminutive wing-half Tom Holford missed, and that moment appeared to change the course of the match. First, Andy scored the equaliser before Charles Lewis gave Arsenal a 2-1 lead. Before they could celebrate a vital away win, however, City were awarded a penalty near the end. Holford, who had earlier missed a second penalty, was again given the responsibility, and this time he scored to earn a point.

In the next match, Charlie Lewis managed to miss a penalty for Arsenal after scoring in open play, but Woolwich were already 3-0 up against Liverpool. Bert Beney, who had made his debut against Manchester City, delighted the Plumstead crowd with a hat-trick before Charlie Satterthwaite scored from the spot to make it 5-0.

March 1909 was a lean month for Arsenal. Without a win, they slipped to 16th in the table and were dragged towards the relegation zone. Leicester Fosse were bottom and certainties to be relegated. Defeat at home to Nottingham Forest had left Bury, in 19th place, just two points behind Arsenal. Another loss, this time to Sunderland, meant that the last month of the season was going to be critical.

It started well with a 1-0 win at home to Sheffield United. In some ways, Arsenal would have felt aggrieved because the match had been replayed after a waterlogged pitch led to an abandonment with Arsenal leading 3-0. However, it was two vital points towards safety.

Two days later, a well-earned point at Chelsea further improved matters. Victories over Blackburn Rovers, The Wednesday and Bradford City lifted the Plumstead team towards safety. Andy provided an assist in the Wednesday match.

The final game of the season was against the newly crowned FA Cup winners, Manchester United, who had won the trophy for the first time in their history. Three second-half goals gave Arsenal a 4-1 victory and propelled them to a sixth-place finish. The final table was testament to the closeness of the league with just six points separating sixth place and 19th, with Manchester City being relegated on goal average.

* * *

Just six days after the United match at Bank Street, Andy was putting on his cricket whites for the first County Championship game of the season. Surrey entertained Northamptonshire at The Oval and Andy's 76-run partnership with Jack Crawford in the second innings helped set up a 106-run win. Crawford also starred with the ball, taking 5-39, as Northamptonshire were bowled out for 94. Andy took two catches in the innings as tight bowling and fielding gave the home team a winning start.

Hampshire were the next visitors and were handsomely beaten by an innings and 468 runs. Surrey's first innings 742, remarkably in just 138.3 overs, was far too many with Ernie Hayes (276) and Jack Hobbs (205) in dominant form; their second-wicket partnership of 371 is still a Surrey record. Andy added 49 before getting out trying to score quickly. Hampshire were bowled out for 129 and 145, with C.B. Fry being the only batsman to look comfortable against the Surrey attack. Fry was already a dual international at this point. Andy took two good catches in the second innings: dismissing Fry at mid-off before pulling off a fantastic catch at fourth slip to remove the captain, Edward Sprot.

FINDING HIS FEET

The rest of May 1909 was frustrating for Andy. After a duck against Warwickshire, he missed two County Championship matches as well as a game against the touring Australians. Scores of 9, 7, 1, 0 and 31 were an underwhelming return. The innings at Trent Bridge was more encouraging despite a heavy defeat for Surrey. Eighteen of the 20 Surrey batsmen were caught as Nottinghamshire secured an innings victory.

Surrey's selection committee were prepared to persist with Andy, and that confidence paid off against Worcestershire at The Oval. In the first innings, he top-scored with 27 as Surrey were bowled out for just 113. However, Worcestershire were soon in trouble and were fielding again before the end of the first day after being bowled out for 52. With the second day lost to rain, day three began with a soft wicket and in dull, overcast weather. Just 500 spectators turned up for the Saturday morning session with a draw looking likely. Surrey batted well in difficult conditions, and Andy's partnership of 46 with debutant Henry Harrison left Surrey with a good lead and Jack Crawford declared to try and force the win inside four hours. They did so easily, as Worcestershire capitulated for 82.

Andy's good form continued against Essex at Leyton, where his 51 not out in an unbeaten 122-run partnership with Ernie Hayes carried Surrey to an eight-wicket victory. Surrey moved on down to Bournemouth to play Hampshire, and Andy was among the runs again. Batting with Jack Hobbs, the pair put on 159 in less than two hours. Hobbs went on to make his fifth century of the season while Andy was out for 88. The first century of his first-class career may have been missed, but Surrey won easily. *The Guardian* reported that Andy had been 'somewhat handicapped until recently by a knee injury sustained in the last match of the football season'.

In the next game, against Northamptonshire, Andy was dismissed twice by paceman George Thompson, who had just been given his first England cap in the first Test against Australia. Andy suffered a similar fate against Lancashire. Express bowler Walter Brearley, who was playing himself into contention for the third Test, picked up Andy's wicket twice at The Oval. Lancashire won by an innings and 35 as a result of Jack Sharp's century. The Everton player would become England's next dual international when called up for the third Test alongside his county colleague, Brearley.

Lancashire would hand Surrey another heavy defeat just two weeks later, this time at Old Trafford, by an innings and 185 runs. Surrey were bowled out for 56 and 96 as their batsmen struggled. Combined with an earlier loss at Sheffield against Yorkshire, bowled out for 62 and 103, Surrey's normally free-scoring run-getters were under pressure.

Next up were the touring Australians, already beaten in a tour match by Surrey in May, back at The Oval and Andy was given the chance to test himself. The Ashes series was tied at 1-1, but Australia fielded a strong side, including captain Monty Noble, Warwick Armstrong, Victor Trumper, and Syd Gregory.

Having won the toss, Noble decided to bat, despite overnight and morning rain. He was soon ruing the decision as the touring team slumped to 29/4. Razor Smith and Ernest Kirk were bowling well, backed up by some excellent fielding. When the fifth wicket fell with the score on 48, Noble joined Trumper at the crease. The captain facilitated the rebuild, including a last-wicket partnership of 43 with Frank Laver, to get the total to 180.

With less than two hours of the day left, Surrey started their response purposefully. They were 87/2 when Andy came out to bat. Armstrong had one wicket already when he trapped Morice Bird lbw. With little time left in the day, Andy misjudged the pace of a delivery in the same over, and was clean bowled. With no play on the second day, the game fizzled out into a draw, with Razor Smith getting the plaudits with 12 wickets. Andy had been found wanting in an important match.

Innings of 28 and 40 against Middlesex at Lord's helped his cause. In the second innings, he batted particularly well with William Davis as the pair put on 74 in 75 minutes to push Surrey towards a sizeable lead. Frank Tarrant's hat-trick, of which Andy was the first victim, pegged Surrey back somewhat, but Middlesex fell 74 runs short in their run chase. Only Warner's hundred, carrying his bat, resisted Ernie Hayes's 7-34.

Monday, 26 July 1909 would go down as a day to remember for Andy, but it wouldn't have been obvious at the start of play. Hayes won the toss and decided to bat against Somerset despite a rain-affected pitch. The captain was making light work of the bowling, but Edward Goatly and William Davis fell cheaply to bring Andy to the crease with the score on 72. When Hayes fell, Henry Harrison followed soon after, but Andy kept on batting. A 52-run partnership with Amos Spring helped Surrey along before Ernie Robson and Talbot Lewis threatened to run through the tail.

Andy had reached his half-century, and with it the milestone of 1,000 County Championship runs, but with two tail-enders left it was looking like another century opportunity would slip through his grasp. Enter Walter Lees, who had two first-class centuries to his name, and the pair put on 98 in less than 50 minutes. Andy was eventually out for 114, but he had finally become a centurion in first-class cricket. With Surrey all out for 305, Somerset's reply was feeble and they were shot out twice in 75 overs with Tom Rushby being the main architect of their demise.

Andy carried his good form in the home match against Nottinghamshire and contributed 58 and 36 in a six-wicket victory. However, there was an incident on the second day that would have been upsetting to Andy. During his innings, he was striking the ball extremely well. Flourishing drives and well-placed cut shots were flying through the dry outfield. With one particular delivery, Andy played a pull shot to a ball bowled short of a length. The square-leg umpire, B.W. Mason, was late in seeing the ball and took evasive action by turning his back. The resultant injury left Mason unable to continue in the match, and a replacement was sent for.

Another half-century against Middlesex, plus more runs in the West Country against Somerset and Gloucestershire, left Andy with one more game left in the County Championship season before joining up with Woolwich Arsenal.

Yorkshire were the visitors and the match, which looked ordinary in prospect, turned into a game that *The Observer* described as 'some of the most amazing play ever seen on the historic Oval or any other ground'. Surrey won the toss and batted first, but lost Tom Hayward and Jack Hobbs early on. Alan Marshal was in no mood to hang around. Andy joined him at the fall of the fourth wicket and held his end up while the Australian reached his century within 90 minutes. Once Marshal was out, Andy took over the mantle of aggressive batting before being caught and bowled by all-rounder George Hirst for 67.

Yorkshire's response was driven by Ben Wilson, David Denton, and James Rothery. Rain on day two, limiting play to just 15 minutes, suggested that the game could descend into a draw. At 200/4 that was very much the case until batting became increasingly difficult. Yorkshire lost their last six wickets for 23 and Surrey had a surprise lead of 50.

Glorious sunshine over The Oval started to dry the pitch out and Surrey's second innings descended into chaos. Some rash shots and bowling in the right areas from Hirst saw the home team all out for 62 in just over an hour and a half. Yorkshire required 113 to win in about 80 minutes, leaving their captain Lord Hawke with the quandary of either chasing the runs on a minefield of a batting strip or batting out time to secure a draw.

The Observer's correspondent had never 'seen a side so utterly helpless'. Within 55 minutes, Surrey had bowled Yorkshire out for 26 to secure a remarkable victory: Tom Rushby took 5-9 and Razor Smith 5-12 as the last five batsmen departed without scoring. Alonzo Drake top-scored with six as Yorkshire were routed. It would be a match that Andy would remember for an awfully long time.

CHAPTER FOUR

On the International Stage
1909–1910

DROPPED: AN unwelcome and chastening experience at any level. Andy experienced that after Woolwich Arsenal's opening-day humiliation at Villa Park in September 1909. A 5-1 defeat by Aston Villa led Woolwich Arsenal manager George Morrell to make changes for the next match at home to Sheffield United. Andy was dropped along with new signing Tom Drain, Archie Gray, and Matt Thomson. Drain's career at Plumstead would run to one more first-team game and a friendly.

Andy's time on the sidelines would last just over a month as a bout of flu delayed his return to the team. By the time he did come back, Arsenal were languishing in the relegation zone. After one win and several heavy defeats, including 7-0 at Blackburn Rovers and 5-1 at Notts County, Andy's experience was required. However, another home defeat would leave Arsenal on the bottom of the table. Andy had played well against Nottingham Forest, but the forwards were not competent in front of goal.

By the time Woolwich Arsenal got to Roker Park, in the middle of October, they were in a slump. Sunderland won 6-2 and the Plumstead men were described by the *London Daily News* as having a 'profound dejection' as they ran on to the pitch before the match.

Despite his team playing badly, Andy was a shining light and was selected for an inter-city match between London and Birmingham.

Along with Gray, he represented Arsenal in the London side. The event was a grand affair with both teams dining at the Norfolk Square Hotel in Paddington. More than 10,000 fans spent their Monday afternoon at Craven Cottage to see Birmingham win 3-1. Unfortunately for Arsenal, both players came back injured: Gray bruised his collarbone while Andy suffered a groin strain.

Andy was out for just under two weeks and returned against Bradford City. Just when it looked like they might get a draw, and a much-needed point, a goalkeeping error lost them the match. Crowd favourite Hugh MacDonald, who was in his second spell for the club, let a shot slip through his grasp to give Bradford the winner. With ten minutes left and Woolwich Arsenal's forwards in such abject form, it was a mortal blow.

The following two games were drawn, with a last-minute equaliser against Bristol City, before a fortuitous winning goal against Bury meant that they were in better form and luck for their next opponents: Tottenham Hotspur. Although the clubs were not geographically as close as they are now, it was still a bitter rivalry.

The match was played at Plumstead, and the pitch was sodden through heavy rain. As the turf cut up, the quality of the match deteriorated, and mistakes were made. Walter Lawrence hit the winning goal, his third of the season, while Andy and his fellow defenders kept the Spurs forwards at bay. Such was the intensity of the game, that Arsenal finished with nine fit players to Spurs' ten.

The Christmas and New Year period proved that Arsenal's recent form had been temporary. Newcastle United were welcomed to Plumstead on Christmas Day and went home with a comfortable 3-0 victory. Liverpool visited two days later, and another point was dropped in a 1-1 draw, Andy's missed penalty proving costly. On New Year's Day, the fixture was reversed, and Woolwich Arsenal travelled to Anfield. The ground was covered in thick fog, but the match went ahead. Liverpool mastered the conditions and won 5-1.

Having been on the receiving end of awful weather, Arsenal used the visit of Middlesbrough in mid-January to test out new football boots. The pitch was frozen due to a hard frost, so the home team wore boots that had felt fitted to the soles. Middlesbrough's players, wearing their studded boots, could not penetrate the pitch and found movement difficult. A 3-0 home win vindicated the innovative decision.

Less than 48 hours after the game, Andy was in action again. This time, he was playing in a trial match for the upcoming Home Internationals. The Football Association called up two teams, the 'Whites' and the 'Stripes', with a view to selecting players for the forthcoming match in Belfast.

The trial was played at Anfield and the pitch, and weather, conspired to make conditions terrible for football. Both teams tried to make the best of it with international selection on the line. Andy was playing for the 'Whites' and was in the half-back line with established international Billy Wedlock and another prospect hoping for the call in Blackburn Rovers' Billy Bradshaw. The threesome put in a good performance for their team despite their forwards not being able to use the ball well. The match ended in a 1-1 draw which was secondary to the news of the selection for the Ireland game. When the line-up was announced, 'DUCAT' was on the team-sheet for Belfast.

Before pulling on his England shirt, Andy was back on club duty and celebrated his call-up with a goal in the 2-0 victory over Bolton Wanderers. Brimming with confidence, according to *The Sporting Life*, Andy 'tricked the defence cleverly, and running through, scored with a strong, low shot'.

On arrival in Belfast, the England team were greeted by incessant rain that had been falling for weeks. By the lunchtime of the game, the rain finally stopped to give the fans a chance to get to the ground without too much discomfort. The trams of Belfast were filled with football fans making their way to the Cliftonville area of the city. The match was being played at the Solitude ground and up to 25,000 spectators squeezed into the stadium. Such was the crush that iron railings used to segregate reserved and unreserved spectators gave way. Many flocked to the reserved part of the ground to get a better view of the action.

As the brass band ended the pre-match entertainment, the players ran on to the soaked and muddy pitch. The teams were:

Ireland

Scott (Everton)

McCann (Belfast Celtic), Burnison (Distillery)

Darling (Linfield), McConnell (The Wednesday), Harris (Everton)

Thompson (Cliftonville), Lacey (Everton), Murray (Motherwell), Murphy (Bradford City), Renneville (Leyton)

England

Hardy (Liverpool)

Cowell (Blackburn Rovers), Morley (Notts County)

Bradshaw (Blackburn Rovers), Wedlock (Bristol City), Ducat (Woolwich Arsenal)

Hall (Aston Villa), Bache (Aston Villa), Woodward (Chelsea), Fleming (Swindon Town), Bond (Bradford City)

The match started with Ireland dealing much better with the conditions that their English counterparts. Also, some of the England players were too meek in their play as the Irish set about their task enthusiastically. England were too keen to play the ball on the ground and some passes failed to reach their intended target due to the pitch being, as the *Northern Whig* described, a 'quagmire'.

Andy and his fellow half-backs slowly rested momentum back and looked to get their forwards into play. The Villa duo of Joe Bache and Albert Hall received many chances but tried to be too intricate. For Ireland, it was English McConnell who caused the visitors the most problems. Not only was McConnell breaking up English attacks, but he was trying to create chances. Sam Hardy,

England's goalkeeper, was kept busy but had saved everything sent his way until two minutes before half-time. A cross from William Renneville, from the right-hand side, was met by Frank Thompson and the debutant beat Hardy with a header.

At the start of the second half, England went in search of an equaliser. Within six minutes, they had achieved parity when Ireland's goalkeeper Billy Scott spilled a ball from Dicky Bond and Harold Fleming managed to bundle it into the net to make the score 1-1. With about 20 minutes to go, Fleming thought he had scored again but the referee disallowed the goal for offside.

The last part of the game took place in ever increasing gloom with the light fading. A 3:30pm kick-off meant that the match was liable to bad light, and so it proved. The Ireland team were playing in dark blue shirts which added to the general confusion. No matter how much England pushed for a winning goal, the home team held firm to secure a draw.

Andy's first international match turned out to be a personal success with *The Guardian* describing him as 'best of the half backs'. It would have been a source of pride to have reached this level at the relatively young age of 23. He would have been able to doubly enjoy his 24th birthday, four days after the match, knowing that he had pretty much secured a second cap the following month against Wales in Cardiff.

The achievement of getting international recognition despite playing in a struggling Woolwich Arsenal team should not be underestimated. Arsenal's financial position was poor and a decline in attendances at Plumstead was making matters worse. A policy of selling meant that the team could not keep players of real worth. The policy would have been known to Andy and the possibility of being sold, as one of the best players at the club, would have been ever-present. An Extraordinary General Meeting was called to discuss the club's dire financial position.

Back in league action, Andy lined up for the home game against Sunderland. In goal for the visitors was none other than

Leigh Roose, who would be winning his 22nd cap for Wales in the upcoming international fixture. Perhaps Andy was trying to lay down a marker but he was inclined to shoot at goal whenever the opportunity arose. One shot had already stung Roose's hands when Andy let fly again. This time, the ball beat Roose and the inside of the post to give the home team the lead. Arsenal took the advantage into the second half and were pushing for a second goal. Andy worked another good shooting position, but Roose pushed his shot out for a corner.

Sunderland pressure led to an equaliser from a corner, but the home team looked to take the lead back. Andy took a free kick, but the ball narrowly went over the bar. Despite the pressure, Sunderland scored again to win the match. Such is the way when teams are fighting for survival and Arsenal found themselves in the relegation zone once again.

Two further draws and a defeat, plus the impending EGM, meant that Andy would travel to Cardiff with England with Arsenal's future looking bleak on and off the pitch. The international match took place on a bright and sunny Monday afternoon with about 20,000 spectators in Cardiff Arms Park. Wales made several changes from their defeat in Scotland in the previous game. The inclusion of George Latham was a late change for Liverpool's Ernest Peake, who was injured. Latham was a Boer War veteran and would go on to win a Military Cross in the First World War. He would also manage Cardiff City when they won the FA Cup in 1927, which is still, at the time of writing, the only time that a team from outside England has won the trophy.

England made five changes to their line-up:

Wales

Roose (Sunderland)

Morris (Derby County), Blew (Wrexham)

Davies (Wrexham), Latham (Southport Central), Hughes (Nottingham Forest)

Evans (Sheffield United), Morris (Nottingham Forest), Jones (Manchester City), Wynn (Manchester City), Meredith (Manchester United)

England

Hardy (Liverpool)

Pennington (West Bromwich Albion), Crompton (Blackburn Rovers)

Bradshaw (Blackburn Rovers), Wedlock (Bristol City), Ducat (Woolwich Arsenal)

Wall (Manchester United), Holley (Sunderland), Parkinson (Liverpool), Fleming (Swindon), Bond (Bradford City)

The home team started the match at high intensity and could have scored in the first minute, but Hardy somehow kept the ball out of the net. England clawed their way back into the game but were guilty of wayward passes. Pennington and Crompton were kept busy at the back. Andy's defensive play was somewhat lacking as he gave Bobby Evans, who would go on to play for England in 1911 and 1912 due to eligibility through birth, far too much room and the Sheffield United man tried to inspire his fellow forwards.

The match remained scoreless well into the second half. Wales were playing well while England had plenty of possession without looking like scoring. About 20 minutes into the second half, England were awarded a corner which was taken by Dicky Bond. The Welsh defence failed to clear the ball and it was left to Andy to drive it into the net to give England the lead.

Straight from the kick-off, England regained possession and swarmed towards the Welsh goal. Having beaten Roose already, Andy tried his luck again with another shot. With Roose beaten, the ball ricocheted off the post back into play. England thought they had a second goal when the ball was put into Roose's goal, but the referee disallowed it for interference with the goalkeeper. Wales tried their hardest to get an equaliser, but England held on to win. The cap that Andy was awarded for the match was sold by Sotheby's in 2013. It was made of red velvet with an embroidered rose emblem and '1910' on the peak, embroidered in gold. The cap sold for £1,320.

The outcome of Woolwich Arsenal's EGM was a resolution to liquidate the old company and form a new one, so that football could be guaranteed for the next season. It was a new beginning for the club but would not address all of the financial issues. A new company would not bring attractive football, or spectators, back to Plumstead. However, it provided a financial lifeline for the short term.

Five days after being the hero for England, Andy played at Bradford City with Arsenal desperate to start winning. They did so with a better performance. Bert Beney netted the winning goal and was close to improving the lead. Andy narrowly missed with a shot over the bar while Bradford were left with very little by the way of chances.

Another away match, on Good Friday, saw Arsenal secure a creditable draw at Newcastle United. The match was of low quality with both sides being profligate in front of goal. The 20,000 spectators were particularly vociferous in letting the players know their displeasure. Newcastle's forward Albert Shepherd was wasteful and was on the receiving end of criticism; such was the ferocity of the barracking that he walked off the pitch. Shepherd was cautioned by the referee before rejoining the game. All would soon be forgiven by player and spectators as Shepherd would go on to score both goals in the FA Cup Final replay a month later to give Newcastle their first win in the competition.

Twenty-four hours later Arsenal were in action again, this time at home to The Wednesday. It was a big ask to play back-to-back after a long return journey from the North East, and Arsenal were beaten 1-0 and dropped back into the relegation places.

On 2 April, more than 100,000 spectators ventured to Hampden Park in Glasgow to witness the match between the Auld Enemies.

Glorious sunshine covered the terraces, with the band and pipers of the Argyll and Sutherland Highlanders providing the soundtrack. England gave debuts to Billy Hibbert and Wally Hardinge. Kent cricketer Hardinge would later become a dual international, as well as the recalled Harry Makepeace, making it three future dual internationals in the England line-up.

Scotland
Brownlie (Third Lanark)
Hay (Celtic), Law (Rangers)
McWilliam (Newcastle United), Thomson (Sunderland), Aitken (Leicester Fosse)
Templeton (Kilmarnock), Quinn (Celtic), McMenemy (Rangers), Higgins (Newcastle United), Bennett (Rangers)

England
Hardy (Liverpool)
Pennington (West Bromwich Albion), Crompton (Blackburn Rovers)
Makepeace (Everton), Wedlock (Bristol City), Ducat (Woolwich Arsenal)
Wall (Manchester United), Hardinge (Sheffield United), Parkinson (Liverpool), Hibbert (Swindon), Bond (Bradford City)

The match started at a great pace, with both teams trying to get a fast start. The pitch was in excellent condition and was conducive to slick, passing football. But the forwards on both teams failed to use the conditions to their advantage. Once the game had settled down, Scotland's half-back trio started to dominate.

England's players were not at their best, but Andy in particular was struggling. Bobby Templeton, Scotland's outside-left (winger), proved to be too fast and tricky for Andy to mark effectively. Templeton had made his Scottish debut in 1902 in the match where 25 supporters were killed; it was rumoured that the stand at Ibrox collapsed when fans surged forward in an effort to see Templeton dribbling with the ball.

In the 20th minute, Hardy failed to hold a shot and Jimmy McMenemy scored, despite Andy's vain attempt to stop the ball on the goal line. From that point, Scotland took charge. Jimmy Quinn, whose shot set up the first goal, scored one himself 12 minutes later. The match, as a spectacle, was over at that point and the game proceeded to an inevitable win for the hosts. As *The Scotsman* succinctly summed up, 'the Scots have beaten the English, and that, after all, is the main thing'.

Andy's third cap had been disastrous, but he needed to pick himself up quickly to help save his club's season. With Arsenal in dire need of a hero, one emerged. The name Charlie McGibbon may not resonate with too many football fans, even Arsenal supporters, but without his goals the season would have ended differently.

McGibbon made his debut for Arsenal in the vital match against fellow strugglers Chelsea. McGibbon was in the army and after being posted to Woolwich was soon 'borrowed', as the *London Daily News* described it, by Woolwich Arsenal. The forward had already scored 19 goals for Southampton that season and was soon on the scoresheet again. The 1-0 win at Chelsea was a massive result.

Champions-elect Aston Villa visited Plumstead and McGibbon contributed the winning goal. At times Arsenal were forced to defend desperately. One occasion saw Andy drop back on the goal line, with the goalkeeper beaten, but Villa shot wide. Another 1-0 win saw Arsenal rise to 14th place with safety almost assured.

That assurance was cemented with a 1-1 draw at rivals Tottenham Hotspur. McGibbon, once again, came up with the priceless goal at White Hart Lane. Tottenham pushed for a winning goal, but the defence held firm. Andy was instrumental with a desperate tackle on Percy Humphreys when it looked like the forward would score.

The final-day defeat against Preston North End was immaterial now, as Arsenal had secured their place in the First Division. It had proved to be a successful season for Andy. He had been awarded a benefit match earlier in the season, at home to Bury, when he received a payment of £250. He was also becoming a celebrity and was featured in an article in *Pearson's Weekly*. The article gave the readers details of his career in football and cricket and commented that he was 'a robust tackler, a splendid placer of the ball to his forwards, and a capital shot at goal … he always seems to be the neatest and cleanest player of the twenty-two on field'.

* * *

Andy's first cricket outing was in the traditional trial match as a precursor to the start of the season. It would be different for Andy this year as his place in the starting line-up, to start with at least, was guaranteed. With Jack Crawford's departure for the sunnier climes of Australia, Andy would get a chance to establish himself in the Surrey batting order. The trial match was successful with a total of 26 runs, a catch, and four wickets.

The County Championship season started on 2 May with the visit of Warwickshire. If Surrey thought that the departure of Tom Rushby, lured by the financial incentive of Lancashire League cricket, might weaken the bowling unit, Razor Smith allayed fears with an impressive outing. Bowling figures of 7-32 and 5-53 saw Warwickshire bowled out cheaply twice to deliver an innings victory.

Derbyshire were the next team to visit The Oval, and were well on the way to suffering a similar fate before the death of Edward VII intervened. The king died of heart problems, late on the Friday night of the match, and the game was abandoned early on the Saturday morning as a mark of respect. Derbyshire had been bowled out for 83 in their first innings and were 74/4, still 40 runs short of making Surrey bat again, before the match was ended.

Surrey were back in action a few days later against Cambridge University but slumped to defeat. Andy hit a season-high 37 in the second innings but it was not good enough individually or collectively.

A visit to Trent Bridge did nothing to help the uncharacteristically fragile Surrey batting. Despite Razor Smith taking 12 wickets in the match, Tom Wass took 14 as Surrey were bowled out for 65 and 96 in a 127-run loss. Andy scored 0 and 10 not out as Surrey's stars, such as Hobbs and Hayes, were helpless.

Back at The Oval, rain clouds delayed the start of the match against Essex, but better weather brought better batting. Andy top-scored in the first innings with 85. Straight from the start, he played positively, driving and cutting the Essex bowlers. Surrey did not have the opportunity to press home their advantage after the loss of the second day due to the king's funeral.

Victory should have been a formality on their trip to the Midlands to play Worcestershire. However, the War Memorial Ground in Stourbridge proved to be history-making for the home team. Having never beaten Surrey in the County Championship, Worcestershire finally won a match against their illustrious opponents with a resounding 316-run victory. Andy had his own issues with the bat; Robert Burrows bowling him twice for low scores.

The match was also the end of the career of Alan Marshal, who had his contract terminated by Surrey immediately afterwards. Marshal had been suspended in 1909 after an incident in Chesterfield, but all appeared to have been forgiven. However, the Surrey committee acted decisively. David Lemmon, in *The History of Surrey County Cricket Club*, offered that, '*Wisden* maintained that Surrey would not have taken such action without good reason. There was talk of irregularities, and it was always suggested that Marshal was not good with money.'

Andy's season had been less than successful so far. A score of 92 against Oxford University could have been a springboard, but two cheap dismissals in another defeat, this time to Gloucestershire, and an injury in the same match saw Andy on the sidelines. He missed three County Championship games with a side strain.

Once back in the team, there was a chance for quick redemption against Worcestershire. However, Burrows had other ideas and clean bowled Andy for the third and fourth time in less than a month. Two more failures, 0 and 23, in the narrow defeat at Horsham against Sussex led to another match on the sidelines. This time it was not due to injury – Andy and Bill Hitch were left out of the team against Lancashire.

Andy returned against Kent, last season's champions, and ran straight into Colin Blythe on a turning wicket. The spinner was already on 48 wickets for the season, but conditions created a spinner's paradise. Intermittent rain and sun made the wicket bite and left Surrey's batsmen defenceless.

Hobbs and Hayward had put Surrey in a decent position, at 98/2, before Blythe's blitz. The first ball of one over saw Fred Huish take the catch to dismiss Hayward. Andy was in next and played awkwardly, almost mesmerised by Blythe, at the next four balls before finally getting bat to ball on the last delivery and steering it, perhaps mercifully, into the hands of James Seymour at second slip. The over is very much reminiscent, albeit a spin version, of Andrew Flintoff's to Ricky Ponting in the 2005 Ashes series.

Blythe eventually took five wickets in ten balls, including a hat-trick, as Surrey capitulated to 133 all out. Kent passed the total for the loss of three wickets before rain washed out some of day two and all of day three to save Surrey from almost certain defeat.

Rain in Manchester would make the game with Lancashire just as difficult, as both sides found batting almost impossible at times. The home side batted first and slumped to 10/4, then partly recovered at 53/6 before James Whitehead and Ralph Heap's partnership elevated them to 182. Surrey started just as badly and were 1/2 before creeping to 100/7. Incessant rain ended play as large pools of water developed on the outfield to rescue both sets of batsmen from more punishment.

Travelling to Bradford, Surrey faced Yorkshire and fared better with the bat. Andy top-scored with 45 as Surrey made 158. In reply, Yorkshire's batters found Razor Smith in fine form and were bowled out for just 89. Surrey started their second innings at the end of the first day and were in control with a 94-run lead with nine wickets in hand.

Day two started well for Yorkshire, with Hayes and Bird out early, before Andy and Jack Hobbs put on 41 in 40 minutes before Andy was run out for 22. From that point on, Surrey's batsmen went into a self-destructive spiral. Yorkshire's bowlers took the last seven wickets for 14 to create a chance of victory. Requiring 157 to win, Wilfred Rhodes provided the innings that was required. The 4,000 spectators were thrilled as Rhodes scored 88 not out to give the home side victory. He sealed the win with a drive down the ground after taking five wickets in Surrey's second innings.

Against Somerset at The Oval, Andy's decent touch with the bat continued with a very good 68. Having been not out overnight on day one, after Somerset were dismissed for 180, Andy added another 40 in less than an hour with a range of off-side strokes described as 'brilliant' by *The Observer*. Surrey's batting, plus Bill Hitch's seven-for, delivered a nine-wicket win.

Andy's dismissal was off the bowling of Ernie Robson, caught by Percy Hardy. Both players would die ahead of their time. Robson succumbed to cancer at the age of 54. Hardy's story is more mysterious. He was found, in 1916, at King's Cross Station with his throat cut and a bloody knife by his side. The idea that Hardy was distraught at returning to the horrors of the Western Front was expounded by David Foot in his history of Somerset CCC.

Further investigation of the Somerset team at The Oval shows that there are two other deaths of note. Prince Hitendra Narayan, the brother of the cricket-loving Maharaja of Cooch Behar, succumbed to flu in 1920 at the young age of 30. The final death is linked to the Curse of Tutankhamun (should you be open to that kind of thinking). Mervyn Herbert was the half-brother to George Herbert, the Fifth Earl of Carnarvon, who discovered the young pharaoh's tomb with Howard Carter. Mervyn Herbert's death in Rome in 1929 was attributed to 'malarial pneumonia'. Although it was almost seven years after the discovery of the tomb, he had travelled to Egypt for the official opening and had been present at the time.

Andy continued to accumulate some impressive scores. Against Sussex, he scored 53 in a rain-affected match. In a demoralising loss to Hampshire, the first one since 1902, he made 39 in the second innings.

Northamptonshire felt the full force of Surrey's disappointment with a comprehensive defeat inside two days. Andy's brilliant 67, in a total of 233, was more than the visitors could muster as a team. Razor Smith's 14 wickets, 6-16 and 8-13, saw Northamptonshire dismissed for 51 in each of their innings. Smith ended the match with a hat-trick and Andy was the safe pair of hands to take the catch that completed his treble.

Less than two weeks later, Surrey visited Northamptonshire and steamrollered them again. Smith took just 11 wickets this time, 7-23 and 4-24, as the helpless batters were bowled out for 105 and 64. Smith recorded his 200th wicket of the season during the second innings as Surrey won again inside two days.

If any aspect of Andy's batting could be criticised, it would have been his inability to go and make big scores. Having passed a century just once, the visit of Yorkshire saw Andy mount a defence against his critics. Playing an array of strokes all round the wicket, he achieved his highest County Championship score. Whether it was driving down the ground, or playing delicate cuts with 'charming absence of effort' according to *The Times*, or hooking with confidence then Yorkshire's bowlers struggled. Although rain made the effort somewhat futile, his 153 would cement his place in the Surrey team for some time to come.

His effort against Yorkshire was followed up with scores of 51 and 45 against Gloucestershire. The match was part of the Cheltenham Festival and spectators witnessed the fall of 23 wickets on the first day. Despite Gilbert Jessop's 124, Surrey were always in control and secured a four-wicket victory.

With second-place in the County Championship still up for grabs, Andy scored a first-innings half-century at Taunton to help Surrey to a 131-run win. The next match, against champions elect Kent, would be key. The game would also serve as a benefit match for the long-serving Oval groundsman Samuel Apted.

It was a low-scoring affair with both sets of bowlers restricting the batsmen. Kent eked out a small first-innings lead, but Andy's 48 helped set up a tantalising fourth-innings target for the visitors to chase. Razor Smith picked up another six wickets to ensure Surrey won comfortably by 71 runs.

Andy's final match of the season was uneventful and Surrey, in his absence, were able to secure second place, mainly thanks to Razor Smith. The bowler topped the Championship averages with 215 wickets at 12.56 with 24 five-wicket innings and eight ten-wicket matches. Andy passed 1,000 runs for the season but would want to average more than 28.35 in the Championship when he the following returned to The Oval next year.

CHAPTER FIVE

Aches and Pains
1910–1912

WOOLWICH ARSENAL were determined not to suffer a similar season to the last one. Their signal of intent to change was securing the signing of Alf Common from Middlesbrough. When Common left Sunderland in 1905, Middlesbrough broke the British transfer record by paying £1,000. Common scored 58 goals in 168 appearances over five years for Middlesbrough and Arsenal were hoping that signing a proven goalscorer was the answer to their problems.

Andy was selected for the first match of the season against Manchester United. Although he was fit, he was lacking in match sharpness. It would take a little time to switch over to football mode. United were in no mood to wait and played confidently to pick up a 2-1 win. They were also in no mood to be messed with by the Football Association. The United players had been instrumental in supporting the Players' Union. Players supporting the fledgling union wore armbands, but the FA had banned the practice. United's players defiantly still wore theirs for the game.

Two days later, Arsenal were playing at Bury when an unfortunate incident occurred that would require Andy to switch positions for a few games. Right-back Duncan McDonald injured his knee ligaments and was taken off on a stretcher. McDonald would not play for the first team again, and Andy slotted into the position as cover until Archie Gray could shake off a less serious injury than McDonald's.

Initially, Andy did well in the makeshift position. Against Sheffield United at home he helped the team keep a clean sheet in a goalless draw. Aston Villa proved to be a sterner test and the Birmingham side ran out 3-0 winners. However, Andy put in a 'sterling effort' according to the *Woolwich Gazette* alongside fellow full-back Joe Shaw. The *Athletic News* was less impressed with Andy's 'ordinary' display against Sunderland, despite another clean sheet. The return of Tim Coleman, in Sunderland's colours, was the main talking point around the game, yet he could not find the back of the net. Another 0-0 draw, at home to Oldham Athletic, was the last game before Gray's recovery and Andy switched back to his preferred position.

By the middle of October, Woolwich Arsenal were still to register a win. As a result, they were sliding down the table and the spectre of relegation was again upon them. Fellow strugglers Blackburn Rovers were beaten, partly due to Andy playing 'wonderfully well' according to *The Observer*, before following up with a 3-2 win at Nottingham Forest.

The welcome victories were a false dawn, as defeats against Manchester City and Everton dragged them back down. Arsenal's form was patchy and defeat to Tottenham Hotspur at the beginning of December signalled a poor run of results.

When teams are in trouble, things tend to go against them, and Middlesbrough's goalkeeper Tim Williamson proved the adage. He was in sparkling form and made, according to *The Daily News*' correspondent, 'twenty-seven saves above the ordinary'. Williamson was even good enough to deny Arsenal from the penalty spot when he saved from Jackie Chalmers. Andy gave the opportunity to take the penalty to the forward which turned out to be an error.

The Christmas period was very mixed for Woolwich Arsenal. Andy was in fine form at home to Notts County and his 'great game', according to the *London Daily News*, helped the home team to a 2-1 victory. Boxing Day was disastrous as Manchester United put Arsenal to the sword with a 5-0 hammering. Fans left Plumstead happy on New Year's Eve as their team edged Bury in a five-goal thriller. Andy set Arsenal on their way from the penalty spot, a lesson learned from the Middlesbrough match, to end the year in 18th place in the table.

Having been beaten at Bramall Lane on the first weekend of the New Year, Arsenal found that the weather was also against them. In their FA Cup first-round match against Clapton Orient, the game was abandoned at half-time due to fog. Despite kicking off in good weather, the referee had no option but to call the game off before the second half began. One week later, Arsenal were 20 minutes away from an invaluable 2-1 victory over Aston Villa when the referee called off the game because of bad light. Andy had scored both goals; the first from the penalty spot, the second a shot from 15 yards out.

Andy might have considered that his luck was out. At Sunderland, his penalty had helped Arsenal to a 2-0 lead before a late, and somewhat dubious, goal secured a draw for the home side. The news that he was omitted from the England team for the match against Ireland was the final piece of evidence. Despite having a fabulous season so far at right-half, and being the incumbent in the position, the FA selection committee had looked elsewhere.

Perhaps Arsenal's poor form had been a factor in the decision. A three-game run without a goal, and just one point from a 'poor game' against Bradford City, did nothing to assuage Andy's worth in the eyes of the FA selection committee. Newspaper correspondents such as in the *Football News* thought that Andy 'is just now certainly better than Ben Warren, and if he is not picked in the next two games I shall be very much surprised'.

Despite scoring against Nottingham Forest, and putting in an excellent performance at Manchester City, Andy was not selected for the next international against Wales. Warren won his 21st cap while Andy was named as a reserve. England went on to win the championship with Warren still preferred at right-half.

While Andy's international career was on hold, Arsenal started to turn things around. Beating Everton at home lifted them off the bottom of the table. A late equaliser at Aston Villa suggested luck was changing.

Next up were Bristol City at home and goals were now easier to find. Three in 17 minutes, including Andy setting up the third, was enough to take the points. Another late goal, this time at Newcastle, suggested that Arsenal would survive the drop again. A win at home to rivals Tottenham, in front of 25,000 spectators, was doubly welcome.

In the line-up for Spurs was Walter Tull. The forward was one of the first players of Afro-Caribbean descent in the league and had been subjected to racism throughout his career. He would soon leave for Northampton Town, but he is remembered most for being the first black officer in the British Army to lead his men into battle. Tull would be killed, in March 1918, by machine-gun fire and his body was never recovered. A sad end for a pioneer, and decent man, who was shamefully treated.

For Andy, his season ended with three matches still to play. Arsenal finished the season with an 11-game unbeaten streak to finish in tenth place. Although it was a false position in many ways, they had something to build on. As long as history didn't repeat itself.

* * *

Despite rain finishing the traditional trial match early, it did not rain on Andy's parade. Unlike in previous years, the switch of sports appeared seamless, and Andy capitalised with a century against a bowling attack including Razor Smith. He made 130, the highest score in the match.

The opening County Championship match, at home to Warwickshire, saw runs less easy to come by. A damp wicket, and chilly conditions, meant that bowlers had the better of the match. Twenty-four wickets fell on day one as Warwickshire were swept aside for 62 before Surrey were bowled out for 195; Andy was joint top-scorer with 37. Warwickshire soon lost their last six wickets on the second day with a marginally better score of 87. Samuel Bates was the bowler who took Andy's wicket. Having claimed Tom Hayward and Jack Hobbs, too, his 3-56 was his best performance.

Bates would claim just three more wickets in his career: he lost his life on the Western Front in 1916.

Leicestershire were next to visit The Oval, but found the home team in imposing form. Despite Cecil Wood and Harry Whitehead's centuries, Surrey fought back from 274/2 to end their innings on 311. Andy's 42 helped Surrey carve out a small lead before Razor Smith and Tom Rushby blew the visitors' batting away to set up a ten-wicket victory.

Andy carried on his good form against Oxford University with 46 and 54 in an easy victory. Again, Surrey were dominant with the ball, but the wickets came from an unlikely source. Jack Hobbs took 7-56 with his medium pace which meant that Surrey would travel to the Midlands to face Worcestershire in fine form.

The match was played at the Bournville ground in Birmingham; it would be the last time Worcestershire used the venue. The game went down to the final afternoon before the home team secured a tight two-wicket victory. For Andy, it was a poor game with two low scores.

He fared better against Essex at The Oval with a welcome second-innings half-century, but it was Frederick Fane who batted superbly for the away team. Fane, an Irish-born batsman who had captained England, scored a tremendous double century to put Surrey under pressure. However, a resolute second innings saw Surrey keep Essex at bay.

Another half-century at Northampton was followed by a hundred in a one-sided win over Gloucestershire. Andy was in fine touch and scored with ease all round the wicket. He was particularly keen to play the ball through the on side to good effect. In his partnership with Harry Bush, or Major Bush as he was described by newspapers, the pair scored 120 runs in an hour.

Such consistent scoring, which had deserted Andy in previous seasons, did not go unnoticed. The England selection committee decided that they would call on Andy to play in the Test trial at Bramall Lane. It had been over 12 months since England had played a Test match, and all eyes were on the MCC tour of Australia during the English winter of 1911/12. If Andy were to be selected, it would cause a dilemma because of his commitment to Woolwich Arsenal.

Andy was selected to play for Pelham Warner's team against Gilbert Jessop's XI. It would have been little surprise that he would represent Warner as the Middlesex stalwart had written favourably of Andy in that year's *Wisden Cricketers' Almanack*. Warner identified Andy as one of the most promising young cricketers in England.

Having decided to bat first, Jessop's XI were soon in trouble as George Hirst used his knowledge of the Sheffield ground to good effect. At 65/6, Jessop strode out to the wicket with his team in trouble. Having scored 4, Jessop square cut a ball, but Andy spilled the catch. It was a huge moment. Jessop made Warner's team pay with an innings of 122 not out. Despite Jessop's score, the Warner XI managed to eke out a lead. Andy put his setback behind him to score 33, but Warner top-scored with 60 not out.

The second key moment came from a piece of misfortune. Leicestershire's Bill Shipman, playing for Jessop's team, was suffering from sunstroke, so the captains agreed that Jack Hearne from Middlesex could replace him. Hearne took full advantage personally and for his team. His 74 not out, batting at No.9 with Surrey's wicketkeeper Herbert Strudwick, who also scored 74, put Jessop's team in a winning position. It also helped Hearne book his place in the touring team to Australia later that year. Warner's team capitulated under pressure, illustrated by Andy's dire three runs, and Jessop's team won by 162 runs. Andy had not batted himself into a moral dilemma just yet.

If Andy had been chastened by the experience at Bramall Lane, he didn't let it show. Although Surrey slipped to defeat at Trent Bridge, he responded well with scores of 21 and 43. With Surrey primed to win at 190/2, chasing 366, it was Andy's wicket that started the collapse. Ex-England captain Arthur Jones dismissed him then Harry Bush straight after. Jones had played rugby union for Leicester until the previous year, and would die of tuberculosis just three years later.

More runs flowed at The Oval against Hampshire with a fluent 65. Andy drove well and hit 11 boundaries. On the last day, with Surrey wrapping up the win, he left the field for treatment on his knee. Fluid had developed on the joint and forced him to rest.

Two weeks later, the injury was still keeping Andy off the field. *The Sportsman* wrote that the knee was 'troublesome', and that Andy was under the care of Dr Thomas Pryce-Jenkins. The physician specialised in sports injuries at his practice just off Oxford Street in London.

Pryce-Jenkins was a former rugby union player who had represented London Welsh as well as winning two Wales caps in 1888.

Andy was back within five weeks. His comeback against Worcestershire at The Oval was inauspicious, with a duck and a single. At Bristol, Andy appeared to be regaining his timing with an assertive 44 against Gloucestershire. Perhaps he was trying to make a point to Gloucestershire's captain Gilbert Jessop, and he was 'tolerably vigorous' according to *The Guardian*.

Scores of 5, 2 and 6 in his next three innings were particularly bad timing. The last innings was telling as three colleagues made big scores: Hayward 202, Bush 135 and Goatly 105. The result was that Andy was left out of the next match against Kent. Goatly was also dropped which seemed particularly harsh.

Andy's replacement, Ion Campbell, made two single-figure scores and Andy was soon back in the batting line-up against Lancashire. Surrey brought 21-year-old Andy Sandham for his

County Championship debut and the young batsman scored 60; a sneak preview of what the future would hold for Sandham.

Although in the team at Taunton, Andy found himself batting at No.7. With the likes of Edward Goatly, Henry Harrison and even young Sandham batting higher, he may have felt pushed out. Somerset won the toss and decided to field first. A rare failure from Jack Hobbs may have appeared to vindicate the decision, but Surrey's batsmen soon recovered. Ernie Hayes scored a century while Goatly and Harrison passed fifty before getting out.

Andy came out to bat on the afternoon of day one with the score sitting at 301/5. It was an ideal time to bat. Somerset's bowlers were tired, and it was a good batting track. Bill Hitch joined Andy with the score on 343 and both set about the wearying bowlers with aplomb. In the last 35 minutes of play, the pair scored 103 runs.

Early on day two, they continued where they had left off. Andy passed the century mark first, before Hitch scored his maiden first-class hundred. He was out straight after, and the declaration came. At 523/7, Surrey were well placed to push for the win. However, rain washed out the final day and saved Somerset from a certain defeat.

More runs flowed against Nottinghamshire where Andy played, according to *The Guardian*, 'excellent cricket' in his 77. The rest of August was less fruitful for all batsmen including Andy. Surrey was beaten inside two days at home to Middlesex before subjecting Leicestershire to the same fate at Aylestone Road, with the home side falling to 4/4 at one point.

The match against Kent was another low-scoring affair with the bowlers in control throughout. Andy scored 12 and 34, notching up 1,000 first-class runs for the season in the process, but the match was all about the bowlers. In Surrey's first innings, Kent only used Colin Blythe and Douglas Carr, with the latter taking 8-67. In response, Kent were bowled out by Razor Smith's 8-31 and were 37 behind. In Surrey's second innings, Andy contributed more than half of his team's total. Frank Woolley initiated an enormous collapse with seven wickets in 24 balls to bowl Surrey out for 63. Kent needed 102 to win but suffered their own collapse. They were coasting at 51/3 before falling agonisingly short by nine runs.

Andy's final match of the season was at Hove, where a half-century and being at the crease when the win was completed might have helped dissuade him from considering that cricket was a bowler's game after all.

* * *

Even though it was a Saturday afternoon in early September, the weather was scorching. With temperatures soaring close to 90°F, the Manor Ground in Plumstead was smothered in searing heat. Liverpool were the visitors and their goalkeeper, Sam Hardy, was having a superb game. Andy was also excelling in the trying conditions, but Percy Sands was not having quite such a good day. The captain was struggling to control the ball and Liverpool were capitalising. With two minutes to go, Liverpool led 2-1 and it looked like Hardy had secured the win before Woolwich Arsenal found an equaliser.

The following week at Villa Park was even more frustrating, with the home side winning comfortably 4-1. Andy showed an unusual lack of discipline to give Aston Villa their fourth goal. Near the end of the match, Villa forward Harry Hampton was bearing down on goal when Andy pushed him and gave away a penalty, which was duly scored. It was uncharacteristic of a sportsman who usually played to the letter of the law. It could have been an aggressive attempt to get the ball after an afternoon of Villa dominance, but the referee ruled foul play.

In the match against Newcastle United at Plumstead, Andy's knee problem flared up again. In the first half, Andy was in fine form and Woolwich Arsenal were a goal to the good. After half-time, Andy did not appear to be himself and eventually left the pitch for treatment. Alf Common dropped back into the right-half position. It was a worrying incident for Andy which resulted in him missing the next three matches. He also missed the annual London v Birmingham match.

He marked his return to the team with three goals in four games. Woolwich Arsenal's forwards won penalties and, as the team's penalty taker, he duly scored them. On his first match back, it was Bradford City's David Taylor who transgressed with an unnecessary handball. Two days later, in the London FA Charity Cup, Fred Taylor of Chelsea was also guilty of handball. Andy's final penalty of the set was in a thrilling 3-3 draw at Manchester City. With just ten minutes remaining, the penalty looked like it had won the game for Arsenal, but the home side found a way through to equalise.

Even though Andy was finding the back of the net, there was clearly something wrong. His performances were not at the same level as previous seasons. It is difficult to know the exact cause, but the troublesome knee must have been a likely reason.

At the beginning of November, Everton won 1-0 at Plumstead and Andy was indirectly responsible for the goal. He was slow to tackle the ball-carrier on an Everton attack, and the player found Frank Jefferis who scored. Even the newspapers were starting to comment. *Lloyd's Weekly Newspaper* described Andy's Everton performance as an 'off day'. By the time The Wednesday left Plumstead with a win at the beginning of December, the same newspaper declared that Andy had been 'off colour for some time'. A defeat against Bury, to give them their first win of the season, did not augur well for the rest of the campaign.

On 25 November an article appeared in *The Football News* headlined 'A Question of Grounds'. The piece discussed different aspects of football grounds from a player's perspective. The author was Andy, and it demonstrated his eloquence and thoughtfulness about the sport. With such insights for readers, expressed so clearly, it's not a surprise that writing would play a part later in his life.

In the week leading up to the home game against Middlesbrough, newspapers were getting wind of a story regarding Arsenal signing a new goalkeeper. Although the target appeared to be signing for

Fulham, he changed his mind and joined the Plumstead club in time to make his debut. It was none other than Leigh Roose.

Roose had already featured against them earlier in the season when he appeared for Aston Villa. Whether it was the Roose factor or just Middlesbrough's poor play, Arsenal won their first match in almost a month.

The victory did not galvanise the team at all. In the ten-day festive period, they had five matches and lost four of them. An in-form Notts County beat them before a massive clash on Christmas Day against Tottenham Hotspur. The official crowd was 47,108, but another 10,000 were turned away from White Hart Lane. The home team won easily, 5-0. Revenge was quick: the reverse fixture was played the next day, with Arsenal overcoming Tottenham, and the heavy rain, 3-1. Further defeats to Liverpool and Manchester United meant that another relegation battle was not too far away.

The start of the new year meant that the Home International season was close, and the FA selection committee would be meeting to decide on the England team. Scouts were sent to Arsenal's home match with Sheffield United. They were looking at three players: Bobby Evans and Albert Trueman from the visitors and Andy.

Andy's defensive game had been called into question in the recent FA Cup defeat against Bolton Wanderers, with the winning goal coming from a corner after sustained pressure from Andy's side of the pitch. Already struggling after a less than exemplary season, Andy did not have a good game. Neither did Evans and Trueman as 'all played below their ordinary form' according to the *Sheffield Daily Telegraph*.

The team was announced two days later and, unsurprisingly, Andy's name was not included. Instead, Tom Brittleton of The Wednesday was to be given his debut at right-half. Brittleton had been a reserve on five previous occasions so it would have been little surprise that he was given his chance.

On the same day as England won their match 6-1, Arsenal started to find some form. Bolton Wanderers were beaten 3-0 and did not muster a shot on goal all game. At Bradford City, a 1-1 draw was secured with Andy having his best match in a while. Two days before the next England team was selected, Arsenal went up to Middlesbrough and inflicted their first home defeat of the season. Andy blasted a penalty and Alf Common scored against his previous employers.

Correlation is not necessarily causation, but Andy and Woolwich Arsenal's mutual improvement was linked. It did not go unnoticed by the FA selection committee and Andy was named as reserve for the match against Wales at Wrexham. Although Brittleton was selected, Andy's inclusion demonstrated that he was still in the thoughts of the powers that be.

A string of three league defeats soon arrested any momentum. Against West Bromwich Albion at home, luck was with the away team. Leigh Roose had a poor game. The combination of the two factors was evident when Andy, trying to clear the ball downfield, only succeeded in cannoning it off Sid Bowser and into the goal. Visits to Sunderland and Everton were also fruitless.

Easter, like Christmas and New Year, was a busy period for a footballer and 1912 was no exception. Arsenal were faced with four matches in eight days, including an evening trip to Sheffield. On Good Friday, Manchester United visited Plumstead and were beaten 2-1.

The Wednesday were entertaining Arsenal the following day and Andy was asked to fill in at right-back due to Joe Shaw not being able to play. It was a difficult day as the home team, buoyed by a headwind in the first half, were soon 2-0 up. Tom Brittleton and George Robertson proved difficult to stop. Andy induced the ire of the 5,000-strong Wednesday following when he put in a heavy challenge on Robertson. *Lloyd's Weekly Newspaper* reported that the tackle 'set the crowd in a roar'. Robertson was particularly favoured by the home fans due to his part in the club's nickname. The player purchased an owl, inspired by the ground's name Owlerton, for the club and it was adopted as a nickname which is still used today.

Easter Monday was a much better day for club and player with a 4-1 thrashing of Preston North End. Andy looked very much like his old self. He set up Alf Common for the first goal with a superb pass, before scoring the second himself from the penalty spot. Five days later, he was on the scoresheet again against Bury, his penalty being the only goal of the game.

Andy's final appearance of the season was at home to Blackburn Rovers. Football was not the only consideration on the day, as the shock following the sinking of the RMS *Titanic* was tangible. It had been one week since the maritime disaster and a collection was made to go towards the Titanic Fund to assist the families affected. It collected £15 which, adjusting for inflation, would equate to well over £1,700 today. The match itself was one sided with Arsenal winning 5-1. However, Andy put through his own net trying to clear a cross from Walter Anthony. It was Andy's final act as an Arsenal player, but he would not know it for several weeks.

* * *

The cricket season started for Andy at The Oval where Northamptonshire were the visitors. Bill Hitch soon found his stride and picked up five wickets to dismiss Northants for 172. By the end of day one, Surrey had reduced the deficit to 45 with eight wickets in hand. Andy was 24 not out with his partner, Ernie Hayes, looking good on 76.

Day two should have been about Surrey dominating, but the visitors' captain Sydney Smith started a collapse. Andy fell one short of his half-century while Hayes reached three figures before losing his wicket. Northamptonshire continued their revival with the bat to end day two with a potentially challenging lead, but rain washed out the third day. Rain would feature predominantly in the summer of 1912.

Next up for Surrey were the visiting South Africans. A change to the Ashes schedule meant that a triangular tournament would take place instead. The Imperial Cricket Conference, the forerunner of the current world governing body of cricket, was formed in 1909 between the three Test-playing nations and agreed to a quadrennial competition between members.

Batting first against Surrey, the South Africans were bowled out for 252 on the first day. However, it left a tricky period in diminishing light during which left-armer Dave Nourse removed Jack Hobbs and Henry Harrison. The following morning was just as tricky for Surrey. Andy played a useful innings of 22 with only Ernie Hayes providing resistance. The first-innings deficit proved to be too great, and Surrey were beaten by 52 runs.

A trip to Dudley to face Worcestershire in another rain-affected County Championship game was sandwiched in between another tour game. This time, it was the Australians who were entertained at The Oval.

Surrey won the toss and decided to bat first against a strong line-up including Syd Gregory, Charlie Macartney, Warren Bardsley and Charlie Kelleway. However, it was uncapped Sid Emery who had too much guile and took 6-54 in Surrey's first innings. The Australians did not have it all their own way when they slumped to 6/2, but Macartney's 123 put the tourists in prime position. Emery's second innings 5-81 left Australia with just 52 to win. Surrey made inroads at 12/3, but Macartney saw his team home. Andy had a match to forget with scores of 1 and 8.

Back in the County Championship, Surrey found that the Gloucestershire bowling unit was far more benign and plundered an innings-and-87-run victory. Andy drove and cut with power and the Gloucestershire bowlers were left helpless. Ably assisted by Bird, the Surrey pair scored all over The Oval with impunity. Andy finally fell for 137, one of George Dennett's seven wickets, after he had scored 14 fours, three fives and two sixes. At the point of dismissal, the scoring rate had been 154 runs in 80 minutes. Bird followed soon after, but Surrey had already put the game beyond Gloucestershire's reach. Ernie Hayes' 8-22 and 5-79 ensured that the visitors were bowled out twice in a day and the win was secured with a day to spare.

The trip to Trent Bridge saw roles reversed as Nottinghamshire's first innings total meant that Surrey were fighting to save the game before picking up a bat. Things started well for Surrey when Tom Rushby bowled George Gunn for a duck. This brought Joe Hardstaff to the wicket. The former England batsman was in sublime form and fell three runs short of a double century. Along with Hardstaff, Nottinghamshire's lower order contributed valuable runs: Jimmy Iremonger (45), Tom Oates (56), and William Riley (43) pushed Nottinghamshire to 444.

Knowing that they needed to bat out almost two days, Surrey's reply fell off sharply. Going well at 160/3, with Hayes set for a century, the situation looked manageable. Then disaster struck, in the form of Nottinghamshire's Tom Wass, and Surrey lost seven wickets for 75 and were required to follow on. Such was the rapid fall of wickets, Andy was third-highest scorer with 22.

Surrey's potential saving grace was that the innings had taken up more than 100 overs, and they needed to bat for the rest of the day to save the match. Wass struck early and removed Hayward and Hayes to leave Surrey 14/2. Andy walked to the crease to join Jack Hobbs. It had been a strange start to the season for Hobbs, who had almost reached the end of May without registering a century. The lure of England's Test summer, and Surrey's predicament, engendered a Hobbs masterclass. Andy played his part in the partnership, but Hobbs was on a mission.

The partnership had reached 124 when Wass returned to shatter Andy's stumps. Out for 43, Andy was replaced by Harry Bush. Hobbs homed in on his century while Bush added 25. Morice Bird joined Hobbs, who completed his hundred before falling for 104. Surrey needed to occupy the crease, but Nottinghamshire kept nicking wickets.

When Surrey lost their final wicket at 277, the target for the home team was 68 in about 45 minutes. The late-afternoon light was starting to dim due to the overcast conditions, making their task even more difficult. Arthur Jones, Nottinghamshire's captain, logged 6 before Razor Smith bowled him. Jones had one more contribution to the game for his team and promoted Ted Alletson as a pinch-hitter. Alletson and George Gunn smashed their way towards victory. More than 4,000 vociferous spectators cheered every run and, with less than ten minutes remaining, 'shouted themselves hoarse' according to *The Guardian* as the winning hit was made.

On returning to The Oval for their next match, against Sussex, Surrey were involved in another close finish. Batting first, Surrey lost Hobbs for a duck, but Hayward hit the ball hard and far. Andy joined him at the fall of the second wicket, with the score on 82, and spent the next hour and three-quarters carving up Sussex's bowling attack. Hayward was out for 125, and Andy for 73, as Surrey posted 312.

Sussex's response was led by the former England batsman Ranjitsinhji, who was now titled the Maharaja of Nawanagar having ascended to the title in 1907. Scores of 59 and 23 from Ranji, and 68 from Robert Relf, saw Sussex leave Surrey needing 75 for an easy victory. Or so they thought. At 29/5, the target looked a long way away. Fortunately for Surrey, Morice Bird made an invaluable 35 and Surrey limped across the line for a three-wicket victory.

After the excitement of the last two matches, Surrey's next encounter was a damp squib. Having travelled up to Sheffield to play Yorkshire at Bramall Lane, three days of rain meant that the game was abandoned without even the toss taking place. Rain also ruined a second match against the South Africans. Less than a day's play was possible before rain stopped play. Surrey were bowled out for 169 on a lively pitch with the South African bowlers extracting movement at will. Andy scored 16 before Sid Pegler, who found prodigious movement at times, bowled him.

The match at Leyton against Essex proved to be far more successful for Andy. Despite scoring 3 in the first innings, he played a far more dominant knock second time around to help set up Surrey for the win. Ernie Hayes would get the plaudits for scores of 143 and 90, but Andy's quick-scoring 73 not out allowed Surrey to push on for the win. Essex needed 347 in just over four hours, but Bill Hitch's 8-38 ensured that the home team were bowled out for just 59. Andy may not have stolen the headlines for his cricket performance, but he was about to dominate the sports news, nonetheless.

CHAPTER SIX

Sold and Broken
1912–1914

ON THE afternoon of 14 June 1912, Aston Villa announced that they had secured the signing of Andy from Woolwich Arsenal. An offer of £1,000 was far too much money for the directors of Woolwich Arsenal to turn down and Andy was transferred. One of the incentives for Andy to sign, apart from Villa's more stable position in the league, was that 15% of the fee was paid to him direct.

Lloyd's Weekly Newspaper summed up why Villa had been so keen to secure Andy's services: 'Ducat is the sort of player that any club in the country would be proud to possess. His form of the last season was not so good as usual, but there must have been some extenuating circumstances which occasioned him to give so many displays that were worthy of merely an ordinary player. His great activity, his calmness of demeanour under the most exciting conditions, his cool-minded dash, and his almost perfect control of the ball, have been the admiration of the followers of the Arsenal club for eight seasons.'

A move north to Birmingham would mean that he would have to leave his family during the football season. In the 1911 Census, Andy was registered as living at 20 Drayton Road, Ealing, with several members of his family. At the time he was living with his parents as well as his aunt, Gertrude, who was classed as the head of the family, and another aunt, Edith. At the age of 26, it was time for Andy to move out. As a professional footballer and cricketer, he would have spent many nights away each year, but the move to Villa gave Andy the opportunity to make a new life.

Before that, he still had to negotiate the rest of his cricket obligations.

* * *

Surrey's next match was against the Australians, who had won their first Triangular Tournament Test against South Africa by an innings and 88 runs. Nine of the victorious tourists were named in a strong line-up. On an overcast day at The Oval, Surrey batted first and initially enjoyed a benign pitch. With Tom Hayward and Jack Hobbs out, Andy and Ernie Hayes played some positive shots before lunch.

On the resumption, batting started to look more difficult as the pitch dried out. Gerry Hazlitt benefited with five wickets, including bowling Andy for 21, as Surrey were bowled out for 190. As the light diminished at the end of the first day, Australia were subjected to some hostile fast bowling from Bill Hitch and Razor Smith.

Australia were lucky to lose just Charlie Kelleway and Warren Bardsley before rain ended play but day two turned out badly for them as the last eight wickets fell for 67. Surrey batted again and were led by Hobbs' imperious 76 and useful scores of 40 from Hayes and Edwin Myers. At 246/5, Surrey had a 327 lead, but Australia claimed the last five wickets for one run to make the game competitive.

Macartney's half-century was the only bright spot as the Australians lost wickets early on the final day. At 112/5, Claude Jennings returned to the crease after retiring hurt on the previous evening. He joined Dave Smith and both batsmen set about winning the match. A wonderful partnership of 176 deserved to win the match, but another collapse saw Surrey home by 21 runs.

Perhaps the impending move to Villa was the cause, or maybe just one of those periods that all batsmen go through, but Andy's form fell off a cliff. Against Lancashire, he scored 16 and 4 as well as being indirectly responsible for Morice Bird's run-out. At Leicester, he scored 5 and 29 not out: robbed of a chance to occupy the crease by a sporting declaration to try to win the match. Things did not improve against Sussex at Horsham, when scores of 0 and 5 did nothing to help Surrey in their 78-run victory. Rain prevented Andy from batting against Hampshire but he may have been saved from the ignominy of dealing with a rain-affected pitch which was getting treacherous. Against Kent, scores of 12 and 3 ratcheted up the pressure. His place in the XI was now precarious.

Surrey's next match was at Northampton and a rain-affected first day saw the visitors start well between interruptions. Then a calamitous collapse saw nine wickets fall for nine runs in just under 30 minutes. From 86/1, Surrey were bowled out for 95. Andy was the first of five ducks; the last thing that county and player required. From there, it was always going to be an arduous task to save the game without the help of rain. That did not materialise, but there was another failure at the crease. As Andy trudged off, trapped in front by medium-pacer Billy East for 5, he must have sensed his fate.

Left out of the team for the match against Lancashire, Andy returned to the Surrey Club and Ground team for their match at Kenley. If the idea were to get some time at the crease, that did not happen as he was bowled for 18. However, he did have a superb match with the ball, taking seven wickets. All of the dismissals were bowled.

While Andy was out of the team results did not improve. Defeats to Lancashire, by ten wickets, and Kent, by an innings and 76 runs, left the Surrey committee short of options in the batting department. Reginald Lagden made his debut but scored just three runs. He did not play for the county again. Ion Campbell was recalled, but to no significant effect.

Andy returned for the match against Leicestershire. With the sun shining down on The Oval for the second day after another wet opening day, Surrey's top order scored well before an all-too-familiar collapse spoiled the day. Andy's 30 accompanied half-centuries from Hayward and Goatly before seven wickets fell for 67. Gerry Campbell joined Lagden in the one county appearance, mustering a single run. Leicestershire easily passed Surrey's total, but more rain ended any prospect of play on the final day.

Next up were Worcestershire, who visited The Oval at the beginning of August. The wet weather continued to disrupt play, but it could not disturb Andy's return to form. The Worcestershire bowlers could not tempt Andy to play loosely, their off-theory tactics proving fruitless, as he set himself for a big score. Worcestershire had batted first and scored 315. In Surrey's reply, John Cuffe removed Jack Hobbs at the end of the day, but the second day belonged to Andy. A rain shower after lunch failed to liven the wicket, but Andy's hitherto watchful innings took on a new life.

His 124 was made in classic Andy style: punishing loose deliveries and working the ball to the on side to great effect. It helped Surrey to a first-innings lead of 86 early on day three. Although a draw was the most likely result, Bill Hitch and Tom Rushby picked up early wickets. When Ernie Hayes bowled a spell of 4-32, Worcestershire were in trouble. Surrey needed 89 to win and achieved their target in less than 16 overs.

The saying 'one swallow doesn't make a summer' was apt because Andy's century did not lead to further improvement with his batting. Against Nottinghamshire, he was out twice to slow left-armer William Riley for scores of 1 and 2. A duck followed against Middlesex but rain saved Surrey from defeat after being bowled out for 67.

In a crossover of his sporting life, Andy travelled up to Birmingham for a charity cricket match for Aston Villa. A benefit match for Billy George, who had retired the year previous after 403 games for the club, took place against Birmingham League cricket team Aston Unity. The team labelled as Aston Villa Football Club

Past and Present called upon Andy to play alongside some of his colleagues and some players from the past.

Included in the team was Jack Devey who was now a director of Aston Villa but had played 268 games before retiring in 1902. Presumably, he was included in the team because of his ability to apply bat to ball. In 1890, a National Baseball League of Great Britain was formed, and Aston Villa entered a team. Devey topped the batting averages at the end of the season.

Aston Unity batted first, and it was another new signing for Villa, Jimmy Harrop, who impressed with the ball. Harrop, who had joined the club from Liverpool, took 5-18 as the Birmingham League team were bowled out for 64. Andy opened for Villa and struck a quickfire 82 as the footballers batted on after passing the target. It was an entertaining innings with seven sixes and four fours. In one over, he scored 24 as he took a liking to the bowling.

Andy missed the next two County Championship matches before featuring one more time for the season at Lord's. It could have been a match that he might not have minded missing as 25 wickets fell on the first day. Batting first, Surrey went from 10/0 to 52 all out. Andy scored a relatively respectable 7, with just Ernie Hayes reaching double figures, as Surrey succumbed on a difficult batting surface.

Middlesex fared slightly better by posting 74 all out. Tom Rushby took 8-31 as the home team found batting no easier. By the end of the day's play, Surrey reached 127/5 in their second innings, but that was the end of the match as the rain returned to end Andy's damp squib of a season.

Surrey finished the season in seventh place, their worst finish since 1904, with Andy's batting average at 24.05. It was not a sufficient return for a player of his ability. Fortunately, any potential replacements were not taking their chances. It must have been a frustrating season to negotiate as rain and bad form blighted his performances. It would have been a goal for Andy to be more consistent when he next padded up for Surrey. What he would not have realised was how long that would eventually be.

* * *

Aston Villa's run up to the 1912/13 season had been about change. The club had been underperforming and the directors decided that a clear-out and acquisition programme was the correct course of action. The summer of 1912 saw Villa release ten players from their squad. At the AGM, chairman Frederick Rinder condemned unacceptable behaviour, 'We may have reasonably expected from certain players in the employment of this club a greater sense of manliness and loyalty than we received.'

The four main pieces of business conducted by Villa were the acquisitions of Andy, Jimmy Harrop and England goalkeeper Sam Hardy from Liverpool, and Harold Halse from Manchester United. At £1,200, Halse was even more expensive than Andy.

Such aggressive transfer tactics enthused the Villa faithful and resulted in a rush for season tickets. With the addition of such quality players to the likes of Harry Hampton, Joe Bache and Clem Stephenson, exciting times, as well as potential success, were expected. For Andy, it was an opportunity to play in a team that was not struggling. He would have been hopeful that England selection was again achievable.

In a pre-season friendly, Andy was soon at ease and put in an impressive performance in his new colours. Halse was also quick off the mark with a brace as the first game of the season, against Chelsea, was just around the corner.

The season started on Monday, 2 September, and over 20,000 spectators witnessed a solid 1-0 win. After five minutes, Stephenson scored the only goal of the game. Villa pushed for a second, but it did not happen. Hardy had to make one good save, but the new-look Villa were off and running.

On the Saturday, Bradford City were the visitors, and they too were caught out with an early goal. This time, it was Halse, notching his first league goal for Villa, who opened the scoring. Bache doubled the lead in the 11th minute and Bradford needed something to get them back in the game. Unfortunately for Andy, it would be him that gave them the opportunity. He tripped Archie Devine, who would go to Andy's old club Woolwich Arsenal for a club record fee 12 months later, to give away a penalty which was scored. It was not a disaster as Villa scored again in the second half to secure the points.

In a ragged game at Oldham Athletic, Andy was a shining light in a mediocre defensive team performance. Villa needed a late penalty to secure a 2-2 draw after Oldham had been afforded plenty of opportunities to extend their lead.

A trip to Hyde Road, to play unbeaten Manchester City, turned out to be a season-defining moment. More than 40,000 packed into the ground to see the home team, fresh from a Manchester derby win at Old Trafford, and were delighted to see George Wynn put his team ahead with a 30-yard blast that Hardy misjudged.

Both teams fought hard to get the next goal, and tempers started to fray. The referee spoke to both sides to try to cool things down. With 15 minutes to go, Manchester City's Sid Hoad was injured and had to leave the pitch. Players were not going to give an inch.

With five minutes remaining, Andy and Lot Jones collided when challenging for the ball and their legs tangled up. The result was a bone snapping in Andy's leg. The crowd were aware that the injury was of a serious nature when ambulance men rushed on to the pitch. Andy received attention before being carried off on a stretcher and taken to the local hospital for treatment. The game restarted after a 15-minute delay and ended in a subdued manner.

Andy was taken to Ancoats Hospital where he was assessed. It was found that he had a fracture to the fibula of his left leg. The bone is the smaller, and outer, one of the two, the other being the tibia, located between the knee and ankle. The prognosis was for the leg to be set in plaster of Paris to protect and immobilise before discharge from the hospital after six weeks. With Andy being single, and a professional sportsman, there was no rush to get out of the hospital.

Over the first few days, the leg was not set in plaster and caused him some discomfort. He was bedridden and only able to lie in one position. In an interview reproduced in the *Express & Star* newspaper, Andy talked frankly. 'I expect I shall be laid up here [Ancoats Hospital] for a week or two and all I want now is to get the limb in plaster of Paris so I can get out of bed,' he said. 'They are awfully good to me here and could do no more for me.'

Andy was quick to absolve Jones of any blame for his accident. He received many gifts, such as books and magazines, from well-wishers. Manchester United sent him a telegram of sympathy and support as news of the injury made its way into newspapers.

In another interview published in *Football News (Nottingham)*, Andy talked of his concern for his future. It is unsurprising that these worries would have dominated his thoughts. Both his livelihoods were at stake if the injury proved to be career-ending. Villa's management would have had similar misgivings. They were quick to make a donation to the hospital and Andy was treated on a private ward. He had plenty of visitors, which would have helped to stop the negative thoughts, including the chairman of Manchester City, who visited to enquire on his welfare and offer commiserations.

Three weeks after the incident, Andy's leg was taken out of plaster and a splint was applied. It was looking positive that the leg was healing, and that Andy would be kicking a ball early in the New Year. There was even discussion that he would be challenging for his place in the team before the season ended.

Just as hope for a quick recovery had begun, it disappeared when a complication was discovered. Leg muscle was preventing the fracture from fusing together and a second operation was required to remove the obstruction. In order to ensure that the bone healed correctly, a plate was inserted to hold the two parts together. Although the operation was successful, it would delay a return to football as well as putting his participation in the 1913 County Championship season for Surrey in jeopardy.

It is important to look at Andy's medical problems through the lens of health care in 1912. X-ray was a new and emerging technology at that point. Ancoats' X-ray department was five years old and the first one in the Manchester area. William Bynum, Professor Emeritus of the History of Medicine at University College London, commented on Andy's case from the materials available. 'It would appear to me that he received pretty standard care,' he said. 'That they missed the fact that his bone could not fuse is unfortunate, but of course imaging techniques were still basic then. Ankle involvement is notoriously complicated, and that could explain the long convalescent period without invoking substandard levels of care.'

Even though it was standard care, and the second operation had gone according to plan, it would do nothing to assuage the possibility of him not playing sport professionally again.

* * *

Up to Andy's injury, his private life did not feature in newspapers because, presumably, there was nothing to report. His time as an inpatient at Ancoats was attributed to being single and not needing to convalesce anywhere else. However, things were about to change. Andy met a woman.

The Holte Hotel was an integral part of the Aston Lower Grounds where Villa were based. Villa Park was part of a large area occupied by the club. If you have visited Villa Park, you may well have seen the impressive Victorian building that was renovated and reopened in 2007. In 1912, it was a place where Villa's players would meet.

The hotel was managed by 48-year-old Horace Barbour, a jovial character who was also involved in the many sports organisations that used the facilities for meetings. Barbour's family would have spent time around the hotel: his wife, Miriam, and his three children, Donald, Vera, and Joyce. It was 21-year-old Vera who would become more than friends with Andy. Perhaps it was not having to play, or travel and play, which made Andy re-evaluate his priorities as the relationship blossomed. With the benefit of hindsight, it was a perfect match for both of them, but in 1912/13 Andy found out that maybe there was more to life than football and cricket.

* * *

By April 1913, seven months after the injury, Andy was limping and needing a stick to walk. Any idea of playing cricket was already out of the question. The thoughts of it being a career-ending injury must have entered his mind regularly.

His Villa team-mates were having an excellent season and were fighting out the league title with Sunderland. The rivals also met in the FA Cup Final, which would have been a bittersweet day for Andy. He must have been pleased for the club that it had a chance for silverware, but desperate that he could not take his place on the pitch.

The final was a bad-tempered affair as animosity prevented the two best teams in England putting on a showpiece match. With 12 minutes left, and the game scoreless, Villa won a corner. Charlie Wallace, who earlier in the match became the first player to miss a penalty in a final, took the kick and Tommy Barber placed his header past Sunderland goalkeeper Joe Butler to score what would be the only goal of the game. Barber was playing in Andy's position at right-half. Sunderland went on to win the league by four points from Villa to end their hopes of the Double. Andy would have been saddened to see Woolwich Arsenal finally relegated as they finished bottom of the table.

The summer of 1913 came and went with Andy missing the entire season. Surrey finished third in the Championship with Jack Hobbs scoring 2,238 runs. By the time the football season started, Andy was close to returning to training. The question remained as to when the leg would be able to cope with the rigours of professional sport, and how long it would take for Andy to get to full fitness.

In November 1913, Andy authored an autobiographical article for the *Illustrated Police News* where he told of how his football career had come about. It also illustrated how frustrated he had become in being out of sport for 13 months.

He wrote, 'I broke my leg, and for more weary months than I care to look back upon I was debarred from following the two games I love, and by which I get my living, viz., football and cricket. I think I could deal out a lot of embroidery on the subject of enforced idleness and the pains and penalties attaching to broken legs, but although it might contain some Anglo Saxon terms, I am advised that the editor's blue pencil would render it valueless as a contribution. I do not want to hear, or see, or write about, or have any connection with broken legs again as long as I live.'

Understandably, Andy's frustration and need to return to sport was at the front of his mind. He still retained his sense of humour, but it was clear that he was desperate to get back on any kind of pitch. Later in the article, he intimated that the main focus was being ready for the cricket season. I suspect that the medical advice was to look to the long term. A season on the cricket field would help stress-test the fibula before being subjected to the physicality of league football. At the end of the football season, Andy made a few appearances for Villa's reserve team to help his fitness for the coming cricket season. He was able to get a full pre-season practice at The Oval, normally restricted by his football obligations, as well as playing in the annual Surrey trial match – 595 days after breaking his leg, Andy was ready to resume professional sport.

* * *

The return of Andy to the Surrey first XI was not the only change as the season began at The Oval. Cyril Wilkinson had taken over the captaincy from Morice Bird. More importantly, with the benefit of hindsight, was the inclusion of Percy Fender. Having played for Sussex since 1910, Fender's legal career had caused him to move to London and his eligibility for Surrey by birth meant that he could keep playing first-class cricket.

Northamptonshire were the visitors for the opening match, and it was their captain, also new to the role, Sydney Smith who made more of an impact. The Trinidad-born player, who also represented his island of birth, posted scores of 66 and 72 not out as well as taking 3-58. Surrey easily came out of the game with a draw. Andy's 36 not out helped settle nerves for both county and player as to his fitness and technique after nearly two years away from the game.

In the next match against Somerset, Andy scored more confidence-building runs. Before that, Fender made his first significant contribution by getting a hat-trick to end the visitors' first innings. With a 127-run first-innings lead, Surrey were in the driving seat. However, their batsmen seemed reticent until Andy joined Ernie Hayes. The pair scored 135 runs in an hour to set up a declaration. The bowlers then did their bit and Somerset were powerless to stop the slide to a 241-run defeat.

In their third successive home fixture, a sad occasion overshadowed the first day of play. The visitors were Worcestershire, and each player wore a black armband in honour of Tip Foster, whose funeral was being held in Malvern. He was a diabetes sufferer and had died at 36. Foster had played for the county from 1899 to 1912, but ill health had forced him out of the game. He was another dual international, who had captained both cricket and football teams.

On the field, Worcestershire batted first and were going well either side of a lunch break that was extended so that play was not taking place during Foster's funeral. Alfred Cliff was set on 57, as part of a 94-run partnership, when he hit the ball in the air down the ground. Andy was the nearest fielder and came running in to take the catch low to the ground. Cliff was gone and the athletic fielder of old was back.

Day two saw things get better for Andy as he scored his first century since August 1912. As fate would have it, Worcestershire had been the opponents then too. The innings started slowly before Andy got the measure of the bowling. He was joined by Bill Hitch, and the pair scored at will. In a 50-minute period, they added 96 to put Surrey in a winning position. The bowlers did their job efficiently to deliver another comprehensive victory.

A trip to Bath, famous for its spas, was anything but curative for batsmen. The picturesque Recreation Ground hosted Somerset and Surrey and with 28 wickets falling on the first day, the match was destined to not last long into the second. Somerset batted first, and lasted 32.2 overs for their 77. Surrey managed eight balls more and eked out a 27-run lead, Billy Abel's contribution of 34 proving vital.

Hitch and Tom Rushby then tore through Somerset for a second time, leaving them on 51/7 before a late afternoon rally took the match into a second day. Finally all out for 108, Somerset left Surrey with a target of 81. Knowing it was anything but a formality, Somerset's 'Farmer' Jack White tried to snatch an unlikely victory for his team. The slow left-armer took five wickets, including Andy for 2, and held on to a catch before Bird and Wilkinson guided Surrey home.

Surrey's unbeaten start to the season continued with a 28-run win over Yorkshire at Bradford. Jack Hobbs' excellent start to the season continued with another century followed by 74 vital runs in the second innings, while Yorkshire fell short in their chase. The game would not have lasted so long, but for an 82-run ninth-wicket partnership between George Hirst and Thomas Birtles in the second innings.

At The Oval, Warwickshire were put to the sword as Surrey registered another comprehensive victory. In response to Warwickshire's 226, Hobbs hit a brilliant 183. Making 50, Andy accompanied Hobbs for the back end of his innings before Fender came to the crease. At that point, the ball started flying to all parts of the ground. In his innings of 140, Fender struck 25 fours and a six. Surrey were intent on batting only once and they did not need anywhere near their lead of 315 as Warwickshire folded meekly. Bobby Abel took 5-38 and Fender picked up 4-21 as the visitors crumbled to 118.

June started with a visit to Trent Bridge. A win at Nottinghamshire's home ground had been elusive for Surrey since 1906. That did not look like changing when they struggled after being put into bat. Had it not been for Fender's invaluable 88, Surrey would have been in trouble. In reply, Nottinghamshire were able to pass Surrey's total, but only by 34. In Surrey's second innings, normality was resumed when Hobbs and Hayward put on 84 for the first wicket. Andy produced an innings in which *The Guardian* described his off-side play as 'brilliant'. He converted a solid start into his second century of the season. It was also just his second first-class century away from The Oval. Here were signs that Andy could go on to score the runs that his talent demanded. The match ended in a draw, but Surrey were starting to mount a challenge for the County Championship.

Despite a first loss, at home to Essex by 323 runs, they soon got back on to the winning trail with victory away to Leicestershire. Revenge for the home defeat was soon achieved when Surrey beat Essex at Leyton. It was interesting to see Wilkinson use himself and Herbert Strudwick as nightwatchmen openers at the end of day one when Essex were bowled out for 309 just before the close. Batting at No.3, Hobbs' 215 was majestic before Hitch and Rushby bowled Surrey into a position to win. Andy (33 not out) and Edward Goatly (26 not out) ensured the victory by seven wickets. It would be 39-year-old Goatly's final first-class appearance as a Surrey player.

Hampshire visited The Oval in mid-June and a reasonable start soon turned sour. C.B. Fry and Alex Bowell reached 33 before Tom Rushby and Bill Hitch made inroads into the visitors' batting line-up. Had it not been for a century from Edward Sprot, Hampshire's total would have been considerably less than the 239 they achieved.

Going into the second day, Hobbs had already scored 40 of Surrey's 53. The opener, enjoying a golden season, batted the Hampshire bowlers into submission. Ernie Hayes played an accompanying role as did Andy as both batsmen reached half-centuries. Andy's athleticism was on show as he scored an all-run seven, and a six, as Hampshire's fielders tired. By the close of play, Surrey were 139 ahead with three wickets in hand.

Before the final day began, Andy reached another milestone. Prior to the start of play on the Saturday morning, he had an appearance at the church of St Stephen in Hounslow for his wedding to Vera. The service appears to be a family affair with both fathers witnessing the marriage certificate.

Details of the wedding were published on the day in many newspapers. The *Evening Despatch* described the nuptials as being 'of the quietest possible nature'. It gave details of the honeymoon taking place in Chelmsford as well as the couple taking 'permanent residence' in Erdington, Birmingham.

As soon as the wedding service was over, and the marriage certificate signed, Andy made his way to The Oval. Surrey scored 25 more runs to reach 403 all out. They took to the field with a lead and another win within their grasp. Before they set about their task, they threw confetti over Andy as he set foot on the outfield. Hampshire safely negotiated the final day, but it was still one to remember for Andy.

After a few days' honeymoon, he was back in action the following Saturday as Middlesex visited The Oval. It was a gloriously sunny day with the prospect of an excellent batting track. A rare failure from Hobbs, dismissed for 4, was a false dawn for Middlesex as the Surrey batsmen scored with impunity. Half-centuries from Hayes and Harrison set a foundation, and Andy made full use of the conditions and state of the match. His 102 was only beaten by his captain. Cyril Wilkinson hammered his maiden first-class century in two hours as Middlesex tired on a long, exhausting, hot day.

A mediocre Middlesex first innings was boosted by Jack Hearne's second-innings 191. Andy picked up the wicket of Leslie Kidd, but Middlesex easily saved the match. During Middlesex's batting, the spectators would have been discussing the events in Sarajevo where Archduke Ferdinand of Austria and his wife were assassinated. Little did they know how events in Europe would spiral out of control from that point.

Rain in Northampton ruined Surrey's next game before they visited Old Trafford. Albert Hornby won the toss for Lancashire but lost his team the game. When batting would have been the sensible option, he decided that fielding first would give him the best chance to force a win due to a predicted change in weather. The change did not come.

Hayward and Hobbs put on 131 for the first wicket before Andy and Ernie Hayes piled on 181 for the fourth. The match was Bill Huddleston's benefit game, and he took six wickets, but he had to bowl 50 overs to get them. Lancashire's batting was not up to chasing 393 and they fell to an innings-and-two-run defeat.

After an almost two-week gap, Surrey's next opponents were Lancashire again. It was a different time and place, but the result was never in doubt. Hobbs made 142, with several cameos including Andy's 44. After posting 402 on day one, Surrey's bowlers were intent on finishing the game inside two days. After just 30.1 overs, Lancashire's openers were walking back out to bat for a second time. It took only another 27.4 overs to finish the match as Lancashire capitulated. The only thing of note from a Lancashire perspective was that it marked the last appearance for the county of Archie MacLaren. Having made his debut in 1890, MacLaren had captained both county and country in an auspicious career.

Andy's summer continued to be impressive when he hit his fourth century of the season against Hampshire at Portsmouth. *The Times* described his innings as 'one of the finest he has ever played'. His first false stroke resulted in his dismissal. Before that he played flawlessly to score 108 in three hours. Surrey won by eight wickets with Percy Fender being equally effective with bat and ball: eight wickets and 60 runs.

A tight win against Sussex was followed up with a draw against Kent which led into the August Bank Holiday fixture at The Oval. While Surrey entertained Nottinghamshire, German forces invaded Belgium and Britain's ultimatum was about to be ignored. More than 14,000 spectators came to see Surrey rack up almost 500 runs in a day. Another Hobbs masterclass set the tone: he hit 226, his eighth hundred of the season and at that point the highest score of his career. Andy scored 76 not out, and passed 1,000 runs for the season, as Surrey made 472/5.

Day two proved uneventful on the pitch, with Nottinghamshire picking up the last five wickets for 70 before batting their way to 283/6. Off the pitch, Britain declared war on Germany which began the First World War. Play was prevented by rain on day three. It would turn out to be the final first-class game at The Oval for almost five years as the war didn't turn out to be over by Christmas.

Cricket became increasingly difficult to play as August wore on. Players across the country received their call-ups for military duty. The Oval was requisitioned for military purposes. There was an increasing amount of pressure for professional cricket and other sports to cease.

Surrey continued their fixture list as the County Championship carried on and travelled to Worcester. Rain ensured that the match would be a draw while Andy maintained his form with scores of 24 and 34 not out. With The Oval out of use, Surrey's next two matches, against Kent and Yorkshire, were moved to Lord's.

The game against Kent was Jack Hobbs' benefit, but the occasion was affected by the circumstances. Around 7,000 people turned up on the first day and they saw Kent quickly slump to 11/4 as Bill Hitch did the main damage. Frank Woolley and Sam Day scored half-centuries, but Kent were bowled out for 140. By the end of the first day, Surrey passed the total for the loss of three wickets as Tom Hayward and Andy shared a century stand.

Day two started much better for Kent as Colin Blythe attempted to turn the match around. His haul of 9-97 limited Surrey to 234. However, Bill Hitch was the destroyer as Kent scored 140 again. Surrey knocked off the target in 13.3 overs, for the loss of two wickets, to secure the win inside two days.

Yorkshire managed to take the game into a third day but were beaten more emphatically. Surrey batted first and ensured that they would bat once only. An opening partnership of 290 between Hayward and Hobbs set the innings up. Hobbs went on to his double century, during which he passed 2,000 County Championship runs for the season as well as 25,000 first-class runs in his career. Hayward scored 116 and Hayes 134 as Surrey relentlessly batted into day two. They finally declared with the score of 549/6, with Andy left on 34 not out, and now aimed to bowl Yorkshire out twice. Another five-for from Hitch made sure that Yorkshire were batting again before the end of the second day. They made a better job of their second innings, Ben Wilson's 95 being the highlight, but they were beaten by an innings and 30 runs.

A trip to Cheltenham was short and sweet as Gloucestershire were beaten in two days. Andy's innings of 74 was the top score in the match as Surrey's bowlers once again proved irresistible. Middlesex proved tougher opposition and tried to force a win with a sporting declaration, but the game was drawn. Andy's final appearance of the season was in a surprise defeat at Warwickshire. The impact of the war could be seen when Warwickshire's Colin Langley missed part of the match; he was a private in the Honourable Artillery Company and had been called up for duty.

Surrey played one more match, an innings win over Gloucestershire, who could only muster ten men, before the season was halted. Surrey had topped the table, comfortably above second-placed Middlesex, but it took another two months before their County Championship victory was ratified. The MCC overruled calls to nullify the season and Surrey received their first title since 1899.

Andy finished ninth in the first-class averages, with 1,370 runs at 42.08, which would have been a psychological fillip. After his enforced absence from cricket, he had found the one thing missing: consistency. Heading for the football season, he was leaving a sport that would have an enforced absence for much longer.

CHAPTER SEVEN

For King and Country
1914–1919

ASTON VILLA'S season started at home to Notts County, but Andy was not in the line-up. Instead, he was getting match fitness for the reserves. Matches against Wednesbury Old Athletic and Dudley gave Andy valuable time on the pitch. Having proved his fitness over the summer, Villa's management were waiting for the opportune moment to reintroduce Andy.

After four matches, including a local derby against West Bromwich Albion, Villa had several injury concerns, including Harry Hampton and Charlie Wallace. It was decided that Andy's comeback would be at Goodison Park against Everton. He led the team out, as captain, to mark his first league game in two years. There appeared to be no signs of rustiness; the *Birmingham Daily Post* commented that Andy was 'as capable as ever'. The match itself was a goalless draw, but for Andy it was the last step back into a life interrupted. The following week saw Chelsea visit Villa Park, which resulted in a 2-1 victory for the home side.

Villa's visit to Bradford City provided a stark reminder that a war was being fought. At half-time, the crowd was addressed by F. Vernon Harcourt of the National Service League (NSL). The NSL had been set up in 1902 as a pressure group to make military training compulsory but suspended its activities at the outbreak of war. At Valley Parade, the purpose of the address was to encourage potential recruits to sign up for the war effort. The match saw a second-half hat-trick from Oscar Fox win the match for the home side 3-0.

The next game was at home to Burnley, and it gave the crowd an exciting, if not high on quality, 3-3 draw. Villa showed resilience after falling 2-0 and 3-1 behind. Andy scored his first league goal since April 1912 when Villa won a penalty. It was Tommy Barber, Andy's cover at right-half, who saved the game with two goals in a minute to complete an unlikely comeback.

An injury to Tom Lyons required Andy to fill in at the back for Newcastle United's visit to Villa Park. It was a gloomy day in Birmingham with a wet pitch to deal with, but Andy was up to the task. He made a key interception in the first half to help Villa to a 2-1 win. Newcastle held the lead at half-time, but a tactical change, moving Harold Edgley to the left wing and Charlie Wallace into the middle, had the desired effect.

Up at Middlesbrough, Andy was called into more defensive action despite reverting to his preferred position. Dick Wynn was a young outside-left for the home team and it took time for Andy to get his measure.

The season was proving to be anything but mundane for Andy, and Villa's game at home to Sheffield United was particularly action-packed. The match was of poor quality, but Villa won a first-half penalty. Andy stepped up to take it but his shot hit the post. He made amends in the second half with a strike from 25 yards. A scrimmage of players occurred on the edge of Sheffield United's penalty area and the ball came out to Andy. The crowd, sensing the opportunity, were baying for a strike on goal. Andy obliged and the ball flew over the melee and dipped under the crossbar. It was the only goal of the game.

Later in November, Villa were involved in a ridiculous scoreline at Anfield. Liverpool had a match to forget while Villa seized their opportunities. Within two minutes, Clem Stephenson took advantage of a mistake at the back to score for Villa. Within four minutes, Liverpool's back line erred again, and Harry Hampton benefited. By half-time, the score read 5-1 to Villa. Liverpool came out in the second half with more invention and closed the gap to 6-3. There was still time for Liverpool to miss a penalty as Robert Crawford failed with a spot kick.

Pressure was increasing on the Football Association, and every player still turning out for their clubs, to abandon the season and take up arms. At the beginning of December, *Reynolds News* reproduced a letter sent from Villa's chairman, Frederick Rinder, to each player:

> In handing you the enclosed circulars from the Football Association and the Voluntary Recruiting League, I and my fellow directors desire to particularly emphasise the call for men therein made, and to remind you of Lord Kitchener's appeal for 'men, and yet more men.' We ask you to let your thoughts dwell for a moment upon the terrible devastation and destruction wrought by the cruel Germans in Belgium and northern France, and to try and picture the sufferings to those thousands of innocent men, women, and little helpless children. If the Germans are victorious then our own beloved country will surely be invaded, our towns and our homes will be destroyed, and our kindred and children will have to endure far worse horrors than have even fallen to the lot of French and Belgians. Let every man ask himself that question. Does my country need my help? Ought I to be serving with colours? And let each one answer as his conscience dictates. For our part we repeat what we said to you in the early part of the season, that in our opinion the best means of helping the country is by joining the colours, and we again promise to pay half the wages of any players who care to enlist.

As the letter was circulated, the First Battle of Ypres had just ended. According to Allan Mallinson's *Fight to the Finish*, the casualty list stood at 86,237. The horrors had just begun, but the idea that the war might be over by Christmas was still being perpetuated. The letter was deliberately emotive yet many men, like Andy, did not take up the call. One can only speculate as to why they did not.

Back on the football field, Bradford Park Avenue made their first trip to Villa Park. The club was formed in 1907 and had won promotion from the Second Division, as runners-up to Notts County, the previous season. A blustery day in Birmingham greeted the Bradford team and they were up against it physically and figuratively in the first half. However, they withstood the storm. Early in the second half, Clem Stephenson headed Villa in front. If the home faithful expected the goals to rain in, it did not happen. In fact, Bradford got back on level terms when Sam Hardy failed to hold on to a shot and it carried on over the line. Sensing an unlikely victory, Bradford pushed on and Tommy Little secured a famous victory five minutes from time.

Bouncing back from defeat, Villa's next two games were both exciting 3-3 draws. The first was against the leaders, Oldham Athletic. Villa came close to losing to Oldham for the first time but Hampton's late equaliser made sure that the points were shared. Manchester United's visit the following week ended in the same score despite an inferior defensive performance from Villa. This time, Hampton scored his seventh and eighth goals of the season to secure a point. In both games, Andy was in majestic form in attacking and defensive play. The *Birmingham Daily Post* commented on his 'unremitting perseverance' as well as being 'easily the most accomplished player on the pitch' against United.

Christmas 1914 proved to be an ultimately frustrating one for Villa and for Andy. Christmas Day was spent at Ewood Park where Villa came back with a 2-1 win. Apart from the strangeness of the festive period taking place under the shadow of war, a death on Christmas Eve further darkened the mood of the 18,000 in attendance. Blackburn's Bob Crompton, who played with Andy in two of his three England games in 1910, lost his father but agreed to play due to a lack of available players. The match was won by a hotly disputed goal.

Boxing Day was an unmitigated disaster as Villa, including Andy, were abysmal. Entertaining Bolton Wanderers, Villa were thrashed 7-1. Bolton's wingers were rampaging down both wings and Andy, moved back to full-back because Lyons was injured, could not cope. Furthermore, Hardy had his worst performance in goal for Villa to exacerbate the one-sidedness of the contest.

During the match, Andy took a kick to the leg. He was able to play on, but it would cause him to miss a few matches. He returned for the FA Cup first-round game against Exeter City, but he then hurt himself in training and missed the home match against The Wednesday. Andy had cut his left hand and required stitches, so was left out as a precaution.

While matters on the pitch were not going well, a piece of PR from Villa tried to help the war effort as well as take away some of the pressure from the players not signed up for military service. Both the *Birmingham Mail* and *Birmingham Daily Gazette* ran the story, including photographs, of Villa's players and staff taking shooting practice at Kingsbury rifle range.

The players caught the train to Kingsbury and then marched to the range carrying Lee Enfield rifles on their shoulders before firing at targets. The article stated that Villa had set up a defence corps, a forerunner to the Home Guard movement during the Second World War and had been providing military training for the players. Colour Sergeant Fox of the Staffordshire Regiment had been tasked to drill the players on the use of rifles. Andy joked that one of his shots had been so poor it had landed in Shropshire.

Back on the pitch, Villa's form continued to slide. Defeat in the derby at West Bromwich Albion was followed by one in the FA Cup at Manchester City. It was the first time that Andy had faced Lot Jones since the accident in which he had broken his leg. The next two games saw Andy on the sidelines again, but this time rested, as Chelsea then Everton beat Villa.

Villa would have to wait until the end of February for their next win. Tottenham Hotspur were beaten 3-1 at Villa Park, their first win in the league since Christmas Day. Middlesbrough were then beaten 5-0 before Andy's recent proclivity for injuries reoccurred. This time it was a side strain and it kept him out for one game.

Fit for the busy Easter period, Andy was instrumental in the winning goal against Blackburn. With the score at 1-1 and time running out, he won the ball out on the touchline and played it to Hampton who, in turn, found Clem Stephenson, who crashed a half-volley home from 15 yards. On the same Good Friday, Manchester United and Liverpool played a match where the home side won to avoid relegation. Eventually, it would be found that a large amount of money had been placed on that scoreline and seven players were banned for life.

Liverpool were welcomed to Villa Park on Easter Saturday and the two teams conspired to produce a match almost as crazy as the reverse fixture at Anfield earlier in the season. Villa selected 22-year-old Harry Nash for his debut and he scored a hat-trick. Hampton also scored three as Liverpool were routed 6-2.

Easter Monday was a more sedate affair with a 1-1 draw at Notts County. In goal for the home side was Albert Iremonger, an ex-county cricketer and brother of Nottinghamshire's James.

Andy's final significant contribution of the season was a penalty at Bradford Park Avenue. His final home game was a resounding 4-1 win over Manchester City. However, he was injured early in the game. He left the pitch for ten minutes while getting attention before returning to see out the match. However, the injury would be enough to rule him out of the last two games. Both were defeats but the futility of the competition, in light of events in Europe, meant that finishing in 14th place was not as disappointing as it would have been in normal times. The Football Association called a halt to professional football. The sport did not disappear from British life, it just changed how it was presented.

* * *

A dark day for Andy and Vera came on 4 December 1915. Horace Barbour, Vera's father, died suddenly at the Holte Hotel. Barbour had managed the hotel for 11 years and was popular among customers. He was connected to many different sporting organisations in the area. He was a keen cyclist and was president of the Ivy Cycle Club. Also, he was a founder of the Birmingham Gymnastics Association and president of the Aston Boxing Club. The funeral took place several days later, with the procession travelling between the Holte Hotel and Handsworth parish church.

Barbour had been a tall, affable character who would be missed by all who had known him. His connection to Villa had gone back to his youth when he had played centre-forward for the reserve team until a double fracture of the leg had prevented any possibility of a football career.

Over the next few months after Barbour's death Andy took on some of the roles he vacated. The *Star Green 'Un* announced that Andy had been 'chosen to succeed his father-in-law, the late Mr Horace Barbour, as manager of the various enterprises connected with the Aston Lower Grounds company'. The article also considered Andy's new connection to Warwickshire CCC, due to his appointment and residing in the county, but this was no more than idle conjecture. The *Sports Argus* announced that Andy had been elected president of the Ivy Cycling Club.

On 10 December, Andy visited recruiting office No.3 in Suffolk Street in the centre of Birmingham and completed his attestation papers to join the Army Reserve. The papers have survived unlike many others that were destroyed during the Second World War. Included in the documents are several items compiled over Andy's service. They give an insight into physical attributes, such as height 5ft 8½in and chest measurement 37½in.

Andy's war effort had started in a munitions factory. Alongside his Villa team-mate, Freddy Miles, Andy spent time in a factory making ammunition such as shells to be used by the artillery. It would have been a useful introduction because when Andy was finally called up to the army in May 1916, he was posted to the Royal Garrison Artillery (RGA). The RGA was responsible for heavy artillery, at the front and at home.

Andy's original posting as a gunner was to 2/8 Company of Hampshire RGA, which was responsible for coastal defences on the eastern side of the country. Within six months, Andy was transferred to 31AA Company which was the Heavy Battery Brigade at Woolwich. The *Star Green 'Un* reported that Andy's commanding officer said that 'there is not a smarter man at a gun in my command'. Having impressed, Andy was promoted to Company Quartermaster Sergeant (CQMS) in June 1917. The CQMS was the second-highest ranked non-commissioned officer in the company, so it came with much responsibility. Andy would have had charge of the stores for the company.

Although Andy was incredibly fit, his war record shows that he did have some problems with his old leg injury. After a medical examination, it was noted that he had 'an old fracture with a plate has caused pain and discomfort'. However, it was not of sufficient severity to stop him serving or to stop him playing in a large number of sporting engagements throughout the war. As the *Star Green 'Un* explained in 1917, Andy was 'always ready for a game of cricket or football and will turn out for anyone if it will oblige them'.

* * *

Although professional football was suspended in 1915, the game was very much alive and played regularly. Andy was one of many sportsmen who balanced their military duty with regular football matches. While Aston Villa had closed down for the duration of the war, Arsenal played regular matches and were more than happy to have Andy back in their colours.

In 1916, England and West Bromwich Albion defender Jesse Pennington captained an England XI, including Andy, in a benefit match made of Midlands-based players. A few weeks later, he joined

Pennington in another benefit match in Birmingham to raise funds for the Soldiers' Tobacco and Cigarette Fund.

One of the more interesting matches that Andy was involved in was his appearance in 1916 for the Black Country factory team Belliss and Morcom. The factory was helping the war effort, like many engineering firms across the country, and a match was arranged against the Footballers' Battalion.

The battalion was originally made up of the 17th Middlesex Regiment which was created in response to a call for footballers to sign up for the war effort. With so many players answering the call, a second football battalion was created: the 23rd Middlesex Regiment. These two regiments are the best-known of the Footballers' Battalions. However, there was a third (the 27th Middlesex) which acted as a backup to the main battalions.

Belliss and Morcom boasted players like Andy as well as Villa colleague Harry Hampton. It was a close-fought game and ended as a 1-1 draw. Andy scored with a 'splendid shot', according to local newspaper the *Smethwick Telephone*, before the Footballers' Battalion equalised. Oscar Linkson, who had played 55 times for Manchester United, was the standout player for the battalion. A few months later, Linkson was transferred to the 17th Regiment and fought in the Somme offensive. During a battle to seize a strategic point at Guillemont, Linkson went missing and his body was never found.

The Football League reappeared as a regional competition from 1915/16 and Andy was made available for Aston Villa's cross-city rivals, Birmingham City in 1916/17. There was controversy around the cost of entry to matches. The British government had raised taxes, via the *Finance (New Duties) Act in 1916*, on entertainment and going to football cost more as a result. The *Evening Despatch* explained it: 'Visitors to the sixpenny side at St Andrew's will be asked to pay sevenpence, the additional penny going to the National Exchequer for war purposes, a contribution football patrons will not grudge.'

* * *

Andy played cricket in the summers during the war and featured regularly for Aston Unity. The club was a founder member of the Birmingham and District Cricket League, which had been suspended, and played matches against other league members as well as facing composite teams such as Syd Santall's XI. Former Warwickshire player Santall engaged professionals such as Willie Quaife. In one such match, raising funds for St Dunstan's Home for Blinded Soldiers, Andy struck a magnificent century in front of a big crowd. The match produced more than 800 runs and didn't finish until 8pm.

With the Australian Imperial Force having many troops in England, it was natural that they would get involved in cricket. Andy featured in a match against an Australian team in 1917. Played at Edgbaston, the Australian team was captained by Test player Charlie Kelleway. Having already taken two wickets, including bowling Andy for 2, Kelleway then achieved a hat-trick during his 5-25 performance.

* * *

November 1917 saw the visit of the 'Front Wanderers' to play matches in England and Scotland. They were a group of Belgian soldiers who had been asked to play fundraising matches. The proceeds went to the British Gifts for Belgian Soldiers fund.

The Front Wanderers played matches at Stamford Bridge, Parkhead, Goodison Park, Old Trafford and Villa Park. The tour started badly with a 4-1 defeat before a 2-1 win in Scotland. Another 2-1 win followed on a misty day in Liverpool before they lost the day after as rain made visibility equally bad in Manchester.

The final official game was held at Villa Park and George Ramsay was asked to pull together a British Army team to face the Belgians. Ramsay talked up the match by saying that 'the teams will be composed mainly of international players', according to the *Birmingham Daily Gazette*, and named a raft of British stars to entice spectators.

Whether it was bravado, or based on promises, Ramsay's declaration proved to be false. Andy, reliable as ever, took his place in the team. Villa colleagues Harry Hampton, who was clearly unfit, and Tommy Weston obliged but Ramsay's team was severely lacking in quality despite his assurances.

The Belgians, on the other hand, boasted several internationals. Up front was Louis van Hege, who had been a prolific goalscorer for AC Milan before the war. Nicknamed 'pallido saettante' meaning 'white lightning', he had scored 97 goals in 91 games in Italy. Defender Oscar Verbeeck was a Belgian international, who had attracted interest from Chelsea and Blackburn Rovers. Two more Belgian internationals were right-winger Hector Goetinck of Club Brugge and Jan van Cant, who had ten caps and had scored seven goals, including a hat-trick.

On the day of the match, the British Army team welcomed Burnley's Teddy Hodgson into the team, but the mismatch was obvious. Around 7,000 spectators were at Villa Park. Before they had even settled down after the kick-off, the Belgians scored. The British Army goalkeeper Gunner Jenner, of the Machine Gun Corps, proved very quickly that he was not up to the task. The *Birmingham Daily Post* described Jenner as 'inexplicably weak'.

The Belgians went 4-0 up before the British Army could even organise themselves. Each attack seemed to lead to a chance as Weston tried to cover the weaknesses in defence. Andy did his best to defend and link up the play with the forwards. However, a combination of sharpness from the opposition and a lack of quality in the British ranks meant the result was never in doubt. In the second half, the Belgians scored two more goals while Gunner Slader of the Royal Garrison Artillery managed a consolation. The match ended 6-1. In the 1920 Olympic football tournament, Belgium would win the gold medal with many of the Front Wanderers playing.

* * *

On 19 January 1918, Vera gave birth to a daughter. Daphne Joyce Ducat was born at the Holte Hotel and was baptised a month later at a local church in Aston. Daphne would be Andy and Vera's only child.

* * *

The London Football Combination was the capital's regional football competition and Andy appeared regularly throughout the war. In the last season, Andy scored for Arsenal against Chelsea and was cheered on in the crowd by old cricketing friends Jack Hobbs and Wally Hardinge.

With the war over, life started to return to something like normal. It couldn't ever be the same after the First World War, with so many lives lost, but everyone had to try. Andy was demobilised in March 1919, and was free to return to professional sport.

CHAPTER EIGHT

One Cup ...
1919–20

THE NUMBER 275 is not a cricket total, but the number of first-class cricketers killed in the First World War according to Nigel McCrery's *Final Wicket: Test and First-Class Cricketers Killed in the Great War*. The game of cricket, like the world, would not be the same as it had been in 1914. As soon as the war ended in November 1918, there were hasty arrangements to bring county cricket back in the summer of 1919. By February, the decision was made to reduce games to two days rather than three. Also, there was a loosening of qualification rules so that any soldiers who had served for a county regiment could play cricket for that county. However, the bureaucratic pen had not been blunted too much by four years of war: qualification based on military service only applied if the soldier had not played for another county previously.

Andy's first post-war appearance for Surrey came at the end of May against the Australian Imperial Forces (AIF) XI at The Oval. It had been decided that a team of Australian servicemen who had fought on the battlefields in Europe would tour the UK in 1919. Trials were held after applications were sought, and the AIF squad started to take shape despite some players carrying injuries from the war.

The AIF was captained by Charlie Kelleway and he opened with Herbie Collins of New South Wales. Surrey made an excellent start to leave the visitors on 3/3. Carl Willis and William Stirling helped to turn the position around, and the AIF were all out for 230. Surrey's response was all about Jack Hobbs, who batted as if he hadn't missed years of first-class cricket. He carried his bat with 205 not out, but the rest of Surrey's batsmen failed to support him. Andy was next highest scorer, with 38, but he fell to a slower ball from Albert Lampard with Kelleway gratefully taking the catch at cover point. Thanks to Hobbs, Surrey had a lead of 114.

AIF's second innings proved to be far more successful. Nip Pellew retired hurt on 106 and Lampard struck 112 before the Australians declared on 554/7. Surrey could not win the game, but they could lose it. Losing Hobbs for 7, then Andy for 12, it looked like they might get defeated, but Henry Harrison and Tom Abel steadied the ship for a draw.

Andy's first County Championship outing came the following week at The Oval against Warwickshire. In the first innings, he had scored 31 before fast bowler Harry Howell beat him for pace with a beautiful delivery that struck the top of the stumps. At the end of day one, both teams had been bowled out and Surrey had a 41-run lead. The following morning saw Warwickshire lose wickets regularly. Cecil Hands hit 36 in 55 minutes at No.11 to hold up Surrey, but partner Len Bates was last man out. Needing 193 to win, Surrey's victory charge was led by Hobbs. A 54-run partnership with Andy Sandham set them on their way. Andy batted at No.3 and put on 113 with Hobbs. Both fell before the target was achieved, but Surrey won the match.

At Trent Bridge, the difficulty of winning matches inside two days on decent batting tracks was demonstrated. George Gunn hit 169 and 185 not out as Nottinghamshire scored 390/7 declared and 338/1. Surrey's 355 in 123.5 overs made sure that the match would constitute batting practice.

At home to Hampshire, Surrey demonstrated how to lose a match in an afternoon. With a lead of two on the first innings, they were bowled out for just 126 in two hours as Alex Kennedy's 7-47 set up the win. Kennedy had proved handy with the bat in the first innings, scoring 48, before Andy took a smart catch on the boundary to remove him.

Another home match saw a severely weakened Sussex team thrashed. Andy was the chief destroyer with a marvellous 190. The bowling was not quite top notch and Andy took full advantage. Sussex had been bowled out for 115 but struck straight away to remove Hobbs. Andy joined Andy Sandham and the runs flowed. They shared a 160-run partnership then Andy and Harry Harrison added 102. When Andy was finally out, he had added another 120 with Alan Peach. There was still time for Cyril Wilkinson and Tom Abel to thrash a century partnership before Surrey declared on 532/6. Sussex made a better fight of the second innings, but still lost by an innings and 189 runs.

In the return fixture against Warwickshire, Surrey managed to hold on for a draw in a low-scoring match. The rain that ended the first day early robbed Warwickshire of valuable overs at the end of the match. Andy had a good game with scores of 40, put down twice in the slips, and 27. Needing 176 to win, Surrey were relieved when stumps were called at 90/6. Frank Field's spell of 5-45 shifted the momentum of the game, but time ran out.

June brought Varsity matches at The Oval, with both Oxford and Cambridge Universities opposing Surrey. In the first match, Cambridge batted first and were thankful for Gerard Rotherham's 72 as they were bowled out for 203. In reply, Surrey lost both Sandham and Hobbs early. Andy consolidated the innings with a patient 56, but Surrey were also grateful for middle order runs. Cyril Wilkinson scored 72 and Frederick Newman hit a half-century on debut to earn a 58-run lead. Cambridge's second innings was played at a higher tempo, almost five runs per over, as they positioned themselves for a declaration. That came at 227/6 and then Surrey almost lost the match chasing the total. Requiring 170 in about 70 minutes, Surrey scored at more than six runs per over but lost wickets regularly. Andy opened with Hobbs and struck two fours and a six before getting out. Hobbs managed to run himself out. Bill Hitch thrashed 55 before falling. With 14 runs to get and five wickets in hand, Australian Gordon Fairbairn picked up three quick wickets. With both sides close to victory, time ran out and the match was drawn.

A week later, Oxford were the visitors. It was a match that Andy would remember for the rest of his life. He punished Oxford's toiling bowlers with an all-round hitting display. In one over, Andy hit Vyvyan Pearse for 25. The South African, who had represented Natal, was hit for five fours and a five. It was a relentless display; Andy gave one chance, at 87, but it was put down by the square-leg fielder.

The runs piled on, mostly from Andy's bat, although wickets fell regularly. The ninth wicket fell with the score on 429 and Andy was past his double century. Tom Rushby provided a platform for Andy to make his score even more memorable. Rushby added 23 in the partnership of 94 which gave Andy an opportunity to score a triple century in one day. He was left on 306 not out and was carried to the pavilion shoulder high. The rest of the match was a foregone conclusion. Oxford were further hampered by the loss of D.J. Knight, playing against his Surrey colleagues, who strained a thigh muscle while fielding. They scored 350 after following on, but still lost by an innings and 47 runs.

Andy had tapped into a rich vein of form. On a visit to Southampton, he proved that he could also produce a large score against a county attack. Hampshire won the toss and batted. In just under 80 overs, they were dismissed for 315. Hobbs and Harrison opened for Surrey and the senior partner fell first with the score on 51. Andy came to the crease with about 90 minutes of play left for the day. In that time, he struck a fabulous century. The Hampshire bowlers were repeatedly smashed through the leg side. He gave a chance on 39, which was not taken. By the end of play, he was 104 not out in a total of 242/2.

Day two started where the previous evening left off. Andy and Ernie Hayes punished bad deliveries, and some good ones too, with ball-striking of the first order. Hampshire's captain Lionel Tennyson brought himself on as his bowlers toiled, but to no great effect. When the partnership was finally broken, it totalled 353. Andy fell for 271 when another ball carved through the leg side was caught on the boundary.

The match petered out to a draw, but Andy had proven that he could make big scores in the County Championship. Also, he had thrived away from the friendly surroundings of The Oval. He passed 1,000 runs for the season during the innings and was becoming one of England's best batsmen.

The Gentlemen v Players match at Lord's was coming up and there was speculation that Andy would be selected. When the Players team was announced, he had been omitted. The batsmen's names were of the highest order: Hobbs, Gunn, Hearne, Mead, Hendren, Woolley. Fine players though they were, on his form in 1919, Andy deserved to be ranked among them. *The Guardian* noted, 'On the side of the Players a place should surely have been found for Ducat, who has the highest aggregate of runs, is third on the list of batsmen, and has played the two biggest innings of the season.' It was a compelling argument.

Andy scored 16 in a draw at Sussex which was not overly helpful. The game marked the County Championship debuts of future England captains Arthur and Harold Gilligan. Arthur was playing for Surrey but would join his brother at Sussex in 1920.

Straight after the Gentlemen versus Players match, Surrey entertained Middlesex in a charity game. The match was in aid of King Edward's Hospital Fund and St Dunstan's, but had first-class status. Middlesex batted first and Jack Hearne scored a century as the visitors piled on 568 in 119 overs. Maybe with a point to prove, Andy produced another fine innings. His defence was sound, and his driving was excellent as he chased down another century. He was finally out for 134, mistiming a shot to mid-off, but he had put together his second hundred in just over a week.

Back in the County Championship, Surrey's grasp on the title was almost gone, with heavy defeats to Yorkshire and Kent. In four innings, Surrey went past 200 just once as the runs dried up. Yorkshire's margin of victory was ten wickets while Kent won by 136 runs. A dull, cold day at Blackheath was brightened by Frank Woolley's 7-36 for Kent. The 4,000 spectators braving the unseasonal July weather witnessed Surrey's capitulation at the hands of Woolley, including a hat-trick to end the first innings.

Although Australia's Ashes tour was two years away, there was already talk of how the England team might look. One of many names being mentioned for possible inclusion was Andy. It was becoming a remarkable upturn in form and recognition fuelled by consistency in run-getting.

Australia's 1919 tourists, the AIF, played a second game against Surrey at The Oval. The match was a decent one for Andy, 33 and 32 not out, but the big story was the return of Jack Crawford to the Surrey team after ten years. Crawford had left Surrey under a cloud and gone to Australia. He played for South Australia for four years before moving to New Zealand. He then played for Otago and Wellington before returning to England. He scored an unbeaten 144 to underline his ability.

August started with a draw at home to Nottinghamshire before a late finish against Middlesex entertained the Bank Holiday crowd at The Oval. Middlesex were struggling from the start. Had it not been for Churchill Gunasekara, the first Sri Lankan to play in the County Championship, and 1918 *Wisden* Cricketer of the Year Greville Stevens, the score would have been much worse than 294 all out. Gunasekara scored 88 not out at No.9. In reply, Surrey scored heavily with Hobbs (84) and Andy (75) giving Andy Sandham support in his 175 not out. Surrey's tail also wagged as Abel hit 73 not out at No.11. Sandham and Abel's partnership added 132 before the declaration came at 582. Middlesex's aim was to bat for the rest of the day in beautiful, scorching conditions. As time ticked on, while wickets fell, the Surrey crowd sensed a tight finish. Almost 11,000 spectators stayed to the finish as the last wicket fell before the 7:30pm close. Surrey secured an innings victory with seconds to spare.

Draws with Yorkshire and Lancashire preceded the match against County Championship leaders Kent. The game was also designated as Jack Hobbs' benefit match to compensate for the 1914 game being affected by the outbreak of the First World War. Andy hit 76 in the first innings as Surrey took a 90-run lead. Kent's second innings lasted 82 overs, but left Surrey enough time to win. Hobbs and Crawford hit the 95 runs to the win the match in 32 minutes. Woolley's six overs went for 54.

With the season drawing to a close, Surrey played Middlesex one more time and Gunasekara proved to be a thorn in Surrey's side once again. He scored 55 batting at No.10 as Middlesex recovered from 95/5 to score 414. Surrey had made 395 so the match finished as a draw.

There was still time for a crazy match at Taunton with 30 wickets falling on the first day. Somerset batted first and slipped from 82/2 to 127 all out. Surrey's reply started badly with Hobbs going for a duck. At 18/4, Somerset's total looked way off before welcome boundaries from Crawford and Hitch pushed Surrey ahead. Somerset's second innings, commencing in the late afternoon, never recovered from 11/4 as Tom Rushby's 6-31 helped dismiss the hosts for 91.

With only 67 required, Surrey's target on day two was an easy one. Except it rained overnight and kept going throughout the morning. The covers came off for a while, but more rain seemed to have robbed Surrey of a win. By 3pm, the weather had cleared and the ground was sufficiently dry to start. Knight and Hobbs fell close together but Andy set his sights on winning the match. Having scored 21, and Surrey needing three to win, he smashed what should have been the winning runs straight at cover who took the catch. Crawford strode to the wicket and smashed the first ball he faced back over the bowler's head. Jim Bridges, fielding on the boundary, made a ham-fisted attempt to catch the ball, dropped it and could only watch it roll gently over the boundary to secure the win for Surrey.

Andy finished the season sixth in the first-class batting averages with 1,695 runs at 52.96. It was easily the best season of his career and further honours seemed within touching distance. His performance does need to be measured against undoubtedly poor quality bowling across the counties. Some of that needs to be put into the context of the loss of bowlers through four years of war. Kent's Colin Blythe is just one example of a quality bowler who did not survive military service. Also, the two-day format produced sporting declarations and sometimes dubious bowling to facilitate them. However, Andy still had to get the runs and he did so consistently.

* * *

Andy's first outing for the 1919/20 football season was a reserve team game at Port Vale. In order to get match fit, Villa decided that an outing at Hanley would help Andy switch over for football. Around 10,000 spectators turned up for the start of the match, and more came as the game progressed, to see Andy. Port Vale started well and took a two-goal lead, but Villa's reserves came back to draw the game. For Andy, it was a frustrating outing because he would miss almost two months due to injury.

While Andy was recovering, Aston Villa's league form was diabolical. In the first 11 matches, they lost eight with two wins and a draw. The bottom of the table was not a place that Villa were accustomed to being.

One of the wins was against Middlesbrough, who provided the opponents for Andy's first game after injury. The league had brought in the concept of teams playing each other home and away on successive weekends as a transitional arrangement while football got back to normal. The match was a lively one with plenty of goals;

not the easiest match to come back into. Villa finally prevailed 5-3, with both teams having a player registering a hat-trick.

Next up for Villa were local rivals West Bromwich Albion. Villa took the honours at The Hawthorns while Albion returned the favour at Villa Park. The match at Villa Park was in front of 60,000 spectators with the stadium bursting at the seams. At one point, hundreds of fans spilled on to the pitch and the game was halted while they were cleared.

Although Villa had found their form, Andy was struggling to find his. At Sheffield United, he looked slow and off the pace. The match was spoiled by the home team's attitude. In one petulant moment, Stan Fazackerley tried to trip up the referee. Villa won 2-1.

By the beginning of December, Andy's form was improving. He was getting into better positions and had a couple of near misses with shots in a 2-0 Villa Park victory against Manchester United. The following week at Old Trafford, Andy helped inspire Villa to a second-half comeback. Along with Frank Barson and Jimmy Harrop, Andy's play helped Villa to a 2-1 win. Barson had been transferred from Barnsley in time for the first Middlesbrough game and revitalised the half-back line. It was his sparkling play that helped Villa to turn their fortunes around.

Against Chelsea on Christmas Day, Andy got on the scoresheet with the final goal in a 5-2 win. He missed the next game at Oldham Athletic, a 3-0 win, as Villa extended their winning streak to seven matches. That streak would end at Newcastle United on New Year's Day, with a defeat, but the poor start to the season was now behind club and player.

At home to Burnley, Andy was tested with a different kind of problem. Villa scored through Clem Stephenson, but Burnley equalised in the 38th minute through Richard Cragg. Villa's goalkeeper Sam Hardy was injured in a collision and needed to leave the pitch for treatment. Andy pulled on the goalkeeper's jersey and managed to keep out Burnley, who were attacking hard to utilise the player advantage. The *Star Green 'Un* commented on Andy being 'very agile' in goal. Hardy could not start the second half, and Andy continued. Within five minutes of the resumption, Villa had taken a 2-1 lead. Hardy returned, much to the crowd's pleasure, but a fumble led to a second equaliser for Burnley.

Two weeks later, Villa visited Burnley and came away with a creditable 0-0 draw. Burnley were in second place and inspired performances by Hardy and Andy secured a point. The *Birmingham Daily Gazette* said that Andy 'played magnificently'. It also said that he 'shone as an intervener, his tackling being clean and clever, while his placing of the ball was praiseworthy in itself'.

Villa's FA Cup campaign had started at home against Queens Park Rangers and despite having most of the possession, they won only 2-1. Billy Walker, who would go on to become one of the club's greatest players, scored twice on his debut.

Before Villa's FA Cup second-round match, they travelled to London to play Arsenal. It was the first time that Andy had faced his old club. Since his departure, they had dropped Woolwich from their name and had moved to Highbury in north London. Around 55,000 spectators witnessed an end-to-end game which was won for Villa by Clem Stephenson's 30-yard daisy-cutter. The game was also a trial for providing commentary to blind people. Twelve soldiers blinded during the war were each given a commentator, called an 'instructor' by the *Weekly Despatch*, who provided details of the action on the pitch.

Villa's cup match at Old Trafford was affected by rain. The conditions, and Manchester United's wasteful nature in front of goal, gave Villa an opportunity that they grabbed. It was Andy who provided the pass for Clem Stephenson to equalise before Walker's winning goal nine minutes from time.

The beginning of February proved to be a busy time for Andy, who played four matches in eight days. On 7 February it was a trip to Goodison Park for a league match with Everton. An inspired performance from Hardy, including a penalty save, helped Villa to a 1-1 draw.

Two days later, Andy was back in an England shirt for a trial match at The Hawthorns. Having been in excellent form for a couple of months, putting in noteworthy displays, he was being given a chance to win more caps. He did not disappoint. He had a good match and played exceedingly well with Sunderland's Charlie Buchan and Liverpool's Jackie Sheldon. The Liverpool player had been the instigator of the betting scandal in 1915, but his life ban was lifted after the war.

With just 48 hours of recuperation, Andy's next outing was a home match against Arsenal. The windy conditions made the game difficult, but Villa won 2-1. Alongside Andy in the half-backs was Jack Pendleton, who was making his debut. Andy's last game of the spell was a draw at home to Everton where another debutant, full back Tommy Smart, made a successful beginning to his Villa career.

Andy's next Villa matches were all FA Cup ties as they continued to progress through the tournament. Although he missed league matches due to illness, Andy was in the team for the cup. Sunderland were the opponents for the third-round match at Villa Park. Andy was on good form again as Villa won 1-0. *The Observer* commented that Andy was 'quite supreme at right-half this season'.

Villa's fourth-round tie was against Tottenham Hotspur at White Hart Lane. Luck was definitely with Villa as the only goal of the game was scored in the seventh minute of the match when Spurs' Tommy Clay scored an own goal trying to clear a ball crossed into the penalty area. As much as Andy, Frank Barson and Jimmy Harrop tried to get their forwards into the game it proved futile. However, Spurs lost their best chance when Bert Bliss missed an open goal. On another occasion, with Hardy beaten, it was left to Andy to clear the ball off the line.

Following the Spurs tie, the England team had been announced for the first match in that year's Home International Championship. After nine years and 348 days, Andy would win another England cap. At that point it was a record time span between appearances.

The match was played at Highbury and the opponents were Wales. Villa had three representatives in the match, a sign of how successful the team was becoming. In the Wales line-up, there was a familiar face. Lot Jones, who had been involved in Andy's accident, was now at Southend United and was winning his 20th cap.

England
Hardy (Aston Villa)

Pennington (West Bromwich Albion), Clay (Tottenham Hotspur)

Grimsdell (Tottenham Hotspur), Barson (Aston Villa), Ducat (Aston Villa)

Quantrill (Derby County), Smith (Bolton Wanderers), Elliott (Middlesbrough), Buchan (Sunderland), Chedgzoy (Everton)

Wales
Peers (Wolverhampton Wanderers)

Russell (Plymouth Argyle), Millership (Rotherham County)

Keenor (Cardiff City), Jones (Stoke), Matthias (Wrexham)

Vizard (Bolton Wanderers), Richards (Wolverhampton Wanderers), Davies (Preston North End), Jones (Southend United), Meredith (Manchester United)

The match started well for England with Charlie Buchan's seventh-minute opener. Dribbling into space, Buchan fired past Teddy Peers in the Welsh goal. Going behind seemed to inspire Wales and they grew into the game. When England captain Jesse Pennington handled the ball, Stan Davies converted the resulting penalty to level the score.

Later in the first half, Wales were gifted a second goal when Pennington slipped, and Dick Richards collected the loose ball and rounded Hardy to score what proved to be the winning goal. Triumphant Welsh captain Billy Meredith spoke positively after the match about Andy. However, several newspapers were critical of his defensive play.

After the disappointment of the Wales game, Andy's next match was the FA Cup semi-final against Chelsea at Bramall Lane. Although the semi-final and final were supposed to be at neutral venues, Stamford Bridge had already been selected as the venue for the final. If they could overcome Villa, Chelsea would be playing at home in the final.

Despite that extra motivating factor, Chelsea never got going. As soon as Villa took the lead, a headed goal from Walker five minutes before half-time, Chelsea lost their composure. Harry Edgley scored a second before Walker put the game beyond Chelsea. A consolation goal was scored near the end as Villa booked their place in the final with a 3-1 win.

As fate would have it, the following week saw Villa and Chelsea face each other in the league. Around 80,000 spectators crammed into Stamford Bridge. Villa took the lead through Billy Kirton. However, it was an incident with Edgley that resulted in a broken leg that soured the game. Chelsea won 2-1, with Villa down to ten men, but Edgley's injury was a contributory factor. The break meant that Edgley would miss the final; a feeling Andy knew all too well from 1913.

In the run-in to the FA Cup Final, *The Globe* ran an interview with Andy. He was asked about the secret of his success and the answer was fruit. Bananas, oranges, pineapples, peaches and apples were noted as being his main foods. Andy's fitness was a known factor, and it is interesting that dietary intake was high on his priorities. He was quoted as saying, 'The semi-raw meat meals of our ancestors are a thing of the past, but even in these days the average professional player consumes a considerable quantity of flesh food. I find fruit a finer fuel, and have yet to be accused of being deficient in stamina.'

Before too many thoughts of the cup final, Andy won his fifth cap against Scotland at Hillsborough.

The teams were:

England

Hardy (Aston Villa)

Pennington (West Bromwich Albion), Longworth (Liverpool)

Grimsdell (Tottenham Hotspur), McCall (Preston North End), Ducat (Aston Villa)

Quantrill (Derby County), Morris (West Bromwich Albion), Cock (Chelsea), Kelly (Burnley), Wallace (Aston Villa)

Scotland

Campbell (Partick Thistle)

Blair (Sheff Wednesday), McNair (Celtic)

Gordon (Rangers), Low (Newcastle United), Bowie (Rangers)

Troup (Dundee), Paterson (Leicester City), Wilson (Dunfermline), Miller (Liverpool), Donaldson (Bolton Wanderers)

The match was an exciting encounter which ended with England winning 5-4. At half-time, that result looked improbable with Scotland having a 4-2 lead and causing the English defence all kinds of trouble. After the match, *The Times* were scathing of Andy's first-half display, describing how 'the failure of Ducat to hold Troup brought three goals for Scotland'.

Alex Troup of Dundee was making his debut for Scotland, playing at outside-left, and was troubling England with his pace down the left wing. It was Andy's tighter marking in the second half that helped England to get hold of the ball and get back into the match. Bob Kelly was the hero for England with two goals on his debut to help win the game.

Prior to the FA Cup Final, Villa travelled to relegation-threatened Blackburn Rovers. The home team, in need of the win, played with intensity in muddy conditions. Perhaps the Villa players were thinking about Stamford Bridge but played well below their best and were handsomely beaten 5-1. A 3-1 win at home to Sheffield Wednesday two days later meant that Villa went into the final on a winning note.

On the morning of 24 April 1920, Aston Villa travelled from New Street station in Birmingham to London for the final. Among the travelling party were dignitaries such as Joseph Ansell (Villa's president), William Cadbury (Lord Mayor of Birmingham), and Evelyn Cecil (MP for Birmingham Aston). Andy travelled knowing that he would be captaining the team. Jimmy Harrop, the regular captain, had failed to recover from injury and would miss out.

Their opponents in the final were Huddersfield Town. Although they were a Second Division team and trying to be the first winner of the FA Cup from outside the top division since Tottenham Hotspur's win as a Southern League club in 1901, Huddersfield went into the game as favourites for many pundits.

Aston Villa
Hardy
Weston, Smart
Moss, Barson, Ducat (capt.)
Dorrell, Stephenson, Walker, Kirton, Wallace

Huddersfield Town
Mutch
Bullock (capt.), Wood
Watson, Wilson, Slade
Islip, Swan, Taylor, Mann, Richardson

The game was played at a fast pace, with Andy and his fellow half-backs playing well. They were stopping Huddersfield in midfield as well as providing quality balls to their forwards. Both teams were reluctant to make a mistake, so scoring chances were few and far between. As the game went on, it was looking more and more likely that a single goal would win the cup.

After 90 minutes the teams were still level so extra time was required for the first time in an FA Cup Final. The deadlock was broken, fortuitously, in the seventh minute of extra time. Andy played the ball to Arthur Dorrell and his attempted cross was put behind for a corner. Dorrell took the resultant kick and Billy Kirton managed to get part of his head on the ball, while beating Tom Wilson in the air, and into the net. Goalkeeper Sandy Mutch could only watch as Villa took a 1-0 lead.

Despite Huddersfield's intense efforts to equalise, Villa defended stoutly and won their sixth FA Cup. Andy led the Villa team up the steps to where Prince Henry awaited with the cup. On receiving the trophy, Andy clung on to it while shaking hands with well-wishers. Even from the grainy footage now available on YouTube, Andy's pride and joy is evident. He remained on the steps after the Villa players had received their medals, and shook the hands of each Huddersfield player.

After the match, a banquet was held at the Great Central Hotel where the day's success was toasted. As captain, Andy responded to the toast and expressed the delight of the team, but also spared a thought for Edgley and Harrop who had missed the match. Before returning to Birmingham, the players visited Edgley as he convalesced in a London hospital. The cup was taken to the hospital and filled with champagne.

The team returned to Birmingham on the Monday afternoon after the final. Inexplicably, they had a league match scheduled against Manchester City later in the day. As the train pulled into New Street station, a band started playing. The public were kept out of the station but had congregated in the streets around. Additional police were required to keep traffic moving. The *Daily Mirror* reported that the players 'went into a hotel for a much-needed cup of tea'.

Around Villa Park, there was a similar sight. Around 45,000 spectators crammed in to see the cup paraded. As Andy led the team on to the pitch, still grasping the trophy, the noise was deafening. The *Birmingham Daily Gazette* commented that 'the cheers were renewed again and again when he [Andy] held up the cup aloft'.

The game itself was a predictable anti-climax with City winning 1-0. The goal was scored inside the first three minutes as Andy handled the ball in the penalty area and the resultant spot kick was scored. Villa had a penalty later, but Frank Barson missed. Villa tried earnestly to equalise, Andy having a good opportunity with a shot, but City held firm. It was a disappointing result but would not diminish the lustre of the winners' medals.

CHAPTER NINE

… One Cap
1920–1921

BEFORE THE cricket season began, Andy's profile had been raised significantly. In the 57th edition of *Wisden Cricketers' Almanack*, he was named one of the Five Cricketers of the Year. Based on his 1919 exploits, Andy was bestowed the honour alongside Yorkshire's Percy Holmes and Herbert Sutcliffe, Middlesex's Patsy Hendren and Ernest Tyldesley of Lancashire.

Even though the season had only just begun, *The Guardian* was speculating on the make-up of England's Ashes team for the home series against Australia and Andy was one of the names put forward. His stock was clearly rising within the cricket fraternity.

The season was less than memorable to start with, as Andy was back in the pavilion before lunch on the first morning of the season. Northamptonshire started well at The Oval, but momentum shifted. Having bowled out Surrey for 266, the visitors were soon struggling and could only muster 140. Hobbs and Sandham opened up the second innings with a 190-run partnership, then Andy scored a swift 39 not out,. Northamptonshire were in huge trouble. It took just 38.3 overs to finish the match, including Andy's 2-5 to wrap Northamptonshire's innings up, with a crushing 299-run win inside two days.

It was an excellent start for the new Surrey captain, Percy Fender. Having missed the whole of 1919, Fender was fully fit after his war injuries and looking to make up for lost time. Warwickshire suffered a similar fate in the next match as Surrey won their second successive match with a day to spare.

Day one was dominated by two forces of nature: rain and Jack Hobbs. The opener was in irresistible form in between rain delays. Andy accompanied him in a 105-run partnership before slow left-arm bowler Edward Illingworth's delightful breaking ball induced a false stroke and bowled him.

Hobbs completed his century on the second day before Fender's cameo half-century helped Surrey to 361. That would be far too many runs, as Warwickshire's batsmen were a shambles. They batted twice in the afternoon and scored 58 and 64 to fall to a humiliating innings-and-239-run defeat.

Having steamrollered their first two opponents, Surrey found that Hampshire were made of sterner stuff. Hampshire batted first and scored 253. In response, Surrey fell to 96/7, with Andy out for 2 and Hobbs for 4. Cyril Wilkinson's century from No.8 ensured that Surrey had parity going into the second innings. Phil Mead backed up his first-innings 86 with 94 as Hampshire set Surrey 241 to win.

Andy took 3-12, plus two catches, to help restrict Hampshire, but he failed again with the bat. He was not the only one, as Surrey slipped to 99/6. Alan Peach's 73, alongside Wilkinson's unbeaten 56, enabled Surrey to win a tight two-wicket victory and maintain their winning start to the season.

The run would end on the first trip away from The Oval when Somerset won by 32 runs at Bath. Andy took 3-23 to help Surrey bowl out Somerset for 223.

A poor batting response would ultimately cost them the match as they were bowled out for 139. Surrey somewhat retrieved the situation when they restricted Somerset to 194 in their second innings. Andy's rich vein of bowling form continued with 3-21, before his batting set Surrey on their way to chasing down their target. He gave a chance on 8, but Somerset put the catch down and he looked like making them pay. However, Norman Hardy bowled him for 71 and Somerset chipped away at the tail to win the match.

Surrey travelled from Bath to Trent Bridge, where they got back to winning ways. The home team collapsed from 152/2 to 200 all out and struggled from there. Percy Fender's 8-66 in the second innings left Surrey with 131 to win and it was achieved at a canter, with Hobbs and Sandham knocking the runs off in 33 overs.

Andy was finding his touch with the bat. Scores of 48 and 37 in the win over Essex were merely the hors d'oeuvre to a feast against Sussex. Joining Hobbs with the score at 14/1, Andy was in fine form. Hobbs fell for 110, 202 runs later, but Andy continued to plunder the bowling. His leg-side hitting was brutal and he passed his double century effortlessly. Having not given a chance, he skied a ball and departed for 203. It was easily his highest score of the season. Sussex had a dreadful start and fell to 24/5 before George Street's invaluable 55 at No.10. Sussex were forced to follow on before making Surrey bat again. However, Surrey secured the match by nine wickets. Andy and the team were playing superb cricket.

At Leicester, the Surrey juggernaut beat the home team and a potentially hazardous pitch. There were no issues for Hobbs, who scored another hundred, but three Leicestershire players were injured, resulting in just eight men batting in the second innings. Rain was the winner in the next match away to Warwickshire, but not before another Hobbs hundred. The opener had taken 5-21 as Warwickshire were bowled out for 70 before his third consecutive hundred. Andy cashed in with a century of his own, but the weather made sure that the game was drawn. Hobbs then recorded his fourth century in four innings to help Surrey beat Yorkshire.

In a brief interlude from the County Championship, Andy scored 40 and 50 in a draw against Oxford University. He was at the crease, scoring 29 not out, with Alan Peach as Essex were beaten by eight wickets at Leyton. Surrey returned to the top of the County Championship.

Andy was selected for the resurrection of the Gentlemen of the South versus Players of the South game at The Oval. The Players' side was stacked with fantastic cricketers, and they showed it, despite it being a benefit match. On the first day, they amassed 551 runs. Jack Hobbs, the captain, scored 115 with Sandham (89), Russell (71), Hendren (68) and Hearne (62) plundering runs. Andy chipped in with 48 as the Gentlemen's bowlers were no match.

Rain rendered the match a draw when the last two days were washed out. It also created the shortest ever first-class career with the unfortunate Percy Herbert not able to bat, bowl, or field. Herbert was the uncle of Percy Fender, the opposing captain, and missed day one completely. Needing an 11th man to bat, Fender called on his 42-year-old relative, but it proved futile and thus created the anomaly of Herbert's non-appearance in his only match.

More rain at Southampton stopped Surrey in their tracks against Hampshire, but not before yet another Hobbs hundred. Leicestershire were beaten inside two days, but it came at a cost as Andy picked up an injury. A thigh strain meant he missed the next three matches. It also saw Surrey's form take a downturn. Against Kent, they were bowled out for 61 and 73 and lost by an innings: their march towards another title had been arrested.

Andy returned against Nottinghamshire, and Surrey took a 64-run lead into the second innings. At 98/1, with Hobbs and Andy set, Surrey looked like creating another winning opportunity. Len Richmond soon changed that. First, he trapped Hobbs leg-before for 44. When Andy played on three runs later, a precipitous decline ensued. Richmond ended with 6-87 and Nottinghamshire required 272 to win. Arthur Carr played a captain's innings to seal victory by three wickets.

Surrey's title aspirations took a further dive when Middlesex won by an innings and 33 runs at The Oval. Jack Hearne's 178 helped the visitors to 377 which was too many for Surrey's now fragile batting. Hobbs top-scored in both innings, but he had little support.

Needing a win at Old Trafford, Surrey batted first and lost wickets regularly on the first day. Harry Dean, in his benefit year, took 8-80 as Surrey were all out for 163. However, Lancashire's abject batting mustered just 87 and Surrey went into the second day in a strong position.

The Surrey players woke up on the second day to find Manchester covered in thick fog. Conditions were too poor to start on time, and it would be 3pm before play could begin. Andy scored 18, but Andy Sandham's century made sure that Surrey had more than enough runs. Their bowlers then wrapped up the match.

Another win, against Kent, put Surrey back in the race for the Championship. However, they suffered a setback when Sussex unexpectedly beat them at Hastings. The batting woes re-emerged as Surrey were bowled out for just 96 in the second innings. Vallance Jupp's 6-30, his best bowling figures, ensured Sussex's success.

Andy's patience was on show against Yorkshire as Surrey tried to be more resolute. Such was his determination to stay at the crease, he took over two hours to score 26 before ending on 62 not out. Surrey had another second-innings collapse, bowled out for 110, but that and their first-innings lead was enough to secure a 31-run win.

Their penultimate match was at The Oval against Northamptonshire and it created a record that would last for 63 years. Surrey scored 619/5 in their first innings, with Percy Fender blasting what was then the fastest hundred on record in 35 minutes. His fifty was achieved in 19 minutes in an extraordinary session of hitting. At one point, 171 runs were added in 42 minutes. Alan Peach ended on 200 not out while Andy added 149. He also took 2-9 in the first innings, as Surrey secured an eight-wicket win.

The title would be decided by two final fixtures: Middlesex v Surrey at Lord's and Lancashire v Worcestershire at Old Trafford. If Middlesex won, they would secure the County Championship in Plum Warner's last match. The contest ebbed and flowed. Warner's 79 saw Middlesex to 268. Andy Sandham played magnificently for 167 not out as Surrey scored 341 before Fender's declaration to try and win the match. Middlesex responded with a 208-run opening partnership and declared midway through the final afternoon.

Surrey were set 244 to win, but lost wickets in their attempt to chase the victory. Andy batted at No.7 and joined Sandham, who had been on the field for every minute of the match. With a draw looking likely, a tired Sandham hit a full toss back at Jack Hearne and was out for 68. Minutes later, Hearne trapped Andy leg-before and Surrey's tail was exposed. At 6:20pm, Middlesex took the final wicket and with it the Championship. As Warner was carried from the pitch by spectators, the Surrey players could only sit and listen to the cacophony of noise celebrating Middlesex's win and wonder how they had let the title slip from their grasp.

* * *

Andy's return to Villa was via the reserves. Having not played any football since April, he got some time on the pitch under his belt before going into the team against Arsenal. Villa had beaten the Gunners 5-0 on the opening day of the season, but a 3-1 defeat at Manchester City meant that a change was required for the trip to London. It worked a treat, with a 1-0 win.

With the fixture list following the pattern of the previous season, Villa put in a better performance at Villa Park against Manchester City, and reversed the result. Andy set up the first goal. A niggling injury kept him and Sam Hardy out of the next game and Villa lost heavily. The following week saw Spurs beaten 2-1 as Villa's form continued to ebb and flow.

The visit of Oldham Athletic witnessed Andy, wearing the captain's armband, lead from the front with a wonderful performance. The *Birmingham Daily Gazette* commented that 'Ducat had to strive like a super-man to cover up the offensive deficiencies.' He played all over the pitch, taking up different positions: wing-half, forward, centre-half. Villa won 3-0 and it was down to Andy's tenacious play as well as his 'comprehensive scheming' as the newspaper explained.

The win over Oldham took Villa to the top of the table in front of newly promoted Huddersfield Town. Andy was forced to miss the following week's match at Oldham due to a shin injury, but he returned at home to Preston North End the next weekend.

The reverse fixture at Preston turned out to be a nightmare for both club and player as Villa were thrashed 6-1. With Villa already losing, Sam Hardy was injured and needed to be replaced in goal. Andy took on the job, but he conceded three goals as Preston took full advantage of the situation. The game had already been troublesome for Andy as Stanley Davies, the Welsh international, had been far too hot to handle.

It was less than ideal preparation for the following week's international at Roker Park. Andy had retained his place in the England team for his sixth cap. The opponents were Ireland, and four new caps were chosen: goalkeeper John Mew, full-backs Dickie Downs and Fred Bullock, and Andy's Villa colleague Billy Walker.

For Andy, it would have been enjoyable to see Bullock, who had captained Huddersfield in the FA Cup Final six months previously. Bullock's story was a sad one. He would not win another cap and retired from football in 1922. He died months later from ammonia poisoning; suicide was suspected.

The teams were:

England

Mew (Manchester United)

Bullock (Huddersfield Town), Downs (Everton)

Grimsdell (Tottenham Hotspur), McCall (Preston North End), Ducat (Aston Villa)

Quantrill (Derby County), Morris (West Bromwich Albion), Walker (Aston Villa), Kelly (Burnley), Chedgzoy (Everton)

Ireland

Scott (Liverpool)

Rollo (Blackburn Rovers), McCracken (Crystal Palace)

Emerson (Glentoran), Lacey (Liverpool), W. McCandless (Linfield)

J. McCandless (Bradford Park Avenue), Gillespie (Sheffield United), Doran (Brighton & Hove Albion), Ferris (Chelsea), Kelly (Manchester City)

The match was a comfortable one for England and they won 2-0. Andy had a solid game, while Billy Walker scored on his debut. It would be several months before the next England game so Andy could concentrate on his league form.

The first match back after the international fixture was away at Sheffield United and Andy was forced to play out of position for most of the second half. Tommy Smart picked up an injury and Andy slotted into the right-back role. Once again, he sacrificed his personal aims for the greater good of the team. Villa managed to hold on to a 0-0 draw.

Villa's indifferent season continued throughout November and December. At home to West Bromwich Albion, another goalless draw resulted from an uninspiring match. The following week at The Hawthorns, Albion won the match 2-1 despite Andy being 'stylish and serene' (*Birmingham Daily Gazette*). A welcome victory at home to Bradford Park Avenue proved to be an outlier as the following week saw Bradford win 4-0.

A trip to the North East saw Villa welcomed with heavy rain and a muddy pitch. Andy mastered the conditions although his colleagues failed to come to terms with the surface. The *Birmingham Daily Gazette* waxed lyrical over Andy's 'wonderful ability in the mud to round a man, rob him then dispose of the ball with unerring accuracy'. Villa still lost 2-1 but Newcastle United's winner was more than slightly fortuitous, but symptomatic of a team's luck in a poor run of games.

Luck was certainly absent at Liverpool for both Andy and Villa. He could not shake off a knock from early in the game at Anfield and had to leave the field. The result of that decision was conceding three goals in 15 minutes and Villa crashed to a 4-1 loss. Andy was on the sidelines for the whole of the Christmas and New Year period.

He returned in early January for the FA Cup match at home to Bristol City. As holders they would have been expecting a tough game, but they would not have expected such a physical encounter. After 12 minutes, the referee called both sets of players together to warn them about the state of play. Bristol City's captain Jock Nicholson, in response to Villa being awarded a penalty, had aimed and landed a kick at Frank Barson. The referee's lack of action against Nicholson, despite the lecture, gave Bristol City licence to use physicality. Villa won 2-0, despite the visitors' tactics, and the *Birmingham Daily Gazette* euphemistically described the match as 'cup-tie-ish'.

Perhaps Andy was brought back too soon and he missed the next match. It seemed that Villa's focus had shifted to defending the FA Cup, with the league already out of reach, and that created its own pressure. Andy and most of the first-team players played in a charity game, against cross-city rivals Birmingham, before taking off to north Wales for a break. The players and staff headed to Rhyl to get away and take in the fresh air and country walks. The medical officer Dr Jessop was particularly enthusiastic about the physical and mental therapeutic properties of the north Wales coast.

The choice of location gave them reasonable proximity by rail to Liverpool where Villa were playing Everton. Despite a 1-1 draw, Villa's performance was excellent and was capped by a superb finish by Billy Kirton. Villa had survived a period of time with Sam Hardy off the pitch due to concussion. Andy took over goalkeeping duties and pulled off two excellent saves before Hardy recovered.

Villa returned to Rhyl after the game and stayed there for several days until travelling to Nottingham for their FA Cup second-round encounter against Notts County at Meadow Lane. Local newspapers were talking up the home team's chances of reaching the final should they beat Villa. Over 50,000 spectators turned up for the highly anticipated encounter. The match was a tight affair with missed chances at both ends. The *Sunday Post* commented on Andy's 'craft' but it could not unlock the match and it ended 0-0. The replay was won by Villa, Billy Walker's free kick being a fine goal to win the tie. Andy could have made the game secure when he dribbled past defenders but chose not to shoot when the goal was in his sights. Nonetheless, it was another excellent performance and a call-up to an England trial game suggested that he was still firmly in the thoughts of the selection committee.

Despite the call, Andy was forced to miss the England game through what the *Pall Mall Gazette* called a 'chill'. He also missed the away match at Burnley where Villa were beaten 7-1. He returned for the home game against Burnley, but the visitors held out for a draw. That result gave Burnley their 23rd unbeaten game in the league, which was a record. It seems that not losing rather than trying to win was the main plan for the visitors.

The next round of the FA Cup was a rerun of the 1920 final when Huddersfield Town visited Villa Park. Unlike the final, Villa scored twice early on and that proved to be enough to progress. After the cup game, a visit to Sunderland came next and a solitary goal brought Villa's first league win in two months. Andy provided the pass, which Sunderland's defenders failed to cut out, and Arthur Dorrell placed the ball into the net.

Things turned decidedly worse in the space of a week with a second England trial and an FA Cup quarter-final. At Burnley, England faced The North but Andy produced a poor performance at the worst possible time. The North ran out 6-1 winners, and Andy was one of many in an England shirt to fail. It resulted in him losing his England place. Then a 1-0 defeat by Tottenham Hotspur at White Hart Lane ended Villa's FA Cup defence. Andy struggled to hold Jimmy Dimmock and the outside-left set up the winning goal. When Jack Thompson had to leave the field with an injury, Andy filled in, which restricted his ability to help Villa get back into the game. It had been a frustrating week.

From that point in the season, Andy featured less regularly in the team. Niggling injuries and selection policy restricted his appearances. When he did play, it appeared that circumstances worked against him. At home to Huddersfield, Tommy Smart left the field with an injury and Andy moved back into his position. It seemed that he was automatically the go-to player whenever a positional shift was required. Perhaps it was testimony to his flexibility, and ability to read games, but it also moved him out of his favoured, and best, position.

Andy's last match came against Derby County and Villa left the Baseball Ground with the points in a thrilling 3-2 win. Derby's forwards were more interested in individual play than linking up as a team. Egyptian forward Tewfik Abdullah was guilty of trying too hard. Villa, on the other hand, did enough to win the match through teamwork. It would be the last time that Andy would pull on a Villa shirt.

Later, it would emerge that Villa's directors were looking to move forward with a younger team. For several months, the policy of rebuilding had been put into place and Andy did not fit into the club's plans. However, age was not the only motivating factor for letting players leave.

Another policy had been put into place about the distance that players could live away from Villa Park. Andy was now residing in London. Clem Stephenson, Sam Hardy, Jimmy Harrop and Frank Barson were also living well away from the Birmingham area. In a 1960 interview in the *Sports Argus*, Barson gave a frank description of being summoned to a board meeting and ordered to move to Birmingham. Barson lasted one more season at Villa, but the rest left the club at the end of the 1920/21 season.

In the press, rumours were circulating about Andy's next destination. At first, it was speculated that Spurs might be interested. Several newspapers were certain that it would be a London club with some running with a Chelsea rumour. In the end, Andy's new club was disclosed in a *Pall Mall Gazette* article written by Chelsea forward, Jack Cock. He said that there was 'every likelihood of Andy Ducat assisting Fulham next season'. Several days later, the transfer was made public.

* * *

Everything in cricket seemed to revolve around the Australian tourists in the Ashes summer of 1921. England's possible team selections received more than their fair share of newspaper column inches. Time has not diminished this obsession. Andy was rumoured to have been working on his bowling technique and was supposed to be developing into a leg-break bowler. A newly formed magazine called *The Cricketer* discussed the possibility of Andy becoming an England all-rounder in the near future.

Andy's first outing for Surrey, after missing the trial match, was against the Australian tourists. After watching Herbie Collins, ably supported by Charlie Macartney, thrash 162, Andy and his colleagues were soon in all sorts of trouble. Australia's captain, the 'Big Ship' Warwick Armstrong was in devastating form with the ball. Among his 12 wickets, he picked up Andy in both innings. His 6-38 and 6-39 ensured that an innings victory was secured by the tourists and their unbeaten start continued.

A few days later, Surrey started their County Championship campaign at home to Warwickshire and found life decidedly easier. Andy, in particular, enjoyed the bowling and scored 131 in the first innings. In the second, he made 32 not out to guide Surrey to a five-wicket victory. It was also the day that the news of his transfer to Fulham was announced.

A trip to Trent Bridge was less successful, with a heavy defeat in two days, but across the East Midlands against Leicestershire Surrey returned to winning ways. Bill Hitch had restricted the home side to 195 before Andy and Alfred Jeacocke put Surrey in the ascendancy. Both scored half-centuries to set up a good first-innings lead. John King, at the age of 50, scored 127, but Leicestershire left Surrey with a gettable total of 128. Andy almost repeated his exploits of the Warwickshire game but was out with eight runs still required.

The month of June 1921 would prove to be, arguably, the most successful period in Andy's cricketing life. By the end of it, he would be so tantalisingly close to the one thing missing from his cricket *palmarès*. Before that, he would score runs. Lots and lots of them.

Hampshire came to The Oval on 1 June, and Andy walked to the crease when Andy Sandham and Alfred Jeacocke's opening partnership was broken on 42. Andy played a wonderful innings of 89 and was the only Surrey batsman to pass fifty. Hampshire batted until the match was safe before Surrey saw out the draw. Andy added a useful 29, but that was just a warm-up.

A few days later, Essex entertained Surrey at Leyton. The home team, weakened by the absence of England captain Johnny Douglas due to family illness, won the toss and were bowled out for 107. Surrey's reply stuttered when William Cook, deputising for Jack Hobbs, was out with the score on 15. Andy was batting at No.3 and made a mockery of the home team's score. By the end of day one, he was 184 not out in Surrey's total of 307/9. Herbert Strudwick's 41 was the only decent score from the rest of the batsmen. Almost at will, Andy hit the ball sweetly through the on side. One over from Joseph Dixon went for 22, including two sixes, as he dominated play.

The second morning saw Andy stride to the wicket with the No.11 batsman. Unfortunately for Essex, it was Sandham, who had been forced to leave the field just after the start of play on the previous day due to illness. The effect of this combination can still be seen, at the time of writing, in Surrey's record books. The tenth-wicket partnership was worth 173; Sandham being run out for 58 to bring the innings to a close. Andy was left stranded on 290 not out but had recorded the highest first-class score of the season so far. Essex failed to make Surrey bat again.

Northamptonshire were the next county to feel the force of Andy's bat. Surrey scored over 600 runs on the first day. Jeacocke and Sandham put on 266 for the first wicket before Andy joined in the runs. With Sandham, he added 247 as the visiting bowlers were powerless to stop Surrey. The declaration came at the end of the first day and the game was wrapped up quickly on the second as Northamptonshire folded under pressure.

Andy was not done with his scoring exploits and a trip to Edgbaston yielded his third consecutive century. A more watchful innings of 120 set up Surrey for another win. Chasing 91, they slipped to 16/3 and 56/5 before getting over the line to register the victory. Importantly for Andy, he had reached 1,000 runs for the season on the way to his century. He was the first batsman to do it in 1921 and it laid a marker down for the Ashes.

The Australians were proving to be an irresistible force. They had already won the first two Tests convincingly: by ten wickets and eight wickets. Having won the previous Ashes series in Australia 5-0, this was seven straight Test wins. Sir Pelham Warner, in his book *Cricket Between Two Wars*, described them as 'as fine a side as has ever visited this country'. Albeit before the 1948 Invincibles, it was high praise for a Test team of distinction.

Straight after the second Test at Lord's, the Australians were in action against Surrey. Jack Gregory rescued the tourists in the first innings with a century, before Surrey replied. With 47 in the first innings and 30 in the second, Andy top-scored in both innings. However, an incident in the run chase in which Andy ran out Jack Crawford upset him. Unhappy that Surrey's final hope of winning the game had disappeared, the crowd made their displeasure known. Andy was disturbed by the reaction and was bowled a little time later, off his glove, by fast bowler Ted McDonald.

In the last week of June, it was announced that Johnny Douglas had been replaced as England captain for the third Test at Headingley by Lionel Tennyson. Also, seven players had been invited to play in the match: Tennyson, Douglas, Hobbs, Hearne, Woolley, Mead and White. There were four more places to fill, and the Gentlemen v Players match at The Oval would help inform the decision. Andy was named in the Players' side. He was on the cusp of selection for England.

He spent day one in the field as the Gentlemen accumulated 404. Middlesex's Clarence Bruce, who would later become Baron Aberdare of Duffryn, dominated with a century. He was assisted by Charles Titchmarsh and the captain, none other than the Honourable Lionel Tennyson. It was an ideal opportunity for Andy to impress the England captain from a close-up viewpoint.

The second day was dominated by the Players' batting and it was not just Andy who made a statement. At 117/2, he joined Jack Hearne. The bowling was not as threatening as it could have been, and he took advantage. Hearne was out, agonisingly, for 99 and was replaced by Wally Hardinge. The pair seized their moment. Andy played slowly to begin with before forcing the pace. Hardinge was more aggressive from the start. With the pair set, Andy tried to turn a single into two and was run out. He had scored 80. Hardinge carried on and was finally out for 127.

The newspapers on the third morning of the match were mentioning that Andy had been asked to report to Headingley for the Test match. The Players won the match, by an innings and three runs, but the result was meaningless in itself. It had been an audition for the third Test and Andy was in the mix.

The *Liverpool Echo* speculated on the final line-up for Headingley. They commented, 'If Ducat and Hardinge play, they will join the small band – which includes Makepeace and Sharp – who have played for England at cricket and football. It will form a rather interesting coincidence, for Ducat and Hardinge also made their debut in the realms of international association football simultaneously.'

On the morning of 2 July, Andy was awarded his cap and became the 200th player to represent England. Also, he became just the eighth England dual international. When congratulated on the achievement, Andy replied in a typically understated manner with, 'It is something to look back on when one's playing days are over.'

The speculation was also correct about Hardinge, and he became number 201, and ninth on the list:

England	Australia
L.H. Tennyson (capt)	W.W. Armstrong (capt)
G. Brown (wk)	T.J.E. Andrews
J.W.H.T. Douglas	W. Bardsley
A. Ducat	H. Carter (wk)
H.T.W. Hardinge	J.M. Gregory
J.W. Hearne	H.S.T.L. Hendry
J.B. Hobbs	C.G. Macartney
V.W.C. Jupp	A.A. Mailey
C.H. Parkin	E.A. McDonald
J.C. White	C.E. Pellew
F.E. Woolley	J.M. Taylor

The weather was perfect. It was a hot, sunny day in Leeds and rain had been absent for a while. However, things started to turn when Armstrong won the toss and made the obvious decision to bat first. Within the first hour of the day, Tennyson split the webbing on his left hand while fielding at silly point. He left the field to have the injury stitched. Later in the day, Jack Hobbs left the field with stomach pains which was diagnosed as appendicitis. Andy had a good day in the field and *The Observer* noted that his fielding had been a 'feature of the game so far'.

Australia scored 407, partly thanks to Charlie Macartney's century, and left England with a tricky period before the close to face pace duo Ted McDonald and Jack Gregory. The pair already had 29 wickets between them in the first two Tests and they soon added to that tally before the close of play as Woolley was bowled by Gregory for a duck and Hearne by McDonald for 7.

Overnight, England were 22/2 with the dual internationals not out. Harding had scored 11 while Andy was on 3. In the morning, another eight runs were added, all from the bat of Hardinge, before one of the most unusual moments in Test cricket occurred. Andy was facing McDonald and attempted to play the ball wide of the slip cordon, through gully, for runs. The ball hit the shoulder of Andy's bat and knocked a piece clean off. The ball flew to Gregory in the slips while the fragment of Andy's bat knocked off a bail. In essence, Andy was out twice but Gregory's catch was recorded as the mode of dismissal. Australia's wicketkeeper Sammy Carter reunited Andy with his bat fragment before he disconsolately returned to the pavilion.

The match, and series, were already in danger. When Vallance Jupp fell, with the score on 67, England had lost their fifth wicket. However, a fighting innings from Douglas, whose wife was ill with appendicitis just like Hobbs, helped the cause. Batting at No.9, Tennyson played one of the strangest, bravest, and most foolhardy innings ever by an England player. With his hand bandaged, he faced the pace duo batting one-handed. Remarkably, he scored 63 before falling to McDonald.

Australia knew that the Ashes were close to being retained and their second innings was all about getting to an unreachable total before letting the pace duo loose again. With England's second innings in a perilous position, Andy came to the wicket at 124/4 knowing that he needed a resolute innings. However, he was enticed out of his crease by Arthur Mailey and Carter did the rest. *The Guardian* described Andy as being 'sorely perplexed' by Mailey's spin and had 'failed most lamentably' to reproduce his county form. With scores of 3 and 2, it was difficult to argue against the assessment. Australia duly won the match, by 219 runs, and had retained the Ashes with two matches left.

From Leeds, Andy headed down south to Taunton for Surrey's County Championship match. Surrey batted first and were in trouble at 76/6. Andy scored 24 before being trapped leg-before by Walter Whiting. Thanks to Fender and Abel, Surrey were able to get a respectable 236. Somerset's response never got going thanks to Tom Rushby, and the Surrey bowler took all ten wickets for 43. Incredibly, the feat had already been achieved twice in 1921. Having been bowled out so cheaply, Somerset were eventually beaten by 229 runs.

Surrey's next match was against Sussex. Despite having a deficit of 139 in the first innings, they were able to turn the match around. Andy had an indifferent match with scores of 1 and 37. For the second successive match, he fell to the same bowler in both innings. This time it was Vallance Jupp, who had played in the Headingley Test with Andy.

Despite his failure in Leeds, Andy was asked to play in the Gentlemen v Players fixture at Lord's. England's selectors needed to stop the run of eight successive Test defeats to Australia and team places were transitory. Phil Mead was one batsman in line to replace Andy and he hit a century to pile pressure on. Andy was demoted to No.7 and managed 24 before being given out to Charles 'Father' Marriott.

The Players got themselves into a winning position, helped by Andy's catch to remove Fender on 101 from a skied delivery, and needed just 42 to win. Hardinge and Andy were promoted to openers, presumably as a final audition, but one of them fluffed their lines. Andy had scored 2 when Marriott bowled him. It must have been obvious, walking back to the pavilion, that he was not going to get the call for the Old Trafford Test.

There was no time for pondering as Middlesex, champions and so far unbeaten in 1921, was the next fixture. Surrey won the toss, batted, and always seemed to be ahead. Andy had another indifferent time with the bat, but Surrey got home by 19 runs and were on the heels on Middlesex in the County Championship.

For the rest of July, it was definitely a batsman's game for Surrey, if not necessarily for Andy. Tom Shepherd hit successive double centuries against Lancashire and Kent, Sandham hit a double century against Somerset. In contrast, Andy had a first-ball duck in the Lancashire match while scoring just 18 at Blackheath. A half-century against Somerset was something, but the high standards of earlier in the season were not being maintained.

Surrey's match with Nottinghamshire ended frustratingly for both county and Andy. For Surrey, an agonising draw meant that an opportunity was missed. For Andy, he was left to sit and watch. Thanks to Sandham, Surrey engineered a 50-run lead on the first innings. In order to get runs quickly, Percy Fender used pinch hitters. Andy was not one of them and was forced to watch Fender, Bill Hitch and John Lockton promoted above him. The tactic was in vain as Nottinghamshire just managed to avoid defeat, as the tenth-wicket partnership of Wilf Payton and Len Richmond held out.

The visit of Kent marked Bill Hitch's benefit, but it was an in-form Sandham who benefited most of all. In the absence of Hobbs, still recovering from appendicitis, Sandham was accumulating his runs like the Master himself. Another century in the first innings, and 95 in the second, helped set up the win. Andy was among the runs too in the second innings and fell just short of a century. Kent made a good attempt at the run chase, but the total was too large, and Surrey kept pace at the top of the Championship. However, rain against Lancashire would undo much of the good work against Kent and the match at Old Trafford was a soggy draw.

The trip to Northampton was far more successful. The home side, deciding to bat first, were all out inside 50 overs for 127. With the score on 175/3, Andy was joined by Surrey debutant Horace Bloomfield. Over the next two hours, the pair scored at will. The partnership yielded 232 before the declaration came. Andy achieved his second double-century of the season, 204 not out, while Bloomfield was unbeaten on 107 in his maiden first-class innings. Having scored over 400, Surrey then bowled out Northamptonshire for a second time to secure the innings victory.

With three matches of the season left, the County Championship race could not have been much tighter. Surrey had a small lead over champions Middlesex. It might come down to the last match of the season, a repeat of last year's decider between Middlesex and Surrey at Lord's.

More rain meant that Surrey could only draw against Yorkshire. However, there was more than an element of fortune about the result. Yorkshire had Surrey in trouble in the second innings. Cognisant of the situation, Andy and Tom Shepherd did their best to play soundly and not make mistakes. In 50 minutes, they scored just 27. Both lost their wickets, and Surrey slipped to 210/8, before rain intervened. Before play began at The Oval, Andy was training at Craven Cottage to get ready for the football season.

Leicestershire must have felt that by restricting Surrey to 228 they had done well; Sandham scored 54, Andy 36, and Douglas Jardine, in his first season playing county cricket, added 37. That feeling soon changed as Fender led from the front and Surrey were 90 runs to the good before batting again. Shepherd's 100 was stand-out, Andy was caught on 49 while Bloomfield ended on 53 not out. Leicestershire required an unlikely 334. Their cause was not helped when Tommy Sidwell arrived late on day three and was not permitted to continue his innings. The seemingly inevitable happened and Surrey won by 88 runs. Their approach was formulaic: first-innings lead, bat quickly to set up the win, take ten wickets.

With the Championship on the line, almost 16,000 spectators attended the first day's play at Lord's. Despite the sight of rain clouds, and the pull of the opening day of the football season, Middlesex and Surrey were supported well. The visitors won the toss and decided to bat. Jack Durston, Middlesex's opening bowler who had also made his only Test appearance earlier in the summer, broke through early with the wicket of D.J. Knight. Soon after, he removed dangerman Andy Sandham, who played on, and Surrey were in a spot of bother at 18/2.

Andy and Tom Shepherd steadied the ship before Hearne's catch sent Andy on his way for 21. Douglas Jardine joined Shepherd and the pair batted through until after tea. Their partnership was worth 144 before Jardine was bowled by Durston for 55. Two more wickets fell quickly as Middlesex fought back. Shepherd batted brilliantly but ran out of partners. Surrey scored 269 and Middlesex negotiated the last few overs of the evening session for the loss of Harry Lee.

Early on day two, Surrey bowlers grabbed the momentum with the collection of key wickets. Jack Hearne and Patsy Hendren both mustered 22 while Frank Mann top-scored with 29. By mid-afternoon, they were 137 runs in front and batting again. The formula was working perfectly.

Durston struck early again and removed both Sandham and Andy. Despite the setback, Surrey were in the box seat at the tea interval with a 240-run lead, Knight and Shepherd looking set, and in position to set up the win with runs on the board. After tea, one piece of inspired cricket turned the game back towards Middlesex. Nigel Haig, another who made an England debut and played just one Test that summer, bowled to Shepherd and pulled off a brilliant caught and bowled. Knight followed a little time later and the rest of the Surrey batting line-up capitulated. Out for 184, Surrey left Middlesex with a lower-than-expected target of 322. Nineteen runs were scored without loss before the close of play. The final day would decide which county would be champions.

Day three started soundly for Middlesex; they reached 48 before Gilly Reay removed Lee for 20. Hearne joined Richard Twining with Surrey's bowlers looking to make inroads. However, that never happened as the Middlesex pair batted with a huge amount of control to steer the home team towards victory. The partnership was worth 229 and it took Middlesex to within 45 runs of their target. Twining scored 135 and Hearne added 106 and it was left to Mann and Hendren to score the winning runs to ensure Middlesex retained their title.

CHAPTER TEN

Fulham Bound
1921–1924

THE DEAL was announced on Friday, 13 May 1921 that Fulham had 'secured the transfer of Andy Ducat, Aston Villa's international right half-back'. Andy had chosen to drop down to the Second Division to play for Fulham, and two individuals that would have been key influences.

First, Sir Henry Norris MP was a director of Fulham. It would have been his membership of Surrey County Cricket Club that would have given him the opportunities to convince Andy to sign. However, more of an influence would have been Fulham's coach, Phil Kelso. What bigger attraction could there have been than the man who had given Andy his start in professional football? Add to that, the location of Craven Cottage, and it was a done deal while Andy was still in his cricket whites.

The 1921/22 season started well for Fulham with two wins in their first two matches. First up was a home game against Coventry City, who had avoided relegation the previous season, and a 5-0 scoreline suggested that the visitors may well have a long season ahead of them. Fulham, on the other hand, had aspirations of promotion and the acquisition of Andy enhanced those ambitions. An improvement on ninth place was the bare minimum for Kelso and Fulham. A visit to Leicester City garnered another win without Fulham's star attraction. It was a positive beginning to life at Craven Cottage for Andy and he was yet to pull on a Fulham shirt.

Andy finally made his debut at Highfield Road in the return match against Coventry. If he was under any illusion of the style of football to be encountered in the Second Division, Andy experienced 'aggressive tactics' according to the *Daily Herald*. In a 2-0 defeat for Fulham, the newspaper attributed the loss to 'bustle, and not by science'.

Two days later, Andy made his home debut for the visit of Leicester. Unsurprisingly, Andy had the most quality on the pitch which manifested itself in accurate passing and excellent reading of the match. Consequentially, he found himself attracting plenty of defenders when in possession. Despite his influence, the kick-and-rush approach dominated, and the game remained goalless.

Andy missed the next game, a defeat at Hull City, due to fluid on the knee. He returned the following week for the return match, and Fulham clicked into gear. Jimmy Torrance missed the Hull game too but his partnership with Andy at home created chances that Fulham took in abundance. The final score was 6-0 with new signing Barney Travers scored a hat-trick.

The match also saw a change of captain for Fulham with Andy being given the role by Torrance, who was the incumbent. With Andy's wealth of experience, Torrance believed that Fulham would be better served by relinquishing the role. The team supported the decision and Andy took over the captaincy.

The next two matches were against Notts County and saw contradictory performances. At Meadow Lane, Andy and Fulham struggled. Andy was 'outpaced and overplayed', said the *Nottingham Journal*, as Notts County's forwards created plenty of opportunities. Despite losing away 3-0, Fulham reversed the result with a 4-0 win the following week. Andy was in much better form as the game was won comfortably.

A visit to Selhurst Park highlighted once again that stylish football was not always effective as Crystal Palace's 'more thrustful' play won over Andy's 'prettier' play. The *Daily Herald* reported on how Andy linked up well with Travers, but Palace scored two more direct goals. A pattern was emerging that Craven Cottage was more amenable to Andy's blend of football than away matches where physicality was winning over.

The trend was bucked with a superb 4-1 win at Hillsborough as Fulham beat The Wednesday comfortably. The reverse match at Craven Cottage saw Fulham win 3-1 which was followed up by another away victory at Bradford Park Avenue. With three wins on the trot, Fulham had moved towards the top of the division.

Unfortunately for Andy, he picked up a leg injury during a London Cup tie and was forced out for almost two months. Just before Christmas, he tried to make a comeback in a London Combination match for the reserves but lasted less than 45 minutes. His leg muscle was not healed and he was forced off for treatment in the first half for 15 minutes. He returned but could not play the second half.

Andy was finally back in the middle of January for the visit of Derby County. The visitors scored within three minutes when goalkeeper Arthur Reynolds tried to punch a shot clear but managed to push the ball on to the post from where it rebounded into the goal. Derby scored again after 25 minutes, and Fulham looked as if they would lose at home for the first time in the season. In the second half, Fulham secured a draw through positive play. Andy and Torrance gelled well as Fulham fought back.

On 28 January, Andy graced the cover of *The Football Favourite* magazine. The article covered cup matches which tied in with Fulham's second-round FA Cup game at Leicester City. Soon after, Andy found himself in another magazine. This time, it was *Sports Fun* which was a new 'weekly comic paper of football and sport'. Despite Andy moving to the Second Division, and his footballing ability starting to wane, his popularity among fans was not diminishing.

Andy was forced to miss two games, including a draw at leaders Nottingham Forest, due to flu. However, he returned for the home match against Forest and impressed with a defensive display. Fulham won 2-0 to aid their promotion push, but it could have been more had two goals not been ruled out by the referee.

Away from football, Andy's new business venture was launched in February. Andy opened up a sports outfitters shop in Southend, and it was managed by an ex-cricket colleague. Undoubtedly, Andy would have been influenced by Jack Hobbs who had opened a shop of his own in 1919. Hobbs' outlet was in Fleet Street, in central London, and sold all kinds of sports gear. Andy's shop was similar, with the front window adorned with cricket bats, pads, racquets and other sporting goods. A large sign declaring 'Andrew Ducat Ltd Sports Outfitters' was visible to all who shopped in London Road in the Westcliff area of Southend. The shop stayed in business until the mid-1930s.

Just as it looked like Fulham might be pushing for promotion, they started losing games. A third defeat in a row, 1-0 away to fellow promotion contenders South Shields, attracted attention from the Football Association and the Football League. Details emerged that Travers had visited the North East three days before the game and had offered a £20 bribe to throw the match in Fulham's favour. The attempted bribe had been discovered prior to the match, so no damage had been done to the integrity of the result. For Travers, it would end in a lifetime ban from football. He was pardoned in 1945, and no other players were implicated in the scandal. There is no doubt that Andy would have been appalled by such conduct.

Fulham's promotion charge ended over Easter 1922 with three successive defeats. The final one, against Leeds United at Craven Cottage, saw Fulham beaten at home for the first time in 15 months. Despite having the run of play, Fulham couldn't score. Leeds scored in the first half and Fulham spent the rest of the game chasing in vain. The match was also Andy's last game of the season as he headed to The Oval with Fulham's promotion hopes dashed for another season.

* * *

The first century of the season for Surrey came in the annual trial match and it was Andy who achieved it. Playing for Percy Fender's team against a side captained by Jack Hobbs, Andy hit an unbeaten 107 before retiring. The *Daily News (London)* was just as interested in a potential batting flaw, 'his persistent flourish of the bat means a waste of much energy', than a finely struck innings.

The County Championship started at home with Somerset being swept aside in two days. Fender's nine wickets set up Hobbs and Andy Sandham to win the game with ease. However, the fact that Surrey's two main bowlers, Bill Hitch and debutant Albert Geary, took just eight wickets between them was a precursor to a flaw that would be evident in the days, weeks, months and years to come.

Fender was equally influential in the next match with a blistering 185 as Surrey won by an innings against Hampshire. Andy scored 19 before offering a simple caught and bowled chance. His trial-match form had not carried through so far, but it would soon show itself with the visit of Essex.

The first day saw more than 15,000 spectators at The Oval. There was royalty of Indian, and cricketing, persuasion with the Maharaja Jam Saheb of Nawanagar (ex-Test cricketer Ranjitsinhji's official title) in attendance. It was Surrey's day, as Essex were bowled out for 265 before Hobbs and Andy carried Surrey to 94/1 at the close. Their partnership yielded 116 before Andy fell for 47 early on day two. Essex fought back and managed to squeeze a two-run lead before batting again. Led by Jack Russell, Essex scored 407/9 declared. However, Andy resisted the charge and scored an unbeaten 108 to secure the draw. With Henry Harrison, Andy was involved in a second century partnership of the match. He scored the majority of the 114 runs as Harrison deferred to his senior partner.

A trip to the South West was successful as Surrey beat Somerset then Gloucestershire comfortably. Andy's scores of 31, 39, 6 and 58 were a decent return. Fender took 18 of the 40 wickets to fall; the captain was covering the inadequacies of his bowling unit.

A second successive half-century for Andy went relatively unnoticed as Sandham and Alfred Jeacocke hammered Sussex's bowlers all over The Oval. Another innings victory was secured as Sussex never recovered from slipping to 27/5 from Bill Hitch's fiery opening spell. At Trent Bridge Andy was more noticeable with a crucial score of 80 as Surrey's usually dependable batsmen were removed cheaply in the first innings. Normality was resumed in the second innings with Hobbs' masterly 151 not out as Surrey cruised to 217/2 and another win.

Surrey's game at Leicestershire was heading for a draw after two days. Surrey had batted first and made 501. Hobbs scored 145, Andy added 72, while Harrison and Abel's half-centuries contributed to a large total. On the morning of the final day, Leicestershire lost their final two wickets to the bowling of Fender. Leicestershire followed on and this time the runs flowed. It smelled of a deal done by Fender and Leicestershire's captain Gustavus Fowke to increase the chances of a victory for either side. The declaration came in the afternoon, leaving Surrey needing 150 to win. Fender swapped his batting order around, moving himself up to No.3 to useful effect, and the win was secured by six wickets. Scoring at well over seven runs an over, Fender's 91 not out had won the game. However, it was felt that a more telling contribution was the discussion with his opposite number before play resumed on the final day.

Surrey travelled to Bradford for a top-of-the-table clash with Yorkshire, but rain was the winner. The game was delicately poised, with Surrey looking to kick on, but the final day's play was washed out. Unsurprisingly, Hobbs and Herbert Sutcliffe had dominated for their respective teams.

In a break from the County Championship, Scotland were touring, and Andy was selected to play despite many other senior players being rested. The match was played with less intensity than a usual first-class match. In the first innings, Andy was bowled going for a slog down the ground. He scored 42 and 41, but the match petered out into a draw.

The summer of 1922 did not have any Test cricket, but that did not stop newspaper speculation over the next England team selections. A winter tour of South Africa was coming up, but *The Guardian* did not rate Andy's chances. They put him in a third XI of possible players; it was a moot point anyway because of his commitment to Fulham.

The article coincided with a slump in Andy's form. Against Gloucestershire, he slapped a ball to mid-on and was dismissed for 12. Surrey scored 478 with Hobbs and Tom Shepherd scoring centuries. Andy fared no better against Cambridge University, 16 and 2, or Sussex with 18 and 6 not out. At the beginning of July, a duck against Essex was the nadir. Rain prevented Surrey closing out the win to doubly frustrate the situation.

Things picked up at Edgbaston when he was promoted to opener on the final day. Surrey had engineered a winning position and required 133 to win. The chase began, but rain soon stopped play. After an agonising wait of an hour and 40 minutes, Surrey were able to continue their innings at 5:40. Still needing another 115, Andy and Hobbs made light work of the total within an hour. Playing shots all around the ground, the batsmen delivered another County Championship win.

After the match, Surrey's players headed for an evening train to Manchester as they were playing Lancashire at Old Trafford the following morning. The match had been designated as Harry Makepeace's benefit, but there was little to celebrate for the opener or his Lancashire colleagues. It was a low-scoring game, but Surrey managed to keep ahead throughout. Andy fell to Cecil Parkin in both innings, for 3 and 8, as his mediocre season continued. *The Guardian*'s report was keen to illustrate the ingenuity and guile of Fender's captaincy. It pointed out how he would 'slyly motion a fieldsman to another place with a hand that waved in a comically surreptitious way behind his back' as a bowler began his run up to bowl.

Even Fender's magic touch couldn't save Surrey from defeat in the next match. Kent's ten-wicket victory was a crushing loss for

Surrey, their first defeat of the season, and allowed Yorkshire to overtake them at the top of the County Championship. History suggested that defeat was inevitable as Surrey had not won in the county since 1897. Furthermore, the Blackheath ground had seen nine successive victories for Kent.

Kent batted first and posted 243 which was mainly due to Frank Woolley's 75. In response, Surrey mustered just two more runs than Woolley as Tich Freeman ran through the hapless visitors' batting and claimed 7-43. From that point, it was only a matter of time before Kent claimed victory. The second innings proved more fruitful for Surrey's batsmen, but defeat was confirmed early on the final day.

After Lancashire had been vanquished for a second time by virtue of Fender's heroics with the ball, Kent visited The Oval. Around 28,000 spectators witnessed Surrey's domination of the game on the first day. Devoid of any fast bowlers in the side, they relied on spin and medium pace, and it worked as Kent were bowled out for 188. In response, Andy Sandham anchored the innings as the other Surrey batsmen attacked.

Andy's 61, before being lured out of his crease by Freeman, was welcome. Fender played one of his trademark innings, thrashing the ball to all parts, as Surrey hit 517. Surrey found their visitors more resolute second time around. Wally Hardinge, James Seymour and Frank Woolley all hit centuries and Kent comfortably earned a draw.

Against Hampshire, Andy took a liking to friendly bowling before Lionel Tennyson astutely brought on the extra pace of George Brown to good effect. Trying to fend off a short ball, Andy could only knock it up into the air and Brown took the catch off his own bowling. Surrey found themselves incredibly lucky to draw the match after another sporting declaration from Fender. Hampshire got within 44 runs of their target when stumps were drawn. It is not clear why the extra half-hour was not offered to them in the situation. Another draw at Nottinghamshire, rain rendering an already soggy pitch unplayable, saw Surrey's title hopes diminishing.

Wins in their next two games, over Middlesex and Leicestershire, set up a massive encounter at The Oval against leaders Yorkshire. Hobbs had been rested against Leicestershire, so his inclusion was a boost. However, Bill Hitch had to withdraw with a leg strain and weakened a bowling attack struggling to take 20 wickets against the better teams.

Around 25,000 spectators turned up on the first day and witnessed Surrey make a solid start to a must-win game. Andy was unluckily out for 49 as the home team scored 315/6. Day two drew an even bigger crowd hoping to see a home victory, but events soon turned the game towards Yorkshire. Surrey lost their last four wickets for 24 then Herbert Sutcliffe put on a performance. Supported by Edgar Oldroyd, Sutcliffe and Yorkshire batted Surrey out of the game and almost out of the County Championship race. Yorkshire finally declared on 539/5, leaving themselves enough time to bowl Surrey out, but the game was easily saved.

Needing a win against Middlesex, and other results to go their way, Surrey started well. Middlesex won the toss and batted first. Fender and John Lockton took wickets regularly and had Middlesex in some trouble at 151/7. Combined with the news from Sussex that Yorkshire had been bowled out for 42, it looked like the cricketing gods were smiling on Surrey.

Events turned when Nigel Haig and Challen Skeet fought back for Middlesex with a 122-run partnership. Also, Sussex managed only 95 and Yorkshire were batting again. Surrey batted all the way through the second day and passed Middlesex's score by virtue of Hobbs' hundred. Andy was among the runs with 84, and his partnership with the Surrey opener was worth 155.

Surrey's inability to take wickets was evident as Frank Mann and Patsy Hendren comfortably scored half-centuries to make sure that Middlesex couldn't lose. Surrey had 15 overs to negotiate at the end of the day, but a draw ended their Championship hopes despite losing just one game. With one round of matches left, Andy was released to play for Fulham.

Andy caught up with correspondence and one such letter is now in my possession. A handwritten note to Louis Frewer, who was a collector of autographs, promised to collect signatures of 'as many of the Surrey Boys as possible' and send them on. Andy apologised for not responding sooner due to mislaying the letter. The note has the address of Ardmore, Branksome Road, Southend-on-Sea so, presumably, this was the main residence for Andy at the time.

Andy was not quite finished with cricket for 1922 as he played in a charity match at Ealing Cricket Club, as part of a festival, for Patsy Hendren's 'All England' team against an Ealing District XVI. With names like Andy, Hendren, Sandham and Hearne in the opposition, Ealing needed more than 11 players to make the game entertaining for spectators. Andy put on a hitting display before skying a ball.

For Andy and Surrey, his average of 34 was not a good enough return. Hobbs topped the batting averages, followed by Sandham. Fender was third with 39.78. More telling was the statistic that he was also the highest wicket-taker with 143; the next nearest wicket-taker was Alan Peach with 60. Surrey needed to look no further than bowling to explain why they only lost one game yet finished third in the table.

* * *

All throughout the cricket season, Andy was subject to speculation about his playing future. There had been rumours of retiring from football to take up a management position. The *Athletic News* was just one of many newspapers to discuss managing a 'seaside League club'. Although the club was not named, Southend United would have to be a firm favourite, given his connection to the town and the club's situation. Southend finished at the bottom of the Third Division (South) and had to rely on re-election to stay in the league.

In an article on 9 July in the *Sunday Illustrated* he confirmed that he had been contemplating retiring but had been persuaded to carry on by 'those at Craven Cottage who hold strong views on

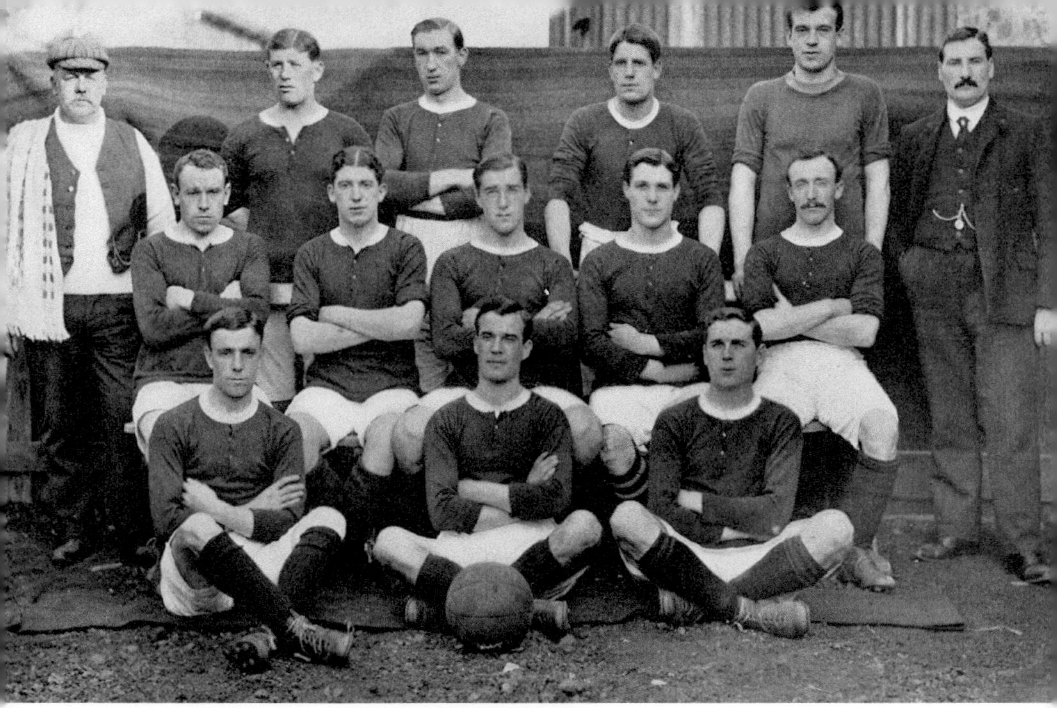

Andy's first team photograph at Woolwich Arsenal in 1905

Andy on staff at Surrey CCC in 1906

England football team in Ireland in 1910.

Surrey team photograph from 1910

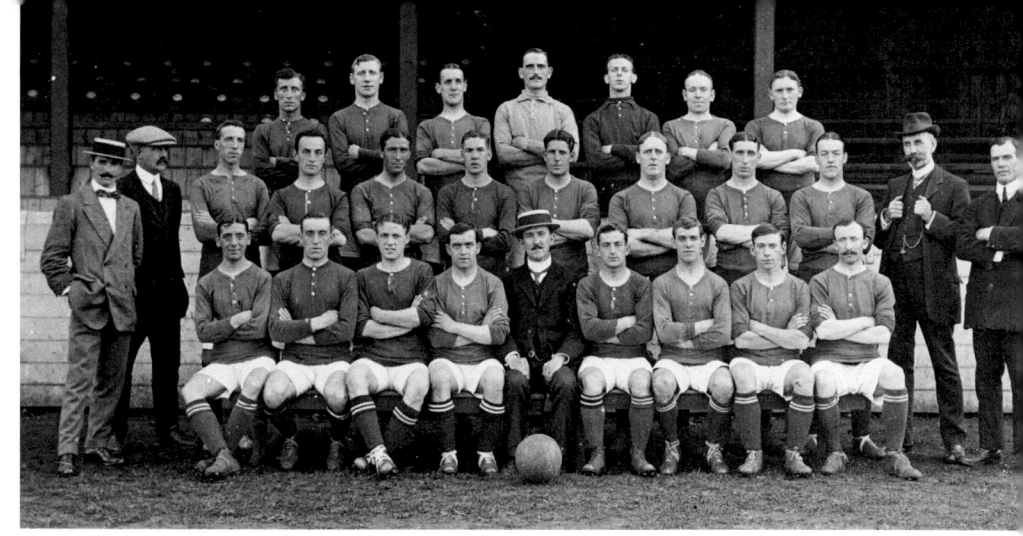

1911/12 Woolwich Arsenal team

A portrait of Andy from 1912

1912–13 Aston Villa team photograph

Meeting Prince Henry before the FA Cup final versus Huddersfield Town in 1920

Aston Villa's 1920 FA Cup winners

Andy in Fulham colours in 1921

A Surrey team photograph from 1922

Andy's benefit match at The Oval in 1923

Appointed as Fulham manager in 1924

A portrait of Andy from 1928　　*Andy batting in 1930*

Coaching at Roehampton in 1932

Umpiring with Herbert Strudwick in 1938

Andy at Lord's on July 23rd, 1942

the subject'. It is not a huge leap to conclude that Phil Kelso would have been a keen advocate for Andy to continue. His was a voice to which Andy attributed much importance. Perhaps not entirely altruistic in his reasoning, Kelso would have argued that Andy still had much to give on the pitch.

The season started with Andy still in cricket whites. Fulham lost just once in eight matches while Andy was trying to get ready for football. Despite playing some matches for the reserves, he did not warrant a place in the team. Andy was the first to recognise this. Harry Bagge was playing well at right-half and, according to the *Derby Daily Telegraph,* Andy 'is the first to deprecate any change being made'. The newspaper also recognised that 'Ducat's attitude marks him once again as a real sportsman.'

Andy's season started in the middle of October for the visit of The Wednesday. Andy had a good game from a defensive perspective. Age seemed to be restricting his forward foraging from midfield, but experience served Andy well in a more defensive role. A similar performance at Old Trafford cemented this style of football.

A 1-0 defeat at home to Barnsley was particularly disappointing as Andy put in another excellent shift defensively. His understanding with Torrance was noteworthy, but others let the team down in front of 20,000 disappointed Fulham fans.

Andy played in a run of games in the period prior to Christmas. It was an indifferent spell for both club and player with just two wins. During a game against Blackpool a female Tangerine fan shouted to Andy to ask what he thought of the 'Barrass/Mee' (Matt Barrass and Georgie Mee) wing partnership, and he responded with 'well, they em-Barrass-Mee'. Not exactly a 'zinger' but telling of Andy's mindset. Rumours of retirement had emerged again, and they seemed to have credence as Andy was showing signs of resignation that his football career was almost over.

Just before Christmas 1922 Andy helped to promote table tennis in the UK. The Table Tennis Association was formed in 1921 as England's national body and worked to grow the game. Bringing

Andy on board would have been a fillip to the cause. The game was growing in Southend and Andy was partly responsible.

The *Daily Mirror* covered the story and noted that 'many athletes, including cricketers, footballers, and boxers, find that table tennis is an excellent method of keeping in training'. They were also sponsoring a table tennis championship to help the sport grow.

In another article, the *Daily Mirror* had photographs of Andy with Jack Hobbs playing table tennis. One of the photographs included the founder of the Table Tennis Association, Ivor Montagu, as referee. Montagu would do much to further table tennis around the world, but he was also a Soviet spy at the same time as Kim Philby, Guy Burgess and Donald MacLean.

Pathé took footage of the game between Andy and Hobbs for cinemagoers. Fortunately, the footage is available on the British Pathé YouTube channel. The film is silent and lasts for just over two minutes. Both men are dressed in waistcoats, ties, trousers and have heavy eye and face makeup which was a feature of 1920s film. There is a mix of slow motion and real time footage clearly designed to leave audiences in wonder at the new game.

Andy returned to the Fulham team in early January for the FA Cup tie with Leicester City. Andy made a crucial interception in the first half before being caught in possession and nearly conceding a goal. Leicester ran away with the match in the second half and Andy uncharacteristically resorted to trying to trip the livewire Percy Tompkin but couldn't make contact.

The visit to Bury saw Andy play much better and Fulham won an away match for the first time in three months. Another win at Rotherham County was followed up by a home defeat in the reverse fixture, and Andy was dropped. Fulham won the next five out of six matches before Andy was slotted in as right-back for the visit to Leicester City. The match was drawn, and Andy was back out of the team for the next match and did not feature again in the 1922/23 season. Retirement from football would have been a serious consideration due to the physicality of playing sport all year round. However, Andy committed to another season at Fulham.

*　*　*

The 1923 cricket season started for Andy in Cardiff. Although Glamorgan had been given first-class status and joined the County Championship in 1921, Surrey had never played against cricket's newest county. There was a minimum number of matches that each county had to play each season, but the make-up of those fixtures was down to the counties themselves. The match at Cardiff Arms Park started well for the home team with Norman Riches scoring 70. Despite being bowled out for 168, Glamorgan had the temerity to remove both openers for 14. Andy's 31 aided the recovery, along with Fender's 39, but Trevor Arnott's 5-50 gave Glamorgan a slender first-innings lead.

Surrey gave two players their debuts in the match, Caryl Thain and Ronald Lowe. Lowe took full advantage of his opportunity and his 5-15 in the second innings contributed to Glamorgan capitulating for just 35. Fender took 4-7 in nine overs as Surrey grabbed the game by the scruff of the neck. Hobbs and Sandham made no mistake in scoring the 46 required for victory.

From south Wales, Surrey headed east to Bath to face Somerset. Surrey found the Recreation Ground tough going after a frustrating first day where just three overs were possible. Hobbs and Sandham were both back in the pavilion with just one on the board. Andy found Somerset's bowlers simple enough while his colleagues failed to get into double figures. Lowe was the final wicket to fall, with the score on 91, leaving Andy 52 not out. Somerset found batting slightly easier but were still bowled out before the end of the second day for 140.

On day three, history was made as Hobbs scored his hundredth hundred. He became the third, after W.G. Grace and Tom Hayward, to achieve the feat. After Hobbs had reached the milestone, Fender soon declared and rolled the dice on winning the match. At one point it looked like the gamble had failed, but last man Ernie Robson nicked Alan Peach to Herbert Strudwick and the trusty wicketkeeper made no mistake. Surrey secured victory by ten runs.

Surrey's final game in their visit to the western counties was against Gloucestershire. The match ended as a draw with Andy returning scores of 9 and 14. The main point of interest was Gloucestershire's 19-year-old opener scoring his maiden century in the first innings. The batsman was Wally Hammond, and he would go on to make another 166 of them in his career. Hammond followed up with 92 in the second innings for good measure.

Andy missed the next three matches with a cold. He returned against Leicestershire, with a solid 30, before scoring 46 in the first innings against Sussex at The Oval. Both matches ended as draws with rain being a contributory factor in both games.

May ended with Andy playing a signature innings. Facing a wayward Glamorgan attack, he knew how to despatch such bowling at The Oval. Robin Baily of the *Daily Herald* recognised that 'once set, the footballer-cricketer hits the ball very hard all round the wicket, and no batsman is more severe on loose bowling, not even Patsy Hendren.' Andy scored 126 including two massive sixes. One of them was described as a 'screamer' in the same *Daily Herald* article, and landed in the pavilion.

Following on from the convincing win over Glamorgan, Surrey beat Essex then Leicestershire by an innings. Both matches ended in their second day as Surrey played some excellent cricket. Essex were swept aside by Sandham's double century whereas Leicestershire were bowled out for 64 and 66. Andy made two single-digit scores.

He played much better in the second innings at Old Trafford a few days later, in a match that Fender was trying to turn into another victory opportunity. Having passed his half-century, Andy flashed at a faster ball from Cecil Parkin. The ball caught the edge and flew like a rocket towards the slips. Dick Tyldesley instinctively threw his large frame towards the ball and caught it no more than an inch from the ground. It was a catch that *The Guardian* labelled as 'miraculous'.

Travelling down to Edgbaston, Surrey faced Warwickshire on a wicket that no batsman enjoyed. On the first day, 20 wickets fell as Warwickshire's Harry Howell then Fender each took seven wickets. Surrey batted first and fell from 59/2, with Hobbs and Andy at the crease, to 103 all out. The home side lasted slightly longer, but a 25-run lead was never going to be enough. Day two witnessed the other 20 wickets fall with Surrey scoring 190 to leave Warwickshire with a tricky total that they never looked like getting.

A trip north to play champions Yorkshire proved to be a chastening experience. Andy's run of single-figure scores continued when his county needed a score from him. Set 183 to win, Surrey comfortably reached 127/2, despite Andy's failure, before Roy Kilner initiated a collapse to secure maximum points for Yorkshire.

Back at The Oval, Andy played himself back into form with an unbeaten 41 against Somerset before facing the friendlier prospect of the bowling attacks of Cambridge University and Oxford University. Cambridge visited The Oval first and rested their key bowlers for the upcoming Varsity match. Despite getting two quick wickets, Cambridge's bowlers were soon dispatched to all parts. Andy was the main protagonist with a century before lunch followed by Jeacocke and Abel reaching the milestone in the afternoon. Declaring overnight on 594/8, Surrey found that the weather was more resistant than the Cambridge batsmen before Bill Sadler's hat-trick wrapped up the win by an innings on day three.

Oxford proved to be far more of a proposition. With Douglas Jardine in their ranks, in the last year of his history degree, as well as others with county cricket experience such as Greville Stevens (Middlesex) and Raymond Robertson-Glasgow (Somerset), Oxford had a good team. Add to that a weakened Surrey selection and the situation was ripe for an upset. The Australian Reg Bettington, studying for a medical degree, took 5-22 as Surrey's last eight batsman failed to get into double figures and Surrey crashed to 100 all out. Andy scored 17 before Stevens trapped him leg before wicket.

In reply, Oxford scored 263 to leave Surrey with a large deficit. Second time around, Surrey batted much better and Andy scored a century. His 134 was scored all around the wicket and helped drive Surrey to a total that they could bowl at. Unfortunately, they could not field to it and a string of errors allowed Oxford to claim a famous victory. They were led by Jardine, who missed the whole of the 1922 season for Surrey due to a knee injury, scoring a far from chanceless 95. Ably assisted by Middlesex's John Guise, who received similar generosity from Surrey's fielders, the pair added 161. Sadler picked up six of the seven wickets to fall but the Dark Blues won the match.

Andy's consistent form carried on back in the County Championship when his third century in as many games helped set up victory against Essex. With Surrey needing 277 to win, Andy along with Tom Shepherd played wonderfully well. Andy couldn't quite see the game to the finish, but Alfred Jeacocke scored 30 of the last 31 required for the win.

Surrey headed north of the border to face Scotland at Hamilton Crescent in Glasgow. Despite dominating the match, they could not quite get the win. As the *Dundee Courier* reported, 'Scotland's lucky draw.' Scotland were nine wickets down when time was called on the match. Both Hobbs and Sandham passed 1,000 runs for the season, while Andy notched his 13,000th first-class run. After Glasgow, Sunderland was the next destination to face Durham. First-class status was still 69 years away for the county and Surrey won easily by an innings and 136 runs. Andy hit 95 as the Minor County struggled to compete with bat and ball.

After a single day off following their journey back from the North East, Surrey welcomed Lancashire at The Oval. Despite giving up a 251-run lead on first innings, Lancashire easily secured the draw with a much-improved second innings. Ernest

Tyldesley's 236 was worthy of the draw alone. The standout moment of the match was Fender's over to Harry Makepeace in the first innings when he bowled an over of slow, dipping deliveries. The over was like something from a T20 game rather than a County Championship match in 1923. Presumably, they were knuckle-ball deliveries which Fender may have taken from baseball. He certainly discussed baseball skills in cricket later in his career. His figures of 6-60 justified what *The Guardian* called his 'subtle arts'.

Later in July, Andy put together a decent run of scores. Against Kent, he punished every short ball he faced until he pulled one to short leg to depart for 35. Away to Hampshire, he played a fine knock of 92 to help make the game safe. A partnership of 134 with Jardine was the standout for Surrey. Even in a game badly affected by rain against Kent, Andy scored a solid 41.

The visit of the touring West Indians, featuring Learie Constantine, proved far more problematic. The express pace of George Francis, without first-class cricket experience prior to the tour, caused Andy distress. Francis bowled to hit the stumps and his pace caught Andy in front for a duck. Francis took 5-31 as Surrey slumped to 87 all out. Francis also proved to be a decent batsman as he supported opener George Challenor, who would be the first West Indian to face a ball in a Test match, to put on 136 for the last wicket. Challenor finished undefeated on 155. Surrey made a better job of the second innings, scoring 336, but Challenor hit 66 not out as the West Indians won by ten wickets.

Prior to his benefit match, Andy warmed up with a half-century against Nottinghamshire. The match was a high-scoring draw. On 11 August, 14,856 people attended the first day of Surrey's game with Middlesex at The Oval. Having been designated as Andy's benefit match, a collection was taken and a sum of £165 19s 4d (around £11,000 in 2022) was realised. Having won the toss, Surrey batted on a fabulous pitch and cashed in. Firstly, Hobbs and Sandham set a new partnership best with an opening stand of 244. Andy then came in and played with, according to *The Observer*, 'form quite worthy of the occasion'. He was out for 75, but Surrey ploughed on and ended the day 482/6.

With an overnight declaration, Fender was looking to get quick wickets. Middlesex withheld the charge, with Patsy Hendren digging in for 86 not out. However, Surrey were batting again before the end of play and looking to set up another victory through weight of runs. When the declaration came, Fender had 428 runs to play with. Despite the best efforts of the Surrey bowlers, Hendren was a thorn in the side once again and his 142 not out secured the draw.

Having been frustrated by Hendren at The Oval, rain proved to be equally influential at Hastings, as Sussex were saved by the weather on the last day. Sussex started the match badly and slipped to 14/4 before scrapping to 164. The Surrey run machine was in full effect in response, and Andy's fifth century of the season helped the visitors to 552/8. A 215-run partnership with Shepherd demoralised a flagging bowling attack. With Sussex at their mercy, rain stopped play for 85 minutes. Within ten minutes of the resumption, the heavens opened again, and no further play was possible.

The season spiralled into an anticlimax with Yorkshire clear winners of the County Championship for the second year running. The final match of the season, against Warwickshire, tailed off into a draw with Surrey apparently having no heart to try to win the game. Andy top-scored with 68 before being bowled by Bob Wyatt, but the game appeared to be gone as a contest before a ball had been bowled.

* * *

Andy returned to Craven Cottage for the 1923/24 season and spent the first few weeks playing for the reserves in London Combination matches. His first match was against Tottenham Hotspur and he played a few other matches including against his 'home' team, Southend United. Despite switching over sports, Andy was still in demand for cricket and featured in a charity game for Patsy Hendren's team at Ealing.

Andy made his first league start of the season for the visit of Coventry City. Fulham's league form had been patchy, including losing their first four games of the season, and Phil Kelso was in need of Andy's experience. Against Coventry, he did not disappoint, playing well defensively and in attack. The *Daily News (London)* noted that, 'The old Villa man has slowed down with the passing of the years, but I am sure that Fulham cannot improve upon him at wing half-back; he used his weight, and he used his experience and generalship and, taken all round, did yeoman service to his side.' Despite his performance, Fulham could only draw 1-1.

Fulham took three points from an available four against fellow strugglers Bristol City but the performances did not improve greatly. Andy gave away a penalty at Craven Cottage to give City an equaliser. He made amends a couple of weeks later with a vintage performance to inspire an injured-ravaged Fulham to beat Southampton 3-2 at home. *The People* noted that Andy had 'rarely given a better display' and made the third goal for Fulham with a run to open up the defence for Jack Papworth to score. The win took Fulham above Hull City, but they were still languishing in 19th place.

Fulham followed up with another 3-2 home victory; this time it was Derby County who were on the wrong end of a five-goal thriller. Andy was not as influential, but still combined well with Torrance to stop Derby's attacks on goal. There was also a desperate block of a goal-bound shot to cement his defensive performance.

Although Fulham's forwards were scoring, their defenders were not performing as well. After two 3-2 wins, they followed with a 3-3 draw at Derby before another 3-2 game at Craven Cottage ended in favour of the visitors Blackpool.

Andy was selected to represent the Football Association for a match against Cambridge University. He was joined by fellow cricketer Patsy Hendren, who played as a forward for Brentford. Unfortunately, the match was called off due to the pitch being unplayable.

Andy was captaining Fulham, but his presence was not enough to change fortunes. A goalless draw against fellow strugglers Nelson, the Lancashire club promoted from the Third Division North, was symptomatic of the malaise at Craven Cottage. Andy played well, trying to inspire from half-back, but a 'most mediocre display of football' according to *Athletic News* saw the 15,000 spectators voice their displeasure.

For the reverse fixture, Andy was switched to full-back. It was a tactic that provided limited success and it needed goalkeeper Arthur Reynolds to save Fulham on several occasions. Fulham drew 1-1 and went into the busy Christmas period without a win in over a month.

Christmas Day saw Hull City visit Craven Cottage and more than 23,000 watched another disappointing draw. Andy was kept at right-back and was responsible for Hull's goal when he handled the ball in the area and the resultant penalty kick was scored. Later in the game, he was beaten by Paddy Mills, but the forward slipped when shooting. After the match, both teams travelled up to Hull for the reverse fixture on Boxing Day. Hull won comfortably 4-2 and Andy was found wanting several times with his slow recovery. A 0-0 draw against Oldham Athletic three days later ended the festive period without a win. Phil Kelso secured the transfer of forward George Reid from Cardiff City and drafted him in against Oldham to get much-needed goals, but he failed to score.

It was the FA Cup first-round encounter that brought Fulham's first win since Derby County. Llanelli AFC were drawn at Craven Cottage and Fulham managed a 2-0 win. Fulham followed up with a 3-1 win over Manchester United in the league. Andy was still at right-back, presumably Kelso thinking this was the best option, and played brilliantly. *Athletic News* commented that Andy was 'as cool, clean, and studied in his methods as he was strong'. Fulham followed up with a 1-1 draw at Manchester United with Andy once again excelling at the back.

Fulham lost their FA Cup second-round match against Burnley after extra time was required in the replay. Both matches were defensive affairs, but Burnley broke away and scored the only goal in the two matches to dump Fulham out of the cup. Andy came out of the match with the plaudits for another performance with the *Daily Mirror* heralding 'Ducat's Great Display'. Andy picked up an injury and missed the next game.

He returned for the visit of Bradford City and struggled as their forwards caused many problems. The match ended 1-1, but an unsavoury incident occurred when Bradford scored. Their goalkeeper, Jimmy McLaren, was showered with pebbles and orange peel. The goalkeeper had been involved in a clash with a Fulham player earlier and the fans took the goal as an opportunity for retribution.

Fulham's performances led to draws at home and defeats away. Andy generally played well during the period but was found wanting at times. When he left the pitch after a 3-0 defeat at Leeds United, he was nursing an injury. An x-ray had revealed a broken bone in a toe and his season was over. It would also bring an end to his playing career and open up a new chapter in Andy's sporting life.

CHAPTER ELEVEN

Into Management
1924–1926

ANDY MISSED Surrey's first game of the County Championship against Glamorgan because of his football injury. A few days after the Welsh county had been beaten inside two days, Andy ventured to The Oval for batting practice. Not long into the practice, with Bill Hitch bowling his fourth delivery, he was hit on the arm by a short ball and left in considerable pain. Andy couldn't get his top hand out of the way and the ball thundered into his forearm just above the wrist.

In no fit state to continue, he left the nets and was taken to have the injury assessed; an x-ray confirmed a break. Photographs of Andy sitting with Hitch were featured in the newspapers. It was an awkwardly posed picture with Andy sitting with his arm in a sling while Hitch looks on.

It was estimated that it would be a minimum of six weeks before Andy was back for Surrey. Little did most people know that events at Craven Cottage would conspire to delay the return for almost 12 months.

* * *

On 11 May, newspapers broke the story that Phil Kelso had resigned as secretary-manager of Fulham. Kelso was leaving football to become a publican at the Grove Tavern at Hammersmith. Andy's name was linked to the job, but no firm decision to take the role had been made. One of the directors had spoken with Andy at The Oval, and the board had met several times.

Once Andy had indicated his interest in the job, Fulham held discussions with Surrey over his cricket contract. In *Beyond Bat and Ball*, David Foot commented that Surrey had been 'rather cross' over Andy's intentions but agreed to his taking the role. They agreed to release him under the stipulation that Andy made himself available for cricket during June and July while still in contract. Fulham agreed, all three parties had an accord and Andy was appointed manager. The appointment was ratified at Fulham's AGM.

One of Andy's first acts as manager, even before the formal approval, was to place an advert in *Athletic News* for new players. Lots of clubs, from Accrington Stanley to York City, advertised for players; Andy was looking for all positions whereas some clubs were specific in their requirements.

His main targets were forwards to get Fulham more goals which they had lacked the previous season. Andy commented in an interview with *The People* that 'because I recognise the strength of our opponents I know how silly one's autumnal optimism may be made to appear in February. Our weakness last campaign was in the forward line.'

Before Andy could get to work in rebuilding the Fulham team, he was struck down by another health issue. His arm was healing, but a nasal problem required an operation and he had to take leave from the new job to get the issue repaired.

Andy's first match in charge was at Valley Parade and his team managed a draw with Bradford City. The home team scored on 13 minutes after Fulham started slowly. The score stayed at 1-0 going into the interval. Andy's first half-time team talk worked wonders as Fulham played much better in the second half and were rewarded with an equaliser with 22 minutes left. Fulham followed that up with another draw, this time at home to South Shields. Andy's first win came at Port Vale with a breakaway goal. After three matches, Fulham were unbeaten.

The unbeaten record soon went with a 5-1 drubbing at Derby County. Andy was still trying to find his best 11 and played Len Oliver at right-half. The player had a torrid time, but Andy provided consolation, according to the *Derby Daily Telegraph*, by saying to Oliver that he should 'not be discouraged, as during the season he would not run up against many left wings like that of Derby'. Clearly, Andy was keen to develop his man-management skills.

With Andy still finding his feet in the world of football management, he chose to dedicate one of his newspaper columns to discussing his expectations. He commented on how his suitability had been questioned by some. Andy showed signs of frustration at people's reaction by saying, 'I do not know whether I should make what is called a good manager or not, but I can assure every individual interested that I took on the job with my eyes open, knowing something of the troubles and difficulties connected with the position.'

By the middle of October, Fulham had lost just twice in eight league matches. Andy was disappointed that the team was not gelling as well as he would have liked. Around the same time, Fulham engaged the services of Fred Spiksley as a coach. The enigmatic ex-player had won an FA Cup winners' medal and seven England caps as well as acting with Charlie Chaplin before coaching teams in Sweden, Germany, France, Switzerland, Mexico and the USA. Spiksley had approached Fulham and demonstrated his coaching techniques, which were years ahead of their time, and was taken on at Craven Cottage.

At the end of the month, Andy faced his first real test as manager, and it was not football related. The Fulham team had just left Craven Cottage in two coaches bound for Tottenham Hotspur for a London Challenge Cup tie, when a lorry pulled out in front of the first coach. The driver swerved to avoid a collision, but the coach toppled over. Two players, William Prouse and Len Oliver, received cuts from broken glass. Trainer Elijah Morse had his arm crushed which resulted in an amputation. Morse required several operations and one of Fulham's players provided blood for a transfusion. It would have been a traumatic incident for all concerned. Morse could not work again and eventually won damages, with Andy required to testify in court, because of the accident.

Andy was affected by the accident and discussed it alongside the concept of 'luck' in his next newspaper column. It was a sympathetic piece, discussing how one of the players had experienced guilt that he had survived the crash without injury. With the memories of the accident still fresh, Fulham were about to receive even darker news.

One of the players involved in the crash was inside-forward Harvey Darvill. Two weeks later, Darvill clashed with Leicester City goalkeeper George Hebden. Darvill lay on the pitch for a while before getting back up. He complained of stomach pains before carrying on. He subsequently played in two more matches, including scoring an equaliser against Stoke, before being rushed into hospital. An operation found a ruptured blood vessel in his stomach, and he died. He was 28 and had been married for six months. Andy and the Fulham team attended the funeral. Such tragedies were putting a huge strain on Andy's personal and professional life.

Fulham's first match after Darvill's death was a 0-0 draw at Oldham. It was testimony to the players that they were able to play. The visit of Middlesbrough, days later, provided the same type of performance and result.

By the end of the year, Fulham were sitting in tenth place. The start of 1925 saw Fulham win 3-1 at Middlesbrough before following up with an FA Cup win at Swindon Town. When Fulham had been drawn against Swindon, their manager Sam Allen was spotted spying on Fulham at their home game against Bradford City. Fulham had already developed a plan to do the same, and Fred Spiksley was sent on an overnight journey to attend Swindon's next match. However, the game was abandoned due to flooding and Spiksley's journey was rendered pointless.

Jimmy Torrance was quoted in the *Coventry Evening Telegraph* as saying that 'we have never before during my long career with the Fulham club been such a happy family as we are today'. Just when it seemed that things were clicking on and off the pitch, Fulham had a run of four straight defeats. Andy had taken the team to Southport for a week's special training, to try and improve his team's away form, yet Fulham continued to do badly away from Craven Cottage.

It was the end of March before Fulham won away from home and it was Prouse who netted the only goal against Coventry City. Reynolds saved a penalty to provide a much-needed win. The game was part of a four-match winning streak for Fulham, but it was followed by losing the next four. The chance of promotion had already gone.

One way in which Andy was thinking of moving Fulham forward was through setting up a youth system. Such an idea seems obvious, and necessary, now but in 1925 it was novel. The *Star Green 'Un* covered the story and reported that Andy was being 'allowed a pet idea of his next season – the formation of a junior team of boys who have just left school. Seeing how promising many schoolboys are, the scheme should be successful, particularly with Fred Spiksley as coach.'

In the last match of the season, Fulham could only draw at Craven Cottage with Port Vale. The *Westminster Gazette* pointed out that 'there was much to admire in the last match of the season at Fulham, and yet before the end the onlookers were inclined to be sarcastic'. Fulham's defence and attack were left wanting. Andy's half-backs in Torrance and Bagge were producing quality, but everywhere else needed improving. With Fulham finishing 12th, 17 points short of promotion, Andy's first season had at least been an improvement on the previous one. Yet there was much to do to deliver Fulham to the First Division for the first time in their history.

* * *

Andy's reintroduction to the Surrey team was via club cricket. He made several appearances for Honor Oak in Dulwich to regain his touch and sharpen his cricket brain after another lengthy lay-off. Alongside Andy in the Honor Oak team was John Lockton, who had played 20 matches for Surrey since 1919.

It was an unsurprisingly positive experience for Andy, who scored plenty of runs as well as nipping out crucial wickets. Against Guy's Hospital, he scored 90 in a comfortable victory. Honor Oak's match with Forest Hill was a tight affair and Andy's 6-30 proved to be the difference as the match was won by one run. At Parson's Green, Andy scored 28 and took a wicket, but that was just a warm-up for the Catford Wanderers' bowlers. His 225 was the highest individual score in London's club cricket that season. It was also a signal that it was time to regain his place in the Surrey ranks.

The match against Cambridge University was chosen for the comeback and, as *The Guardian* reported, it was a 'successful return to the team'. It was like almost two years had not passed as he joined Jack Hobbs and the pair scored almost at will. In a 171-run partnership, Andy made 91 to mark his return emphatically. Hobbs scored a century in both innings, but Cambridge secured a remarkable victory by scoring 427 in the fourth innings. Future England players Eddie Dawson and K.S. Duleepsinhji batted brilliantly to set up the win.

Andy's County Championship return proved to be even more successful with a century and an innings win against Somerset. Andy and Hobbs shared another century partnership before he was joined by Shepherd. The pair scored 180 in 95 minutes as inferior bowling and poor fielding were punished. Andy offered catches on 87 and 111, disproving superstitious cricket fans from Australia and the United Kingdom, and finally perished on 128. Shepherd completed his century as Surrey amassed 477, which proved too much for Somerset.

Andy's first away match in nearly two years was not a successful one. At Edgbaston, scores of 3 and 2 did nothing to help Surrey, although Hobbs' 215 set up a five-wicket win. The visit to Bradford resulted in a resounding defeat. Yorkshire had won the past three County Championships and were looking for an unprecedented fourth in a row. At lunch on the first day, Surrey had scored 87/3. Hobbs, Sandham and Andy had all got starts then got out. After lunch, Surrey imploded and lost their last seven wickets for 24. It was a blow that they could not recover from and, despite an improved second innings, Percy Holmes and Herbert Sutcliffe easily knocked off the runs to secure a ten-wicket victory.

After missing several matches, Andy returned for the game away to Hampshire. He passed 14,000 first-class runs in the match to help Surrey to victory. A 94-run partnership with Sandham gave Surrey momentum, but the match was won by Albert Geary's bowling in the fourth innings.

Andy's final Championship match of the season, before resuming his Fulham duties, was the visit to Gloucester. The match was played at the Wagon Works Ground, owned by the Gloucester Railway Carriage and Wagon Company, and was the first time that Surrey had played there. Andy scored 65 and 39 before Gloucestershire crumbled to Percy Fender's bowling. Andy ended the season with an average of 41.09 from 11 innings. Surrey finished second in the table to record-breaking Yorkshire, who were unbeaten.

Despite returning to Craven Cottage, Andy could not put his cricket whites away for winter. A cricket competition between some of London's football teams, for the *London Evening News* Cricket Cup, saw Andy playing for Fulham. In the opening round, Fulham and Chelsea met and Andy was on sparkling form. He opened the batting with Bert White, who had played eight times for Warwickshire, and the pair easily put on 109 before White was bowled for 34. George Utley, who was a cricket coach when not coaching Fulham, supported Andy, who was crashing the ball around the Parsons Green ground. When Utley was out for 16, Andy declared. The score was 193/2 and Andy had scored 142 of the runs. However, rain had been falling regularly and washed the game out soon after Chelsea attempted their almost impossible run chase. The abandoned game was played a few days later and Fulham won by 70 runs. Andy was not quite as emphatic with the bat; Utley did the damage with the ball with a 7-38 haul. More than 3,000 people packed into the ground to witness the match.

In the semi-final, Fulham faced Crystal Palace, and Andy was again in good form with the bat. White opened with Andy and a partnership of more than 150 was achieved before George Clarke removed them both. Fulham set Crystal Palace 196 to win, and the total was too much despite Tom Crosskey, who would play for Scotland against the 1948 Australian Invincibles, carrying his bat for 66 not out. Andy took 3-8 as Fulham eased into the final.

The final was a massive anticlimax for Andy and Fulham as a poor display saw underdogs Millwall collect the cup by 35 runs. Andy, White and Bob Gregory, another Surrey cricketer who Andy had signed for Fulham earlier in the summer, all failed with the bat. Gregory took a hat-trick with the ball, but Millwall were fair value for their win. Jack Hobbs presented the cup in front of 5,000 spectators at the Army Sports Ground in Leyton. The *Westminster and Pimlico News* reported that Hobbs 'jokingly remarked that his friend, Andy Ducat, had persuaded him to sign on for Fulham for next season in order that he might take part in the competition himself'.

* * *

Andy's focus for the 1925/26 season included a change to the offside law. The change was anticipated to bring more goals, due to the position that defenders would need to get into to invoke the offside rule, and Andy was a fan of the change. What he, and others would not realise to begin with, was that the tried and tested 2-3-5 formation would become redundant as teams found ways to exploit the change to the law.

In between Fulham's cricketing exploits, the new season started away to The Wednesday. Ominously, Fulham were 1-0 down within three minutes when Alex Chaplin conceded a penalty. Andy used three new players in his line-up and the team tried hard, but Wednesday's forwards were more clinical and scored twice more for a comprehensive win.

Two days later, Second Division newcomers Swansea Town visited Craven Cottage and scored six minutes from time to nick the match 1-0. When Fulham lost their third match, Andy changed the team. Albert Barrett, who had just signed, came in for the trip to Oldham. Despite Fulham putting in a sterling effort, Oldham won 4-0.

Despite losing the first four matches, Andy still managed to 'smile through his troubles' reported the *Daily Mirror*. By keeping positive, Andy finally got his first victory of the season with a 1-0 win over Stockport County. But it was a false dawn as Fulham lost the next four matches. Scores of 6-0, 4-0, 5-2 and 2-1 left Fulham in trouble, and Andy needing to turn the problems around quickly.

He brought in two new forwards, Albert Pape and Joseph Harris, and a 2-1 win at home against Preston North End released some pressure. The following week saw Leyton Orient visit and win 2-0. To make matters worse, a note appeared in the match programme stating that 'we wish to make it known, once and for all, that the directors have not been responsible for selecting the team. The choosing has been done by Mr Andy Ducat, our manager.' No matter how well intentioned the note was, it was clearly putting the current position of the club at Andy's door. Andy's response, printed in the *Derby Daily Telegraph*, stated that 'he [Andy] is quite willing to stand or fall by his own judgement'.

November 1925 saw Andy receive a welcome distraction from Fulham's plight. He had turned inventor and launched his table football game in time for the Christmas market. The game was designed for tabletops and was 4ft 6in in length and 3ft 2in wide. The 'footballers' were actually metal scoops attached to cross rods. Each goal was netted, and the ball was 'celluloid' so would probably have been inspired by Andy's interest in table tennis.

INTO MANAGEMENT

The foosball design we know today was not commonplace until the 1930s. Andy's design was certainly not unique but would have been unknown to many at the time. There were three rods per team and the game was designed for a player to control each rod.

A press gathering was organised to announce the 'Andy Ducat Football Game' and took place at Anderton's Hotel in Fleet Street. Andy was joined by Charlie Buchan, George Edmonds and Jack Hobbs. Buchan was playing at Arsenal, after joining them from Sunderland, but had started his career there in 1909 as an amateur. He would have known Andy from then and the pair were friends. As a Fulham player, Edmonds was supporting his manager. And for Hobbs, his endorsement would have been perceived as a massive boost to the reach of the product.

At the gathering, a game was played between three journalists and Andy with Buchan and Edmonds. The footballers won 6-2 while Hobbs acted as referee. The price of the game was 50 shillings (more than £150 in 2021) but was supplied to the British Legion for 42 shillings. It is impossible to know how well the game was adopted by families in the UK. An advert in *The Guardian* early in 1926 called for a salesman in the Lancashire area to sell the game on a commission basis only.

The game was not the first time that Andy had turned inventor. He had patented his 'Ducat' football boot with a 'shock absorber' on the front. The toes were covered by a sponge and rubber casing. They were marketed as the 'football boot of the future'. The boots were regularly advertised in newspapers up to the late 1930s.

At the end of the month, an unfortunate accident meant that Andy required an emergency operation to remove a bone from his throat. Andy had eaten some food several days earlier which had lodged and prevented him from eating. He could only drink and, after consulting with Fulham's club doctor, an x-ray revealed the problem was a chicken bone.

Beyond Bat and Ball asserts that Andy was distracted and that was the cause. We will never know, but it seems certain that he would have been fixated by Fulham's plight. In a season when promotion was the goal, a relegation battle was on, and it was on Andy's shoulders. He would not have it any other way, but that would have brought no comfort from the stresses and strains of club management. Furthermore, the hospitalisation and recovery process removed him from the situation when Fulham needed him most.

While Andy recovered, Fulham continued to struggle. A defeat at Blackpool was followed by draws against Port Vale and Bradford City. Christmas Day brought a welcome victory over Middlesbrough, but Fulham still lay one place off the bottom of the table. Middlesbrough took their revenge in the reverse fixture on Boxing Day with an emphatic 4-0 scoreline.

January brought entry into the FA Cup and although it was a distraction, it proved to be a positive one. In the third round, Fulham had been drawn away to First Division Everton. At Goodison Park, Fulham secured a 1-1 draw despite going behind to a goal from prolific marksman Dixie Dean. Andy set Fulham up to play a long-ball game and it upset Everton's play. In the replay, with Craven Cottage blanketed in snow, a second-half breakaway goal was enough for Fulham to progress.

The fourth round saw Fulham pitched against Liverpool with the odds in favour of the First Division team. Around 35,000 spectators packed into Craven Cottage and Fulham scored within the first three minutes and won the match 3-1. Fulham's fifth-round opponents were again from the First Division. Drawn away at Notts County, Fulham would have gone into the game feeling confident. Living up to the giant-killer tag, William Prouse scored with three minutes of the game to go to secure a place in the sixth round.

Manchester United were the sixth-round opponents, the fourth successive First Division team Fulham had faced. Andy would have been pleased to see one of United's players, ex-Villa colleague Frank Barson. However, it was Barson who had a very good game as United ended Fulham's cup run with a 2-1 win at Craven Cottage.

One aspect of the run that would have pleased Andy was how it had a positive effect on league form. In the period of their progress, ending at the beginning of March, Fulham won three games while drawing one and losing two. One of the ways that Andy tried to keep his team on track was to take a trip to the theatre as a distraction. He took the players to the newly opened Vaudeville Theatre in the West End of London to watch a play starring his sister-in-law, Joyce Barbour.

Despite a period of resurgence, a 2-1 defeat at Preston North End started another run of poor results. Andy's body language after the match did not augur well for Fulham. The *Lancashire Evening Post* summed up the situation, 'Fulham's shortcomings were so glaring that there were very few moments when their play conveyed the impression of the ability to earn the points they so greatly needed. Andy Ducat, the old football and cricket international, who is their manager, wore a very gloomy expression at the close of this uneven game with a frolicsome ball, and well he might, for his team had chances enough – easy ones at that – to win.'

After losing five of the next six matches, Andy's expression would have deteriorated as rapidly as Fulham's league position. It was not just Andy who was suffering because of Fulham's form. After a 2-0 defeat at home to Nottingham Forest, many supporters demonstrated against the referee as he blew the final whistle. Clearly projecting their anger, the protesting spectators started to get hostile. Andy decided that he would intervene and appealed to the crowd but, as the *Nottingham Journal* commented, 'Andy Ducat's persuasive powers had little effect and eventually the referee made his exit unobserved under the protection of a cordon of police and the Forest team.'

The UK was about to enter the General Strike, and feelings were running high. The demonstration at Craven Cottage would have appalled Andy despite the tension in the country. In the last five matches of the season, Fulham avoided defeat. That, combined with the poor form of Stoke City and Stockport County, enabled Fulham to retain their Second Division status by two points. Although avoiding relegation was an achievement of sorts, Andy's job as manager of Fulham was hanging by a thread, and it was a matter of time as to which party would sever the tie first.

The question of whether Andy was sacked or resigned appears to be answered by the discussion at Fulham's AGM nearly three months after the end of the season. It was said that 'only when they [the directors] felt that the club was on the precipice did they take action'. Even after such a poor outcome from his management of the team, Fulham chairman John Dean said that Andy was 'one of the finest men he had ever known, and his honesty was unimpeachable'. Another director summed up the problem when he said that Andy was 'too kind and too lenient'.

Whatever the circumstance that led to Andy leaving Fulham, it brought down the curtain on his professional football career. Although he would be linked to other jobs in the game, he would not go back. Andy had been a fantastic servant to football in England despite his foray into management not being successful.

Despite finishing professionally, Andy had not entirely quit playing and joined the Casuals. The team, who merged with Corinthians in 1939 to become Corinthian-Casuals, played in the Isthmian League, but as an ex-professional Andy was barred from playing. However, the FA allowed him to appear in friendly matches. Also, his inclusion was a compliment as usually membership of the team was limited to university and former public-school players. Andy provided coaching as well.

CHAPTER TWELVE

Time at the Crease
1926–1928

PERHAPS IT was inevitable given his departure from Fulham, but Andy missed the first three matches of the season. His first game was against Gloucestershire at The Oval and the mix of home ground and an attack bereft of pace, apart from the ineffectual Tom Goddard, resulted in a fine start. Andy scored 97 before Charlie Parker, another to play his only Test match in the 1921 Ashes series, lured him out of his crease and Harry Smith completed the stumping. Surrey were well on the way to a big total at that point, courtesy of a Hobbs hundred, and completed the victory by an innings without the third day being required.

A few days later against Essex, Andy found himself demoted to bat at No.6 as Surrey put out a strong XI at Leyton. It was a powerful batting line-up in front of Andy: Hobbs, Andy Sandham, Alfred Jeacocke, Tom Shepherd and Douglas Jardine. All five scored half-centuries, justifying their places in the order, while Andy was bowled for 32. Like Gloucestershire, Essex had too many runs to chase and were beaten inside two days. Only Fred Nicholas, grandfather of future Hampshire captain and TV commentator, Mark Nicholas, was able to resist with a century and a half-century.

Back at The Oval, Surrey experienced defeat there for the first time since August 1920 when Sussex prevailed by 92 runs. The game was lost when Surrey gave up a first-innings lead of 96 with a poor batting performance. Andy scored 2 in the first innings, which was symptomatic of the line-up not firing. The innings started well enough with Hobbs and Sandham putting on 43 for the first wicket, but the last nine fell for 92. Surrey still had a chance to win on the final day; set 380 to win, they reached 234/5 before wickets fell regularly. Maurice Tate was chief destroyer with four out of the last five wickets to fall. Tate finished with 7-90 while Andy was left on 37 not out when he ran out of partners.

Andy was promoted to No.3 in a weakened Surrey team at Leicestershire, and scored a half-century. It was a morale boost for the next match at Old Trafford, as Andy would have to face his bowling nemesis from Headingley in 1921: Ted McDonald.

McDonald had moved to England and had been playing in the Lancashire League until he qualified to play for Lancashire. The Australian was immensely fast, as seen in 1921 with several instances of pure pace causing mental and physical anguish. McDonald had played Australian Rules football, a physically demanding sport, for Essendon and Fitzroy in the Victorian Football League, which would have contributed to his ability to find life in benign batting pitches through sheer speed.

Lancashire batted first and played negative cricket on a dead pitch. In the 110 overs they batted on the first day, before being bowled out for 181, 44 were maidens. Surrey had to bat with the light deteriorating and McDonald with the ball in his hand. Unsurprisingly, he sent back both openers with just 13 on the board. Sandham was 'palpably lbw', according to *The Guardian*, which left Andy to face McDonald steaming in. Andy's plan was 'cultivating easeful defensive batting'. Along with Tom Shepherd, the pair played each ball on its merit, not worrying if McDonald beat the outside edge. Soon, batting became easier as McDonald tired and they saw out the rest of the day unbeaten.

Day two saw more of the same before Andy came out of his shell and scored his first century of the season. With a first innings lead of 95, Surrey would have expected to force a winning position.

However, a spectacular batting collapse when needing 159 to win saw Lancashire take the match on the last ball. At 111/3, the match was almost won before Surrey lost three wickets without scoring a run and a fourth just one run later. Dick Tyldesley bowled the final over and Stanley Fenley needed to keep him out, but the final ball struck his pad and the umpire gave the decision. Old Trafford erupted with joy and relief, as the home team had secured a win after a session of nervous cricket.

Two weeks later, Andy hit another century. This one was at The Oval against Essex after the first day had been washed out. Perhaps influenced by his watchful century against McDonald, Andy started very slowly and carefully. In the first 35 minutes of his innings, Andy accumulated three runs. After two hours, his score had moved on to 37. At that point, Andy accelerated as the Essex bowlers started to tire. When Andy lashed a drive at Laurie Eastman into the hands of John Freeman, he was out for 121 of Surrey's 230. They reached 306, but a result was always unlikely. Essex easily batted out the final day.

Andy missed the rest of June and returned for the match at Hampshire. Day one was spent in the field and day two was spent watching Hobbs and Geary dominate the bowlers before watching rain fall all day to cap a frustrating return. When Andy did get to the crease, it was productive with 67 against Lancashire and 44 against Kent.

Against Sussex at Eastbourne, Andy provided two contrasting innings. The first was as an opener when he scored 8 before nicking Clement Gibson to Duleepsinhji in the slips. Gibson was Argentinian-born and captained a South American team on a tour to England in 1932. He had no luck in the second innings as Duleepsinhji dropped Andy twice. Taking his good fortune and running with it, Andy scored 61 to help Surrey save the match after they had been bowled out for 112 on the first day. An 83-run partnership with Jardine steadied the second innings after Sandham went early.

Andy's more watchful approach continued as the season wore on. In a rain-affected game against Kent, he was again reluctant to play his shots. Against Nottinghamshire at The Oval, Hobbs' second benefit match, his measured approach was noticeable. Andy was at the crease when the match was won, despite Harold Larwood blasting out Jeacocke and Shepherd, as Surrey marked Hobbs' milestone with a victory.

The month of August started disappointingly as Andy struggled. The visit of Middlesex was all about Hendren, out for 199, and Hobbs, unbeaten on 176, while Andy fell for 8. He fared slightly better at Weston-super-Mare, with 22 and 18, but rain saved Somerset. From there, Surrey travelled to Cheltenham and prevailed in a low-scoring contest. Andy's scores of 4 and 2 were symptomatic of a deteriorating pitch where 25 wickets fell on the second day to wrap the match up.

Edgbaston was where Andy found his touch, but not before a first-innings duck. Bob Wyatt removed Bob Gregory, opening with Sandham, without scoring before finding a way through Andy's defences to leave Surrey 1/2. It was Jardine who turned the innings around with a big century as Surrey posted 328. Warwickshire's response was boosted by centuries from Norman Kilner and Len Bates. After threatening to set up Surrey for a struggle to save the match on the third day, Warwickshire collapsed from 300/2 to 364 all out. Surrey still had to bat their way to safety on the final day, with a windy and wet Birmingham day to navigate too, but Andy played wonderfully to score 130 not out. Despite several stoppages for rain, and a vicious wind blowing across the ground, Andy applied himself to ensure that Surrey would not capitulate as they had done earlier in the season.

Andy left his best knock for the season until the penultimate match with a double century. On the way to 235, Andy passed 1,000 runs for the season. His method was, again, watchful as Leicestershire's bowlers toiled. His fifty took ten minutes shy of two hours. It was another hour before he reached his century before doubling his score in 65 minutes. A 261-run stand for the third wicket with Jeacocke demonstrated the pair's dominance. It could have ended far earlier, but Andy was dropped on 33 and took full advantage of Leicestershire's error.

The final match of the season was at Lord's where Surrey ended the season on a high with an innings-and-63-run victory. It was dominated by Hobbs' triple century which, remarkably when you consider the 45,500 runs he had scored to this point, was his first in first-class cricket. Andy crafted 41, reverting to his more aggressive style, before Jardine added a century of his own to see Surrey to 579/5 declared. Middlesex fought as best they could, but Surrey wore the batsmen down to secure the win. Andy finished the season with an average of 46.11 as well as a method of grinding out scores to add to the aggressive strokeplay in his armoury.

* * *

In preparation for the 1927 season, Andy spent some time in Acton at an indoor cricket school run by Patsy Hendren. Although he had to bat on matting, Andy commented to *The Illustrated Sporting and Dramatic News* that it 'keeps your eye in' and it was 'getting your cricket muscles into working order'. Andy was so enamoured by the indoor cricket school that he was running one of his own at the Pleasure Beach Hall in Southend by December of the same year.

Andy's first outdoor cricket was at Lord's as Surrey faced MCC. Andy fared well against a strong team captained by Freddie Calthorpe, who would die of cancer just eight years later, with scores of 27 and 48 not out. The second innings was particularly impressive as Andy was the only Surrey batsman to resist Calthorpe and Jack Hearne's bowling. Rain then sunshine made batting increasingly difficult, but Andy applied himself to his task despite MCC forging towards victory.

A week later, Andy hit his first century of the season against Gloucestershire. His batting was not symptomatic of his usual style. His timing with off but he maximised his time at the crease. Andy has scored just a single when he offered a chance, but the catch went down, and he ploughed on to take advantage of his opportunity. With Tom Shepherd, himself on his way to a double century, he added 289, Andy scoring 142 of them. The match was drawn after Wally Hammond scored centuries in both innings for the visitors. Hammond was in prodigious form, and he would pass 1,000 runs before the end of May, becoming the third batsman to achieve the feat after W.G. Grace and Tom Hayward.

More runs flowed at Taunton with a dichotomous innings of 73 not out. Andy started off with a flourish, but Jack White was getting serious turn and a more reserved approach was required. It worked well as another big partnership was constructed with Shepherd. Surrey declared at 466/4 early on day two, and Somerset struggled. Stanley Fenley and Percy Fender took 15 of the 20 wickets to fall as Surrey secured an innings victory.

Back at The Oval, Glamorgan put up a spirited performance. Although Surrey prevailed, the Welsh county kept pace nearly all the way through the match. Andy carried on his fine form with scores of 54 and 64 as Surrey set Glamorgan 413 to win. Expecting a procession of wickets, Glamorgan did not oblige and got within 37 runs of victory. One curious fact from the match was the debut of Joe O'Gorman. With the first ball he bowled in first-class cricket, O'Gorman took the wicket of Eddie Bates. O'Gorman played just two more matches for the first XI. He was already well known as a comedian, in a double act with his brother, and would go on to appear in films and in the Royal Variety Show after the Second World War.

Andy hit his fourth successive fifty, in an innings victory over Essex, before travelling north to feature in a match against Durham for Shrimp Leveson-Gower's XI. Andy was a late replacement for Middlesex's Gerald Crutchley and although he did not score many runs, he gained credit for his solid batting. The *Newcastle Journal* noted Andy's 'defensive batsmanship reduced to a fine art' as Durham had their illustrious opponents in significant bother on the last afternoon. However, Andy was steadfast to ensure no late wickets fell.

For the next game, Andy and his Surrey colleagues faced the mighty Yorkshire who had won five out of the eight County Championships since the end of the First World War. Predictably, Surrey suffered a ten-wicket loss. Herbert Sutcliffe surpassed Surrey's first innings score on his own as Yorkshire outplayed the visitors. Andy received lavish praise for his second-innings 59 while the rest of the team struggled, with *The Guardian* commenting, 'he examined every ball, judged the length and spin to a nicety, and never made a stroke against the break. In defence, and offence his bat made beautiful movements. Here was a most skilful, stylish, reliant, and vigilant cricketer in a bad hour for his side.'

June started less favourably with scores of 16, 0, 10 and 6. Those last two were courtesy of Harold Larwood as the Nottinghamshire paceman clean bowled Andy twice. Despite his low score in the first innings, it was still part of a 62-run partnership with Shepherd. Andy had developed a knack to stay at the crease even if the runs were not flowing. At 41, it was probably too late to have any hope of an England recall. It was just a shame that this new-found skill had not been discovered earlier.

More pace was awaiting at Lancashire with Ted McDonald. The Lancashire fast bowler struck both Sandham and Tom Barling, opening for Surrey, within ten minutes. Bowling several of what *The Guardian* described as 'sinister bumpers … at killing speed', McDonald was definitely aiming for the body. Andy came to the crease at 90/3 and was soon joined by Jardine. The pair knew that McDonald would tire, and waited for the inevitable. It was a plan that worked, and the pair added 88. McDonald finally got them, both bowled, but not before Andy scored 39 and Jardine notched an impressive 143. Surrey could not take wickets early and Lancashire, like the current champions they were, scored more than 500, but the game was destined to be a draw.

Warwickshire tried to deal Surrey some of their own medicine when they won the toss, batted first, and racked up almost 500. Then Surrey, filling the part that the visitors usually played at The Oval, were dismissed in less than three hours for 153. In serious trouble, Surrey pulled off what turned out to be a master stroke. Andy was asked to open the innings with Tom Barling, and the pair batted as if the earlier collapse hadn't happened. Harry Howell's pace, which had been so troublesome, was rendered innocuous. Willie Quaife's change of pace lacked menace, and Surrey took full advantage. Both batsmen passed their centuries before Barling fell, near the end of play, after an expansive drive was taken by Reg Santall. Andy finally fell for 166 on the final afternoon after rain had delayed the start for hours. The game had been easily saved.

After the annual matches against Oxford and Cambridge, rain again caused a County Championship draw. This time, the match against Somerset did not get through each side's first innings before weather put paid to the contest. Next up was a visit to Essex, where Fender's inspired declaration sent Essex into a tailspin which ended with them bowled out for 94.

At Kent, it was Hobbs who starred with his hundredth century for Surrey. Andy, on the other hand, had problems with Tich Freeman. The bowler had Andy caught behind in both innings with John Evans, yet another of the 1921 one-cap wonders, taking the dismissals for scores of 15 and 36.

Light relief came with an appearance in a charity match for the Actors' Orphanage in Buckinghamshire. Names such as Patsy Hendren, Jack Hearne, Wilf Rhodes and Andy Sandham joined Andy in a match against representatives from the orphanage. More than 800 spectators paid to see such quality cricketers on show. Along with some top-class cricket, plenty of light-hearted play occurred such as Hendren bowling left-handed.

The visit of Lancashire to The Oval gave Andy the opportunity to pass 1,000 runs for the season, but not much else went right.

Scores of 1 and 23 were not overly inspiring with slow left-armer Jack Iddon causing Andy plenty of problems. In addition, Andy dropped Harry Makepeace when he was on 79 and he went on to hit 152. It was a sharp chance at short leg, but one that Andy would have expected to take.

A change of batting position, due to Surrey's England hopefuls missing the match against Kent, led to an upturn in Andy's form. Being asked to open, as Surrey's senior batsman, saw Andy put together scores of 89 and 56 to help secure a 114-run win. In the first innings, a 175-run partnership for the third wicket with Shepherd set Surrey on their way. In the second innings, a 108-run opening partnership with Tom Barling gave a firm foundation to kick on and set up the declaration.

Scores of 32 and 36 at Sussex and 58 against Nottinghamshire were further proof of Andy's change in fortunes. In the Nottinghamshire match, Hobbs and Sandham were back, and Surrey scored 522 on the first day. Unfortunately, rain washed out the second day and rendered the strong position futile.

August started well for Andy with a cricketing first: a century against an international touring team. The New Zealanders were playing 26 first-class matches on their tour, and they visited The Oval to play Surrey. At this point, New Zealand did not have Test status but their showing on the tour convinced the International Cricket Council to convey the honour.

The tourists batted first and scored 313 thanks to a Jack Mills hundred. In reply, Surrey started well with an opening partnership of 180 between Hobbs and Sandham. Andy scored 32, and the New Zealanders fought back but still faced a deficit of 64. Inspired by batting sensation Stewie Dempster, the New Zealanders set a total of 306 for Surrey to chase in just over three hours. Herb McGirr picked up Hobbs for a duck which brought Andy to the crease. With Sandham, he added 105 in just over an hour before the loss of the opener started an unwelcome run of wickets. Andy completed his century in two hours then was immediately out, exposing Surrey to potential defeat. However, Tom Barling's spirited 78 not out secured a creditable draw.

Andy followed his century with another against Middlesex; his first back-to-back centuries since 1921. Andy accompanied Sandham as the pair added 186 for the second wicket as Surrey looked set for a big total. However, rain washed out day two before Patsy Hendren prevented Surrey creating a collapse. Hendren made 86 while the next best Middlesex batsman scored 17. Without that, Surrey could have pressed for a win.

The rest of August was blighted by rain, with matches against Gloucestershire, Warwickshire, Yorkshire and Leicestershire all losing the vast majority of days available. On the first day of the match against Yorkshire, which was rained off, all other County Championship games starting on the day suffered the same fate, except Somerset who did get 50 minutes of play before weather intervened.

The rain was most welcome for Surrey in their match against Glamorgan. It was Swansea Cricket Week, and the County Championship match was the culmination. Day one was mostly rained off and Glamorgan started the second on 11/1. They reached 158 then Surrey had to bat on what was a difficult wicket. As Surrey struggled, Trevor Arnott and Jack Mercer bowled unchanged for 34 overs. The result was a disastrous 55 all out with Andy top-scoring with 14. However, rain fell heavily and put the wicket under water to end the match early. Glamorgan had lost the chance of an almost inevitable win and suffered financial losses at a time when they least needed it.

The final match of the season was at Lord's against Middlesex and it was wicketkeeper Herbert Strudwick's last match before retirement. Victory was almost secured on the first morning as Middlesex suffered an ignominious collapse and were bowled out for 54. Percy Fender took a remarkable 7-10: four wickets in five balls, five in seven and six in eleven as Middlesex slipped from 46/3. Their second innings fared much better with a Jack Hearne century leaving Surrey with a potentially tricky run chase. Hobbs, Sandham and Andy all scored half-centuries to set up the win. Andy's 51 was particularly painstaking with no boundaries scored and two all-run fours demonstrating his determination not to play unnecessarily aggressive shots.

October 1927 saw Andy invited to an unusual banquet hosted by the Mayor of London, Sir Rowland Blades. Being well known for his love of sport, Blades hosted the dinner 'in honour of cricket'. It was attended by several of the game's stars, such as Hobbs, Fender, Frank Woolley, Maurice Tate and the Gilligan brothers. Past greats such as C.B. Fry and Plum Warner were also there.

* * *

The 1928 season started late for Andy when an ankle injury required minor surgery. Fluid had built up around the joint and required aspiration to aid recovery. Andy missed the season opener against MCC as well as four County Championship games and a match against the West Indian touring team. Andy's luck seemed to be out because alongside the injured ankle, he had been involved in an accident when the car he was driving collided with a lorry in Southend. Fortunately, he was not hurt.

Andy's first game was against Sussex, and, for the first two days, he could only sit and watch the rain fall on The Oval. When play did get underway, Sussex batted for 54 overs before declaring to give Surrey some time in the middle.

Andy Sandham was out early so Andy did bat but scored just 11 before getting out. With Andy needing time at the crease, it was an opportunity missed.

The next game was at Trent Bridge, and it turned out to be remarkable for several reasons. Nottinghamshire batted first and they were boosted by a remarkable stand from their No.8 and No.9 batsmen. Fred Barratt and Arthur Staples put together a 167-run partnership with both scoring nineties to help the home side to 457 all out.

In response, Surrey had Andy and Hobbs get them off to a good start despite the loss of Sandham. Andy's timing was lacking, but he played a watchful innings for 44. Hobbs struck the 150th century of his career, but Surrey were bowled out for 288. Nottinghamshire captain Arthur Carr decided not to enforce the follow-on despite there being just 35 minutes of play left to bat in bad light. It would be a decision he would rue. By the close, he was at the crease with his team at 15/4. Nottinghamshire's batsmen continued to fall on the following morning and were soon bowled out for a miserable 50. Surrey needed 220 to win and, despite losing Hobbs and Andy, who lost his middle stump with three runs on the board, it was completed fairly easily. It had been a remarkable turnaround of fortune.

A visit to Aylestone Road, to play Leicestershire, gave Andy an opportunity to get some time at the crease and he scored his first half-century of the season. It was perfect preparation for a trip to the champions, Lancashire, and old adversary Ted McDonald. Old Trafford was bathed in sunshine and more than 20,000 packed in to see Surrey in fine batting form. Despite losing Hobbs to McDonald early on, Andy joined Sandham, and the pair started defensively before coming out after lunch with far more attacking intent. Described by *The Guardian* as a 'violent offensive', the pair took McDonald head on. Andy was looking to put the ball through the on side with, as *The Guardian* journalist described it, the possibility of 'hearty human fallibility in Ducat suddenly exposed under his gay finery of skill'. Even if Andy was fallible, as had been demonstrated many times against sheer pace, he still scored his first century of the season. The partnership with Sandham was worth 299 as Surrey scored almost 500 in a day. Sandham retired ill, on 282, early on the morning of day two and Surrey posted 567. Lancashire's response was equally emphatic, with Frank Watson scoring 300 not out.

Andy's second century of the season came in the next game. Visitors Warwickshire bowled and fielded badly, as demonstrated by Andy being dropped with just a single to his name. He scored 179 not out as Warwickshire's hapless bowlers were punished. A

299-run stand with Tom Shepherd ensued, as Surrey scored at will. Fender's declaration came in the late afternoon, with a 363-run lead. However, the quick wickets did not come as Warwickshire's batsmen dug their team out of the hole. Bob Wyatt's 159 not out ensured that Surrey would remain winless at The Oval for a little while longer.

The trip to Hove was a personal triumph for Andy, as he completed three consecutive centuries. Another unbeaten hundred for Andy had to be tempered with a Surrey batting collapse which let Sussex back into the match. The home team batted well and left Surrey with a tricky period late on day two, and all of day three, to negotiate. Surrey slipped to 60/4 and Andy, along with Percy Fender, went into defensive mode to try to bat out the day. Andy batted for two and a half hours for 42, but the fall of his wicket started a collapse and Surrey lost their first match of the season.

Next up was a trip to Leyton to play Essex. It was Jack Russell's benefit match, but Essex failed to mark the occasion with a good performance. Day one saw Essex bat all day for 220 as Surrey kept the bowling tight and only Johnny Douglas managed a score of note. On the second day, Surrey were far less encumbered and scored more than 500 runs. Andy hit a masterly 208; he was reserved at first before playing his expansive hitting game. Shepherd joined him and the pair, according to *The Guardian*, were 'sending the ball to all parts of the field' in their 317-run partnership. Essex could not get anywhere near Surrey's total, and lost by an innings and 149 runs.

Andy's rich vein of form ended against Cambridge University, but not before he had hit another half-century. It was not chanceless, offering a catch to slip before he had scored, but Andy was utilising any second chances offered. It was ankle trouble, which had already caused him to miss the start of the season, that led to another spell on the sidelines. He was struck on the ankle by a ball when batting and it meant he could not bat in the second innings as well as the next couple of matches.

It was a real shame for Andy to be injured when being in such good touch. He had 837 runs to his name, at a phenomenal average of 104.62, with a double century, three centuries, and two half-centuries so far.

He came back into the team for the match at Southampton which was the benefit match for Hampshire's opener George Brown. Both teams cancelled each other out and the match petered out into a draw after rain intervened. Andy's scores of 19 and 28 were symptomatic of someone returning from injury which was unsurprising under the circumstances. The match gave an opportunity for Surrey to give a debut to wicketkeeper Woolf Barnato. Apart from having such a fabulous name, Barnato was a racing driver and had recently won the 24 Hours of Le Mans race. He was a financier and owned car manufacturer Bentley, and would drive one of their cars to victory at Le Mans in 1929 and 1930.

The visit of Somerset to The Oval saw Fender at his finest with creative captaincy throughout. Having won the toss, Fender asked the visitors to bat which was unusual, but not unique. The tactic fell somewhat flat when Somerset batted all day. However, Andy and Douglas Jardine wrested the momentum back with a 171-run stand. Andy went on to his fourth hundred of the summer before Fender rolled the dice again with a declaration. With a 45-run lead, Fender was hoping that the bowlers would do what they failed to do in the first innings. However, Somerset resisted to leave Surrey still awaiting their first home victory.

Surrey's inability to win matches continued with draws against Yorkshire and Kent. For Andy, it was a lean period as well as enduring plenty of travel between matches. He represented Shrimp Leveson-Gower's team in Durham again between Championship matches. Travels continued with a match in Northampton, the first meeting of the two counties since 1921. Surrey were able to include Hobbs who, naturally, scored a century as Surrey amassed 530/9. Andy hit a half-century, sharing a partnership of 110 with Hobbs, as Surrey won by ten wickets.

Having got the better of Ted McDonald in recent encounters, Andy and Surrey felt the full force of the Australian bowler when Lancashire visited The Oval. Had it not been for Alan Peach's 94 not out, batting at No.8, Surrey would have posted far less than the 219 they did. McDonald bowled two overs then changed ends and soon had Sandham caught behind. Andy came in next and fell to the same dismissal soon after without scoring. Dick Tyldesley got in on the act as Surrey's batsmen fell cheaply. McDonald was denied a hat-trick by Barnato but picked up his third wicket of the over next ball. He finished with 6-99 from 18 blistering overs.

Lancashire's batting was far more competent, with Jack Iddon's 184 being exemplary, before Surrey had to face McDonald again with a deficit of 267. Andy suffered the ignominy of a pair when nicking Frank Sibbles to George Duckworth. McDonald took 6-98 this time round as Surrey crashed to an innings-and-nine-run defeat.

The more docile bowling attack of Northamptonshire was welcome respite from the Championship-winning attack of Lancashire. Surrey cashed in, Andy scoring a half-century, one of four batsmen to do so, and finally won a match with Hobbs captaining in Fender's absence. Fender picked up his first win of the season in the next match as Kent imploded from 64/0, chasing 131 to win, to lose by 14 runs. Fender took 5-53 to facilitate a win from an unlikely position.

The last month of the season started well for Andy with scores of 56 against Nottinghamshire, 71 against Warwickshire, and 46 away to Glamorgan. Andy's 55 in the second innings against Gloucestershire at Cheltenham was in a rearguard action, but he could not prevent defeat. It would have been harsh on Wally Hammond if he saved the match after the Gloucestershire player scored 139 and 143 while taking ten catches in the match and grabbing the wicket of Jack Hobbs in the first innings. Five of his six second-innings catches came off the bowling of Charlie Parker.

Another period of defiant batting to save a match came at home to Middlesex, and this time it proved successful. Andy scored 82, but more importantly occupied the crease for three hours and 40 minutes. He was supported by Shepherd and Barling, with each partnership adding 68 runs, as Middlesex's hold on the game slipped away. Bob Gregory and Monty Garland-Wells both hit half-centuries as Surrey found, according to *The Guardian*, a 'handsome way of avoiding defeat'.

Yorkshire found Andy again in a resolute mood when they visited The Oval. An unbeaten 70, only ended by rain on the final day, was scored in a slow, methodical way. The game finished as a draw, as did the last two matches of the season, as Surrey's lack of ability to bowl teams out twice was underlined.

Andy's season was an impressive one with 1,660 runs at an average of 55.33. It was an even better season than his *annus mirabilis* of 1919. It posed the question as to whether another England cap was a possibility. Age could not be a factor as Hobbs was three years older. It was a question of whether he would be trusted to test his ability on the highest stage.

CHAPTER THIRTEEN

Season in the Sun
1929–1930

APART FROM readying himself for the start of the cricket season, Andy was imparting his knowledge for the benefit of young cricketers. The picture of Andy demonstrating a forward defensive stroke at Roehampton adorned the cover on the *Daily Mirror* in early April.

The cricket season started on 1 May and MCC visited The Oval to play Surrey. The game was played under experimental new playing conditions with the stumps being wider and taller. This caused several batsmen to make errors of judgement and be trapped leg-before. Surrey had the better of the match until the fourth innings when Johnny Douglas' side bowled them out cheaply to secure the win. Andy returned scores of 32 and 4 in a low-scoring affair.

The opening County Championship match of the season, in which Hampshire visited The Oval, was a different matter, as Surrey scored 490 on the first day. Jack Hobbs received many of the plaudits with 154, but Andy stuck a magnificent 171. The pair put on 176 before Hobbs departed. Tom Shepherd and Tom Barling came and went before Andy was joined by Percy Fender. In 55 minutes, the pair slammed 133 before Andy lobbed an easy caught and bowled chance to Lewis Harfield. Unfortunately, no play was possible on the second day due to bad weather and the match was drawn.

Andy's next opportunity to impress was against the touring South Africans. Surrey inflicted the first defeat of the summer on the tourists after an impressive first-innings bowling display. Fender played excellently with bat and ball while Andy struggled. It was a similar story against Warwickshire, with Fender excelling while Andy did not contribute much.

The visit of Sussex to The Oval turned out to be a tight affair, but that did not look likely to be the case when the visitors were bowled out for 60 on the first day. However, they clawed their way back into the game and were positioned for an unlikely victory until Andy switched tactics with the bat. Needing just 164 to win, Surrey lost wickets regularly. Andy came to the crease with the score at 26/1 and played a watchful innings. He punished the bad balls but did nothing to give his wicket away. At 125/8, Surrey looked out of the match. Andy decided that he couldn't rely on Ted Brooks to stay with him, so he forced the game. Feeling the momentum swinging back, Sussex started making errors, including conceding nine off one ball via overthrows. Fittingly, it was Andy who hit the winning run. He had scored 89 not out; the next-highest score was 13.

In the matches at Trent Bridge and Old Trafford, Andy had mixed results against quick bowlers. Nottinghamshire's Bill Voce, who would be one of Douglas Jardine's Bodyline bowlers in 1932/33, got Andy out twice. Playing Lancashire meant facing Ted McDonald, and Andy played well for 42, out of a total of 102, but as *The Guardian* reported, he 'obviously did not like McDonald'. Both matches were heavy defeats for Surrey.

Andy's first century of the season came at the beginning of June against Essex at The Oval. Surrey had already earned a 175-run first-innings lead. Andy Sandham fell on 24, but when Andy joined Hobbs the pair scored quickly. Andy's half-century was achieved in 45 minutes while Hobbs took double the time for his. Another 40 minutes later and Andy had his century before the close of play. Resuming on the final morning, Andy added four to his score before getting out for 105. Hobbs achieved his century then the declaration came, but Essex easily held on for a draw.

A week later saw Andy captain Surrey against Northamptonshire at Kettering. With Hobbs and Fender at Lord's for the Test Trial, Andy was given the opportunity to take on the leadership role. Northamptonshire won the toss and batted, but Surrey soon got the upper hand with three quick wickets. Bert Lock, whose middle name was Christmas, got rid of both openers before Alan Peach picked up the third. Jack Timms and Austin Matthews fought back, and Northamptonshire scored 281. Surrey ended the first day at 33/1 with Sandham and Andy at the crease.

Day two started after the obligatory Sunday rest day and Northamptonshire's captain Vallance Jupp could not take the field due to an accident at home. Maybe Andy thought his luck was in, but after making his fifty he was bowled, and the momentum started to shift inexorably towards the home side. Surrey gave up a 73-run lead which was built on by Northamptonshire with patient batting.

Northants batted on into the final day before declaring after the lead extended to 300. With two sessions to negotiate, Andy must have thought that a draw was possible. However, Nobby Clark had other ideas and took six wickets. Andy scored just 7, as Surrey slipped to defeat for the first time against Northamptonshire since 1912. Having the captaincy for this defeat would have been a disappointing experience.

Surrey and Andy soon made amends with a comprehensive innings and 70-run win over Glamorgan. The Welsh county won the toss and batted; it proved a costly error of judgement, as Surrey bowled them out for 37 in 29 overs. Maurice Allom and Albert Geary picked up five wickets each, as three wickets fell before a run had been scored. Surrey found batting far more pleasurable and Sandham's 187, ably assisted by Andy's 70, put the match beyond Glamorgan.

Andy continued his run-scoring exploits against Cambridge University at The Oval. His first-innings score of 42 was creditable, but his second innings was much better. He scored 168 not out and did not give the Cambridge bowlers, who had fared well in the first innings, any chances. He shared a 159-run partnership with Tom Shepherd as well as passing 1,000 runs for the season during the innings. Surrey could not force the win, but it was a fine batting effort.

Stiffer opposition from the South Africans in the second tour match was next, but scores of 42 and 62 not out underlined where Andy was as a batsman. The captaincy issue was in the past and Andy was seeing the ball well. Oxford University's bowlers found this out first hand with Andy scoring his fourth century of the season in the next match as Surrey won by an innings.

Andy passed 20,000 first-class runs during the innings and was sitting in sixth place in the first-class batting averages with 1,323 runs at 50.88. From here, Andy's season declined as runs became more difficult to accumulate. Also, his bad luck would rear its head again.

Andy was batting at Southampton on the opening day of the match against Hampshire when he was dismissed in an unusual manner. Bob Gregory had departed already, bringing Andy to the crease without a run on the board, when Alex Kennedy got a ball through Andy's defences. The ball struck the wickets and 'removed the bail from its groove, and it remained on top of the stumps', according to *The Guardian*. It was given out, but if that happened in the modern game then law 29.1.2 would apply and it would be not out. Surrey's defeat in the match was not down to bad luck, however, but a capitulation in the second innings. Bowled out for 95, Surrey were beaten inside two days.

Rain in Birmingham ruined the encounter with Warwickshire and washed out the first day of the match against Yorkshire. It was Herbert Sutcliffe's benefit. When Surrey did bat, they slipped to 65/6 before a lower-order fightback took the total to 156. Yorkshire declared on 324/9, but Surrey held firm. Andy's unbeaten 54 helped save the match.

Andy travelled back down to London straight afterwards because he had been selected for the Gentlemen v Players match at The Oval, starting the following morning. The Gentlemen, captained by Fender, batted first and spent the whole of the first day and part of the second at the crease. When Andy finally came in to bat, he shared a 90-run partnership with Nottinghamshire's Arthur Staples to dig the Players out of a hole. Andy was dismissed for a duck in the second innings, but the Players batted out for a draw.

Surrey's visit to Kent yielded plenty of runs for both teams, but Andy bagged two single-figure scores. In the second innings, he fell to old friend Wally Hardinge for 5, nicking him to wicketkeeper Geoffrey Legge. Against Somerset, Andy scored a half-century before having to face his Aussie-Lancastrian nemesis again.

Lancashire batted first and McDonald spent the first day and a half watching his colleagues score 526/7. Once the declaration came, he was soon making life uncomfortable for Hobbs by hitting him sharply in the leg with a fast cutter. However, Hobbs and Sandham weathered the initial storm and added 83 before McDonald made the breakthrough. Andy came in next and made 3 before playing a careless shot. He tried to pull a short, fast ball from McDonald but could only find the safe hands of Jack Iddon at mid-on. Sandham got out to the exact same shot, and McDonald was on a roll. He eventually took 7-104 as Surrey capitulated for 210. With most of the day to bat again, Surrey set about saving the game. McDonald's exertions meant that his pace was blunted, and the game was saved. Andy fell cheaply again; this time deceived by Dick Tyldesley, and was bowled meekly off his pads.

Surrey's match against Kent was all about Hobbs. The Master scored his 165th century as Surrey piled on 400 on the first day. Bob Gregory shared a 50-run stand with Hobbs before getting out and Andy came to the crease. The pair then added 102, with Andy playing a subservient role with 36, as Hobbs headed towards another milestone. Tom Shepherd and Ernest Wilson scored half-centuries. Kent's reply was led by Les Ames' 109, but a lack of partners saw Kent follow on before the second day was out. Kent made a better fist of their second innings, with Ames agonisingly out for 99, leaving Surrey needing 180 to win. With the score on 29, Bill Ashdown took two wickets in an over, including Andy for 0, but that was as good as it got for the visitors. Hobbs and Shepherd drove Surrey on to victory.

Rain ruined the next match, with Andy in need of time at the crease, as the visit of Gloucestershire saw just 51 overs of cricket in three days. Bad weather would bring an early end to the visit of Nottinghamshire as well, but Andy got some welcome runs beforehand. The visitors batted first and had the better of the first day and were 363/3 before Maurice Allom, who had been awarded his county cap during the previous match, initiated a collapse. Despite Surrey conceding 409 runs the previous day, more than 20,000 spectators crammed into The Oval for day two. After a rare Hobbs failure, Andy joined Sandham for a 161-run partnership. Keeping Larwood and Voce at bay, the Surrey pair scored all round the wicket with a fine array of strokes. Finally, Larwood broke the partnership with the new ball. Andy was on 68 when trying to cut Larwood away but he picked out Arthur Carr at backward point. Larwood then bowled Sandham for 119, but Shepherd's century allowed Surrey to pass Nottinghamshire's total before the end of play. Rain prevented any play on the final day with the game interestingly poised.

Having been hammered by Sussex, another heavy defeat was on the cards with the visit of Middlesex. The visitors batted first and amassed 514/5 declared with Harry Lee (225) and Gubby Allen (155) punishing a toothless bowling display. Surrey then found themselves bamboozled by Ian Peebles' leg spin and were forced to follow on 343 runs adrift. Needing to bat for well over a day to save the game, Surrey soon lost Sandham to illness. It brought Andy to the wicket late in the afternoon, but the first test was passed when Surrey finished day two on 94/0 with Hobbs 65 not out and key to Surrey's fate. Day three started well enough, with 34 added to the total when Walter Robins managed to sneak a ball through to bowl Andy. Robins then removed Hobbs, and later Gregory, as Surrey's task became more and more difficult. Stan Squires batted well for an unbeaten 58 but had little support. Surrey managed to get past Middlesex's total but the visitors, with the help of claiming the extra half-hour, won by eight wickets.

The absence of Sandham from the trip to Weston-super-Mare meant that Andy was pushed up the order to open with Hobbs against Somerset. Morning rain did little to spice up the wicket, but Andy was out early while Hobbs powered to yet another century. Somerset captain Jack White made the most of his decision to field by taking 8-113. Surrey posted 321 while Somerset found batting more problematic with Ulick Considine, a Bath and England rugby union player, being the only one to reach 50. With batting getting increasingly difficult, Surrey set 277 for Somerset to chase and they fell 161 runs short. Andy had a second failure as opener in a forgettable game for him. The experiment was tried again at Cheltenham, this time opening with Sandham, but Andy failed once more in the draw against Gloucestershire.

Around the same time as the Somerset match, newspapers ran with the story that Andy had been offered the role of coach of Queensland Cricket Association (QCA), and he had accepted the position. He would leave England at the beginning of September to set sail for Brisbane and take up the job before the end of October. It would be quite a physical challenge. After playing all summer in England, he would be playing and coaching during the Australian summer before returning home to begin the new English season. Andy's only respite would be on the outgoing and return journeys, each lasting six weeks, which would bring their own issues with maintaining fitness.

Andy's season ended with three matches where he batted once. In the innings-and-56-run win over Glamorgan, Andy was bowled for 11 after Hobbs and Sandham scored 207 for the first wicket. At The Oval, Andy achieved the same score against Yorkshire as Edgar

Oldroyd, Percy Holmes, Herbert Sutcliffe and Sandham all scored big hundreds. Andy's final appearance was against Leicestershire, where he scored 27 in a draw. Surrey's final position in the County Championship was tenth, the lowest since 1904.

As Andy left Surrey for the warmer climes of Brisbane, the final averages bore out how his season had declined. An average of 35.12 was his worst performance since 1922 and was vastly inferior to Hobbs and Sandham. It must have crossed Andy's mind more than once on the journey to Australia and back, that a repeat of the second half of the season in 1930 would soon see him surplus to Surrey's requirements.

* * *

Andy's appointment as cricket coach, from a shortlist of six candidates, had come as a surprise to many in Queensland. Despite being the preferred candidate of the president, John Silvester 'Jack' Hutcheon, the local press rounded on the choice of Andy. *The Truth* newspaper decried the appointment by announcing 'Eleven Thousand Miles for a Cricket Coach!' and 'Local Champions Ignored'.

Hutcheon stood resolute in his defence of Andy, who had not yet left England at this point. At the Annual General Meeting of the QCA on 20 August, Hutcheon talked of the 'ungenerous criticisms' of Andy and defended his choice.

Queensland's new coach set sail from London on the SS *Mongolia* two weeks later, bound for Brisbane. The details of Andy's contract made sure he would not have time to be idle. Along with an intensive programme of coaching, he would provide a series of talks on various aspects of cricket. Also, he would be responsible for the Colts, who played in Brisbane's Grade competition. There was no possibility of playing for Queensland in the Sheffield Shield due to his registration being held by Surrey. His remuneration for the period, which was for one season only, would be £500, from which he had to pay his travel expenses.

Andy's coaching programme encompassed schoolboys through to university students as well as the Colts. One thousand individuals per month were estimated to receive coaching from Andy. Most of this would be at the Exhibition Ground in Brisbane. The detailed schedule included sessions every weekday morning and afternoon, Saturday morning sessions before Colts matches as well as other sessions to accommodate the university and Colts players.

Throughout his sporting life, Andy wrote many newspaper articles on football and cricket. His time in Queensland would be no different. Also, Andy's opinion was sought by newspapers on the upcoming MCC tour of Australia and New Zealand as well as Australia's Ashes tour to England in 1930.

Andy was interviewed as he reached each port in Australia. The SS *Mongolia* was a mail boat, stopping at major ports, and journalists were keen to speak with Queensland's new coach. In Fremantle, his opinion of the Ashes was of interest. In Adelaide, his view was sought about the changes to the lbw law.

When he reached Sydney, Andy travelled to the Sydney Cricket Ground where he met some players he had played against in England such as Bert Oldfield, Warren Bardsley, Charlie Kelleway and Monty Noble. He also met some of Australia's new players in Archie Jackson, Alan Fairfax and Don Bradman.

On arrival in Brisbane on 21 October, Andy started his employment at Country Carnival week. The players he would be working with were introduced to him, but he also pulled on his whites. In the Country v Metropolis match, he batted at No.8 and scored a slow 14 before being bowled by up-and-coming Queenslander Ron Oxenham. The bowler had played three Tests in the 1928/29 Ashes. Andy may not have impressed with his batting but his 'brand new hat' was well received. The Metropolis team won handsomely by an innings and 262 runs, but this would have been little surprise as most of their players also represented Queensland in the Sheffield Shield.

Andy's lectures started at the same time as the carnival and 'fielding efficiency' was the first topic. On 6 November, he presided over a talk on 'batting principles' where he used lantern slides to illuminate his lecture. Slides of W.G. Grace, Clem Hill and Monty Noble in batting poses allowed Andy to demonstrate how to play shots. When taking questions at the end of the lecture, one particular question caused amusement. A keen individual asked how to score from a yorker which provoked laughter from around the room. Andy's answer, as he was always looking to be instructive, was, 'If you use your feet properly [then] no ball would be a yorker.'

November would see Andy play plenty of cricket alongside his coaching duties. Representing the Colts against Western Suburbs, over two weekends, Andy showed his class in both innings. On 16 November, he played a patient innings of 71 not out after the Colts dismissed their opponents for 123. Opening the batting, Andy took more than 30 minutes to score his first three runs before demonstrating his obvious class. Andy's on-side shots were particularly good, and he scored nine boundaries in his 109-minute innings.

If the Western Suburbs bowlers thought they had seen the Surrey man's ability, he surpassed himself the following weekend. During a hot early-summer Queensland afternoon, Andy played an aggressive innings with shots on both sides of the wicket. His clean hitting, combined with powerful drives, produced an excellent score of 153 not out. Western Suburbs could only watch the ball flayed around on a fabulous day for batting as Andy accumulated 20 fours and two sixes. Mick Brew also scored a century but Andy's innings was the highest score of the day across the Grade fixtures.

After producing two scores of quality, Andy's services were required by the touring MCC team before they headed off for Test matches in New Zealand. Not only was the MCC touring Australasia, but they were also sending a squad for a series of Test matches against West Indies. The problem the tourists faced was that injuries were mounting up leading to a shortage of players. Andy's potential availability was of interest.

Initially, MCC captain Harold Gilligan was looking for the match to be cancelled. He appealed to the New Zealand Cricket Council, the board of control for MCC'S tour, but they deferred to the local authority, the Australian Board of Control, and QCA were incensed by the request.

The response of QCA secretary R.T. Stephens was, 'Unless the Englishmen refuse point blank to come to Brisbane, the cricket match between Marylebone Cricket Club and a Queensland eleven must take place. If they do refuse to come, it will be a sad reflection on English sportsmanship.' Having been beaten by Victoria and struggled with the ball in a draw with New South Wales, MCC were already finding Australian conditions challenging.

The Brisbane press were speculating about Frank Woolley's participation. Woolley played in Brisbane in 1911 but had missed the match in 1924 which fuelled resentment by the press. *The Telegraph* claimed that Woolley had 'pleaded illness'. In the end, 1929 was no different as the batsman was injured during an innings of 219 against New South Wales and headed straight to New Zealand.

With MCC down to 14 players, Andy agreed to play for them. Although he made more runs than his solitary Test appearance in 1921, scores of 13 and 10 did little to persuade anyone that he could represent his country again. Queensland deserved their victory, by five wickets, with some fine batting and bowling. Frank Gough, who was the first bowler to dismiss Bradman for a duck in first-class cricket, starred with the bat with 52 and 104.

If the match had been a disappointment for Andy, he let out his frustration with a belligerent effort against South Brisbane. His innings ended on 145, but not before he had thrashed 18 fours and four sixes. Two of those sixes scattered spectators in the grandstand. Taking one bowler, Frewin, for 23 runs in an over and another, Sherry, for 18, Andy played an innings akin to a T20 match.

After the distraction of the MCC match at the Exhibition Ground, Andy got back into his day job with a series of lectures, as well as coaching sessions and school visits. One of the facets of Australian batting that Andy highlighted was the grips that schoolboys adopted when batting. After visiting 20 schools in Brisbane, he noted that the boys did not grip the handle with their hands close together, which counteracted the wrist action required. He followed this up in early January as part of an article on batting and timing. The piece was instructional on the positions needed to play shots.

An earlier newspaper article focused on attacking fielding at cover point and in the slips. Having played for more than 20 seasons for Surrey, Andy had seen many exceptional fielders, but it was good friend and county colleague Jack Hobbs who was advocated as a 'most destructive cover point'. Also, Patsy Hendren was given the description of an 'all-round fieldsman'. Andy's detailed description of positional play, and technique, would have been avid reading for cricket fans.

Andy must have been immensely proud when one of the Colts players, Ken Mossop, gained selection to play Sheffield Shield cricket for Queensland in January. Mossop had opened the batting with Andy against South Brisbane and was showing a significant improvement over the season. He was selected to play against South Australia. A first-innings score of 1 would have been a disappointment, but 66 in the second innings against a bowling attack including Clarrie Grimmett was an impressive start to first-class cricket. The South Australian leg-spinner took his 50th wicket of the season in the match, so Mossop's half-century was well earned.

As the season drew to a close, Andy decided that he would not be returning the following year. He said that 'for private reasons, it will be impossible for me to renew [my contract] next season'. One can only surmise what those reasons were, but 11-year-old daughter, Daphne, did not appear to have joined Andy and Vera in Australia.

Passenger lists for the ship show that only Andy and Vera travelled back from Brisbane. Presumably, the decision had been made that she should stay in England with grandparents so as not to miss schooling. Also, Andy had business ventures such as his sports shop in Southend to consider.

The decision to return to England and not come back was met with much sadness. QCA president Hutcheon 'regretted' the decision, saying that the tenure had been 'very successful' and that it was with 'regret that they would say goodbye'.

At the last Colts game, Andy was presented with a silver cigarette case as a mark of appreciation. On the eve of departure, QCA presented Andy with a bridge set and a walking stick. The coach said that he 'regretted' not being able to continue and said that Queensland was 'too far from England'.

He departed for England, via Sydney, on 1 March. He left Australia having grown a reputation for being a knowledgeable cricketer, impressive coach and after winning over doubting critics. There was quite a gathering at the dock for the departure; it was a telling sign of how much Andy had impressed as Queensland's coach.

Andy's average of 92 left him second in the Brisbane grade averages while the Colts were a better team for the tutelage. Andy had left a lasting impression on the cricketers he coached. It was a shame for them that he did not come back to build on his summer in the Queensland sun.

Before leaving Queensland, Andy may well have been instrumental in starting the career of the much-maligned Aboriginal cricketer Eddie Gilbert. A few days after Andy departed, *The Brisbane Courier* ran a story about Gilbert having a trial in the nets at the Exhibition Ground in the previous week. It goes without saying that QCA would have wanted Andy to see the much-talked-about fast bowler first-hand to be able to offer an opinion.

The story of Gilbert is a sad one because of the way he was treated and how he was ostracised from cricket. Undoubtedly, his skin colour was a factor. His bowling action raised questions about its legitimacy, but the 'chucker' label was applied far too easily. It would stay with Gilbert throughout his life and played a part in contributing to his mental health issues.

Gilbert's bowling style was not too dissimilar, in some ways, to Jofra Archer's: an easy, unhurried run-up to the stumps then the ball was launched at ferocious pace towards the unwitting batsman. Don Bradman was said to credit Gilbert as the fastest bowler he ever faced. In a Sheffield Shield match in 1931, Gilbert famously put Bradman on his backside before dismissing Australia's greatest batsman for a duck with a lightning quick ball that was caught behind.

Back at the end of February, Gilbert was invited to Brisbane for a trial. He had to be accompanied by a chaperone because *the Aboriginals Protection and Restriction of the Sale of Opium Act 1897* forbade Aboriginals to leave their settlement without one. It was a pernicious piece of legislation passed by the government of Queensland to control movement of first nations people in the state.

Gilbert left Barambah (now called Cherbourg) by train, travelling overnight, and arrived the next day to bowl in the nets. Officials, presumably including Andy, and reporters witnessed a hostile spell of bowling. Three batsmen were hit as Gilbert's raw pace and slingy action caused problems.

After the session, Gilbert returned to his settlement but received an invite to play for the Colts the following November. As coach of QCA, and the Colts in particular, it's not a huge leap of imagination to see that Andy would have suggested this course of action. He had seen, and faced, some of the fastest bowlers such as Harold Larwood and Ted McDonald, and Gilbert would have impressed him with his speed and ability to put batsmen in trouble.

*　*　*

As soon as Andy had arrived back in England, he had to report back at The Oval for Surrey's first County Championship match of the season. Glamorgan batted first and posted an impressive total of 474. The response was led, of course, by Hobbs with a century. Andy shared a 79-run partnership with the opener, but Surrey still fell 141 runs short. When Surrey batted again, they could only lose the match. Hobbs followed up with another century to ensure the draw but Andy was dismissed for a duck.

Worcestershire were next to visit The Oval, but they had a less than productive time. Batting first, the visitors lost their first three wickets with just a single on the board. Eric Stroud, in his second match for Surrey, took 4-17 as Worcestershire collapsed to 40 all out. If they had any hope of saving the game, that soon disappeared when Hobbs and Andy Sandham hit a century opening stand. When Andy came to the crease, he played his shots through the leg side with aplomb. After Tom Shepherd joined Andy, the pair accelerated the scoring with 179 runs in just under two hours. Andy was finally out for 125, but the game was over as a competitive match and Surrey won by an innings.

The knock against Worcestershire seemed to kick-start Andy. Against MCC at Lord's, he hit 76 and 100 not out. In the first innings, he joined Hobbs in a 120-run partnership. The second innings was described as a 'great hundred' by *The Guardian*. It was a typical Andy century: driving well, pulling and cutting, and scoring through the leg side often.

The next four innings were less than inspiring, with only 51 runs including two ducks, but he scored runs again when needed. Warwickshire had taken control of the match at The Oval, mainly thanks to Derek Foster's 7-42, and Surrey needed to bat out the rest of the final day after being forced to follow on. Bob Wyatt removed Sandham on 36, to bring Andy out to join Hobbs. The opener always looked to punish bad balls and continued to do so, despite the position of the match, with powerful drives and pulls. Andy slipped easily into support mode while Hobbs scored freely. With the score on 127, Hobbs was given out, somewhat controversially, stumped by Tiger Smith at the second attempt after a bail had been removed. Shepherd was next in and scored quickly. Both Shepherd and Andy looked comfortable, and the game was easily saved. The pair reached unbeaten centuries.

In their next home match, Surrey entertained the touring Australians. It was an impressive line-up at The Oval: Bill Woodfull, Archie Jackson, Don Bradman, Vic Richardson, Bill Ponsford, Stan McCabe, Alan Fairfax, Bill Oldfield, Percy Hornibrook, Tom Wall and Clarrie Grimmett. But the spectators got only one day's play due to rain. In that day, they saw the Australians score 379, with Bradman hitting 252. It was a precursor to the Ashes series, as Bradman scored 974 runs, including 334 at Headingley, and amassed just shy of 3,000 runs on the tour at an average of 98.66. Unsurprisingly, the Australians won the Test series.

Surrey's County Championship campaign had stalled before it had really started. The brief interlude against the tourists did nothing to reboot their inability to win games. In fact, things got worse against Gloucestershire and it needed rain to prevent a home defeat. Away to Essex, Surrey slipped to 8/3 and 35/4 before Andy scored a welcome 65 to help turn the position around. Even bowling Sussex out for 72 in their first innings could not be taken advantage of, as another match was drawn. It required useful scores from Hobbs, Sandham and Andy to prevent an embarrassing defeat.

Winning the toss and batting on a 'perfect wicket', as *The Observer* described it, at Trent Bridge was advantageous. Surrey certainly capitalised, despite facing Harold Larwood and Bill Voce, as Nottinghamshire's bowlers conceded 477 runs on the first day. Larwood bowled Hobbs for 5 then watched helplessly as Sandham and Andy put on 281 for the second wicket. As Larwood and Voce erred on length, Andy drove them to the boundary imperiously. After Sandham, Shepherd and Barling fell, Andy found company in Percy Fender and added another 133 runs in just over an hour. Andy was out for 218 as Surrey amassed 501 in their first innings. Despite making the home team bat again, a win eluded Surrey when rain prevented them getting the last three wickets.

On the back of a defeat against Leicestershire, Surrey travelled to Old Trafford to face Lancashire for Dick Tyldesley's benefit match. Meeting Lancashire meant another opportunity, if such a word is applicable in this instance, to face Ted McDonald. However, the Australian was suffering from fluid on his knee and bowled 13 overs before seeking medical assistance. Andy scored 60 including a 'delectable sweep', according to *The Guardian*, off Jack Iddon before having his stumps rearranged by Frank Sibbles. The bowler had found some vicious, late swing with the new ball and Andy received one of those deliveries that you just can't do anything about. The match finished as another draw.

During Lancashire's second innings, Andy was fielding when he received a telegram to inform him of the sad news that his 77-year-old father had passed away. Andy left the field immediately and was replaced by Alf Gover. He returned to Southend straight away and the funeral took place several days later.

Andy missed the second tour match against the Australians before returning for the visit of Essex. Surrey batted first and scored a big total then the visitors played as if a draw was their only concern. Sandham hit 176 while Andy added 70 with a signature batting display, featuring shots all round the wicket. With 491 on the board, Surrey knew they would not be batting again. By the end of the second day, Essex had been forced to follow on and had to survive a full day. It was a task that they achieved, much to the chagrin of paying spectators, by stonewalling. In 113 overs, 58 were maidens. Only 161 runs were scored, but just two wickets fell.

Andy's next two appearances saw him used as an opener against Cambridge and Oxford Universities. He featured in two century opening partnerships with Barling as well as sharing a 205-run partnership with Shepherd. Scores of 49, 61, 56 and 87 were a good return from high-scoring matches. The triple Le Mans-winning Woolf Barnato played his last match for Surrey against Oxford, just over a week after his latest triumph on the track. The matches ended as draws.

Confidence after the Varsity matches was high and Andy followed up with two half-centuries at Derby. A 96-run partnership with Hobbs helped Surrey to a first-innings lead, but Surrey could not find a way to force a victory. Andy was in a good place with his batting and more impressive still when considering that he was now batting in glasses. His eyesight had deteriorated to the point that spectacles were required. Batting with glasses without the safety of a helmet would have been an interesting proposition.

After travelling north to play Yorkshire in Emmott Robinson's benefit match, Andy scored a century. *The Guardian* commented, 'Curious how these old players can still go on, holding their own with the young men, and also keeping back time.' Yorkshire's bowlers did little to threaten, and Andy, along with Shepherd, collected runs at their own pace. Surrey posted 438/9 before managing to bowl Yorkshire out twice to win by an innings.

Mediocre scores in draws against Kent, Somerset and Lancashire preceded Andy taking the captaincy once again. At The Oval, Derbyshire won the toss and batted. Andy utilised the bowling of Shepherd and Bert Lock well in the afternoon session to restrict the visitors to 162. With Hobbs playing for England, Andy stepped in to open and made 35. However, only Shepherd and Barling managed decent scores and Surrey fell four runs short of Derbyshire. In their second innings, the visitors' top order fired with two centuries and a half century to leave Surrey needing 310 to win in four hours. Andy was the first wicket to fall, and it created a precipitous collapse. Surrey slumped to 110 all out, which resulted in a first defeat at The Oval for the season.

Andy retained the captaincy for the visit of Kent. The visitors batted first and preceded to lose wickets in batches. At 219/9, Andy would have been hopeful of wrapping up the innings and getting to bat on a decent wicket in fine weather. Annoyingly, the tenth-wicket partnership garnered 63 runs. When Surrey did bat, Andy led off with 51 before Stan Squires and Ted Brooks added half-centuries of their own to squeeze out a 21-run lead. Any chance of a win was extinguished by Frank Woolley's fine 109 and rain that washed out play after lunch. It was the closest that Andy had come to a victory as captain of Surrey, and there was still a lot to do to secure that.

By the beginning of August, Andy was sitting third in the batting averages with only Duleepsinhji and Sutcliffe holding a better average than 52.38. It was an impressive turnaround from the previous season. When considering his age, getting used to spectacles, intermittent captaincy and makeshift opening, then it was even more remarkable.

The trip to Sussex saw Andy return to batting at No.3. He was out for a duck, before scoring 71 not out in the second innings after returning to opening. He stayed as opener for the trip to Gloucestershire, scoring 15 and 33, in a heavy loss which was created by Charlie Parker's superb match figures of 15-91. More runs flowed at Warwickshire in a 142-run opening partnership with Sandham, who went on to score 204 in a drawn game. At Worcester, Andy scored another half-century, but the home team secured a ten-wicket victory courtesy of another Surrey batting collapse.

Before the season was out, Andy scored two more half-centuries to pass 2,000 runs for the season. Both Hobbs and Sandham finished higher than Andy in the averages, but he had finished the season in a far better position than he had started. If the Surrey selection committee had any thoughts of not retaining Andy, they would not have any qualms in bringing him back for his 20th season.

CHAPTER FOURTEEN

Stumps
1931–1942

ANDY SPENT the winter at the indoor cricket school in Upminster where he performed the duties of senior coach. The school was an impressive facility with four full-size pitches allowing bowlers to take a full run-up due to the length of the main hall. One of the coaches assisting Andy was 22-year-old Essex bowler Peter Smith, who had made his debut in 1929. At the time of writing, Smith still holds the record for the highest first-class score by a No.11 with 163 in 1947.

The marriage of sister-in-law Joyce Barbour to fellow actor Richard Bird took place in March. Andy's attendance at the wedding appeared to be almost as newsworthy as the nuptials. A heavy snowstorm covered St Pancras Register Office as Bird arrived with Andy before the bride's arrival. As soon as the ceremony was over, Bird departed for Elstree where he was working on a film while Joyce Barbour was due to perform in a play at the Adelphi Theatre.

In a *Daily Mirror* article a few months later, it was revealed that Andy had performed the duty of best man at the wedding. The article included a photograph of their wedding present to each other, a bulldog called Bill, purchased on Andy's advice. It's an aspect of his life that there is little information about, but Andy was a dog lover, and he had a bulldog of his own called Dan.

The 1931 season started at The Oval with the visit of Gloucestershire. On the first day Surrey were bowled out for 258 with Charlie Parker taking 7-128. Parker received help with indifferent bounce; Andy was one who was caught in front of the stumps by a ball keeping low. Day two was ruined by rain and Gloucestershire scored just 42 runs for the loss of one wicket.

The third day threatened to descend into a benign draw until Gloucestershire captain Bev Lyon declared just after lunch with a deficit of 83. *The Guardian* described it as 'the boldest captaincy in 23 years'. Percy Fender, always one to look for a tactical declaration, played his part and instructed his team to score quickly because the game was on. Andy top-scored with 22, with Surrey then declaring at 60/6 to leave a total of 145 as the target for Gloucestershire. With Wally Hammond at the crease, anything was possible and his partnership with New Zealander Ces Dacre brought quick runs. When Dacre was out, Gloucestershire lost wickets at regular intervals. But Hammond maintained his resolve and it was fitting that he hit the winning boundary with three wickets in hand to complete Lyon's plan.

A visit to Lord's to play MCC was also plagued by rain. Patsy Hendren's hundred bolstered MCC. Another sporting declaration saw Surrey successfully hold off MCC without trying for the win. Andy combined with Jack Hobbs to make the game safe.

When Derbyshire visited The Oval, Surrey batted first and struggled to find a partnership before losing their last four wickets for nine runs. Derbyshire took the opportunity to create a lead before Surrey struggled once again. However, Fender and Alan Peach rescued them before a declaration was easily defended by Derbyshire. Fender then gave part-time bowlers most of the overs; Andy bowled 11 without taking a wicket.

Andy's first score of note came against Somerset at The Oval. Somerset batted first and posted a good total of 338. In response, Surrey's batsmen were unstoppable and piled on more than 500 runs on day two. Hobbs and Sandham started with a signature opening partnership of 231. Andy joined in with 80, most notably scoring on the leg side, and sharing a century partnership with Douglas Jardine. Fender came in later on and smashed the tiring bowlers all over the ground. The match was ideally poised for a declaration and a whole day to bowl Somerset out a second time, but rain had other ideas and the game was drawn.

Carrying on from his half-century against Somerset, Andy batted well for scores of 45 and 34 not out against Hampshire. Surrey took two full days for their first innings as rain continued to blight English cricket in May. The final day was then set alight by more sporting declarations, this time Fender conspiring with Hampshire captain Stephen Fry to try to engineer a positive result. Andy was pushed up to open with Surrey trying to score quickly. But Hampshire did not make too much of an effort to win after losing two early wickets.

In another home match, Surrey were their own worst enemies. Batting first against Sussex, Surrey reached 202/2 before collapsing at the hands of Maurice Tate. Hobbs had another century and Sandham reached his half-century before the innings disintegrated. Andy scored 20 before Tate lured him out of his crease. The rest fell cheaply as Surrey were all out for 232. Sussex had no such problems, led by centurions in Ted Bowley and Duleepsinhji, and declared late on day two. With a difficult spell to face, Andy was asked to open with Sandham. Presumably, Hobbs was being kept back to bat for a long time on the final day. The tactic failed as Tich Cornford caught Andy off the bowling of Bert Wensley for a duck. Tom Shepherd fell three runs later to leave Surrey in a precarious position overnight. However, more rain washed a difficult situation away and no further play was possible on the final day.

After five straight home matches in the County Championship, Surrey headed to Trent Bridge. Nottinghamshire won the toss and batted but soon found life difficult. Bob Gregory's 5-28 helped Surrey bowl out the home side for 130. In response, Surrey got to 22/0 before rain started to fall heavily. It rained all through the rest day on Sunday and did not resume until midway through Monday afternoon. Batting was now a whole lot more difficult than on Saturday. When Andy finally got to the crease, the ball was turning acutely, and bounce was far from true. He applied himself, as Sandham was doing, and the pair added 58. Early on the final morning, Nottinghamshire had to bat again and lasted 59 overs. Surrey had an opportunity to win, but when they needed another 103, with nine wickets in hand, a heavy rainstorm hit and frustratingly prevented more play. The good fortune against Sussex had already been repaid.

More good luck was to be had away to Leicestershire, when Sandham batted more than three hours for 40 runs to prevent defeat. Andy had a poor game, but Sandham's dogged approach and more rain resulted in another drawn match.

Moving on to Old Trafford meant another clash with Ted McDonald. The Lancashire bowler had noticeably lost some pace but was still able to cause problems with his mastery of line and length. In the first innings, McDonald was ineffectual as Surrey scored 311. Andy made 41 while Sandham, Shepherd and Jardine hit half-centuries. Lancashire passed Surrey's score by virtue of Len Hopwood's 165 not out before McDonald came back to haunt Andy once more. Sandham was first to go, trapped leg-before by McDonald, after showing a distinct lack of footwork. Andy came out to bat and McDonald struck him on the pads first ball. The umpire was unmoved. With the next ball, he was struck again and this time he was gone for a second-ball duck. It was the sixth time that McDonald had claimed Andy's wicket and the second time for a duck. Shepherd and Jardine steered Surrey away from calamity before rain ended yet another match early.

In need of a big score, Andy duly obliged during the visit of Warwickshire. The visitors had batted first and struggled to 139 then Surrey set about amassing a big total. Sandham went cheaply and Andy joined Hobbs with the score on 19/1. Andy was cautious at first and took 40 minutes to score 5. By the end of the first day, Hobbs was 79 not out and Andy was on 60.

The pair resumed on day two and continued to score well. Both converted their positions to centuries and Hobbs was the first to fall, with the score on 267, for 147, his 178th first-class hundred. Andy was out for 125 before Shepherd and Barling took Surrey past 500. It was Andy's first century for 11 months and his first at The Oval for more than a year. The last one, in May 1930, was also against Warwickshire. Needing 365 to make Surrey bat again, Warwickshire failed. Only Bob Wyatt and Reg Santall put up resistance, but Surrey claimed their first win of the season on 5 June.

After another rain-affected draw, this time with Essex, Surrey headed to Horsham for their match with Sussex. Andy struggled in the first innings but played a patient knock in the second to set up a chance for a win. Surrey had an 82-run lead, but lost Sandham early. Andy joined Hobbs and adopted a no-risk approach. *The Guardian* described it as 'subdued' as Andy took two and three-quarter hours to score 57. Hobbs had made 57 before departing and Jardine added his own half-century before Fender declared to give Sussex a target of 338 to win. Duleepsinhji and Tate led the way, but Sussex fell 12 agonising runs short.

Andy was among the runs again when Surrey visited Essex. The home team won the toss and batted first but were bowled out for 162. In reply, Surrey reached 121/1 at the close of the first day. Day two was all about Surrey, with Sandham and Andy leading the way. Andy shared an 82-run partnership with Shepherd, before departing for 62. Ted Sheffield's unexpected 64 not out, batting at No.9, allowed Surrey to reach 394. In reply, Essex struggled and only just managed to take the match into the final day. Twelve balls into the third morning, Surrey had secured a victory by an innings and 80 runs.

Surrey's next two matches were against Oxford and Cambridge Universities and wholesale changes were made. Andy was rested alongside other senior players and Surrey's youngsters were given the opportunity to shine. Against Cambridge, 21-year-old Stan Squires did exactly that. A sparkling innings of 200 not out gave the selection committee a nudge.

When the team was selected for the match against Derbyshire at Chesterfield, Surrey made one change to the team which had beaten Essex. Squires was brought into the team at the expense of Andy. On the third day, Andy came on as a substitute fielder which must have been a chastening experience for a player with such seniority.

Surrey's next match was at Bradford to face Yorkshire. The game also represented Yorkshire bowler George Macaulay's benefit match. Andy was restored to the side in his usual position at No.3 with Squires pushed down the order. Surrey batted first and found the wicket problematic. Bill Bowes extracted acute bounce which was difficult to play. Andy top-scored with 42, including a partnership of 59 with Squires, as Surrey limped to 165 all out. The Yorkshire crowd were displeased with Andy's slow scoring: he took nearly three hours to score 20, before speeding up his play.

Yorkshire's response was blighted by rain on day two, and a draw looked the most likely result at the start of the final day. Maurice Leyland struck a hundred, ably assisted by Edgar Oldroyd and Yorkshire captain Frank Greenwood, who then declared with a 116-run lead. With about two hours of the match remaining, Surrey had to occupy the crease. However, Hedley Verity bowled a superb spell to spin Surrey to defeat. His 6-11, alongside Bowes' 4-32, saw Surrey routed in under two hours to complete a remarkable Yorkshire victory.

While batting against Yorkshire, Andy had been struck on the ribcage but played on. He did not suffer any problems in the match, but during the lead-up to the next game he thought that he should report that he did not think he would be fit due to discomfort. On examination, it was found that he had a broken rib. It was brave, or foolhardy, to continue playing with such an injury. As a result, Andy needed a period of time to allow the rib to heal.

It would be six matches before he was reintroduced to the team. He came back against Nottinghamshire at The Oval, but looked unsettled and scored 10 and 1 in a defeat. Surrey collapsed from 65/2 to 82 all out and Nottinghamshire duly completed the victory with ease.

Andy found himself doing 12th man duties again before being selected for the Cheltenham Festival match against Gloucestershire. Just 50 minutes of play was possible on day one and day two was washed out completely. The final day saw the home side bowled out for 135 before Surrey slipped to 98/8. Andy scored 17 as the game ended tamely.

Andy retained his place at Taunton. Somerset batted first and spent all day compiling 240/8. In keeping with much of the season, rain washed out day two completely. On the final day, Somerset added another 40 before their innings ended. Hobbs and Sandham opened for Surrey and batted the rest of the day without losing a wicket. In 93 overs, Surrey scored 193 as the great opening duo added another partnership of quality to their list of achievements.

Andy would have sat in the pavilion padded up waiting for the first wicket to fall. Although he knew nothing about it, that would be his final act as a Surrey player, and first-class cricketer. That news would be delivered to Andy by Surrey on the following morning. However, it would take almost a week before the news was released. On Friday, 27 August, the following statement was issued by Surrey:

> The Surrey County Cricket Club, being faced with the prospect of a serious deficit at the end of the current year, recently appointed a special committee to examine and report as to the possibility of effecting economies in the management of the club.
>
> This committee recommended that a saving of at least £2,000 should be made, and that their recommendations included, among other economies, the reduction of the

number of professionals engaged on the staff and a limitation of second eleven and club and ground games to eight and 14 respectively.

Acting on the report the General Committee decided that the engagements of six professionals, including Ducat and Peach, should not be renewed, the preference being given to younger players in the interests of future Surrey cricket.

The committee recognises that Ducat and Peach have both rendered great service to the club. Both have received benefits.

One can imagine that the Surrey committee would have sat and discussed cuts and rationalised that old 'Mac', as he was known throughout the cricket world, would understand. However, that was not the case. As soon as the news broke, journalists sought Andy out for his reaction. At first, he was not inclined to comment. When Andy did finally speak about his treatment by Surrey, he was uncharacteristically blunt. In the *Daily News (London)*, he said that he was in 'shock after so many happy years at Surrey'. Newspapers such as the *Sheffield Independent* carried Andy's more detailed comments:

'Until last Saturday morning, I had not the faintest idea that anything like this was about to occur. It came as a complete surprise to me, for having been told nothing all the season I naturally expected that my services would be required next summer.

'It means that I have had practically a week's notice. It is eight years since I had a benefit and, without being at all optimistic, I was rather looking forward shortly to another benefit, because none of the younger members of the side had played long enough to qualify for one, and if a benefit had to be given I was next on the list for it.'

It is worth stopping to consider whether Andy had any valid points in his rebuttal of Surrey's decision. The point that holds the most merit is that of the notice period. It does seem to be rather short for a loyal player of 25 years. The financial situation of the club was clearly serious and reducing staff would have been an obvious place to make savings. Also, Surrey would have been considering their personnel for 1932 earlier than August. Andy deserved a conversation about not being part of their future plans.

But he could be accused of naivete for not considering that he wasn't going to be retained. He would have been aware that his form was considerably poorer than in 1930, and his lack of playing time in August should have alerted him to something going on. Perhaps he was in denial. It poses the question whether Andy should have raised the subject when he was out of favour in the second half of the season.

Surrey were perfectly entitled to not retain Andy, and his 1931 record suggested that his decline would continue. Where Surrey let themselves and Andy down, in my opinion, was not to have dialogue with a loyal and long-serving member of the staff. However, the decision was made, and Andy's cricket career was at an end. Newspaper rumours circulated that he would take a coaching role with Essex, or even return as a player for the county, but there was no substance to the reports.

* * *

During the 1930s, Andy was employed as a journalist for the *Daily Sketch*. He would provide match reports for the newspaper. It was a natural extension to the writing he did in the 1920s. As David Foot commented, Andy was not opinionated in his pieces because he wasn't that way inclined. He did bring an astute sporting brain to the analysis of matches. Andy would love catching up with old friends in the press box who had also turned their hands to journalism and to talk about sport. It was said that Aston Villa was Andy's real love in football and he would look out for their results first. I'm sure that Arsenal and Fulham would not be too far behind because of Andy's sense of propriety in such matters.

In 1933 Andy's instructional book called *Cricket* was published. The publisher, Hutchinson & Co., decided to use a ghostwriter which, quite rightly, attracted the ire of David Foot. The book comes alive when Andy's voice is allowed to come through. Little nuggets of information that young boys and girls reading would have ingested word for word gave a window on Andy's philosophy on the game. These include, 'If the batsman can secure his runs in an attractive manner he will naturally obtain greater pleasure from the game in addition to providing a pleasing spectacle for the onlookers.'

Andy's sense of fair play can be found throughout and he clearly thought it important that future cricketers had the right mindset. When considering getting out, Andy said, 'There is nothing disgraceful in being bowled by a ball that beats you fairly and squarely, and batsmen who harp everlastingly on this excuse are likely to come to believe it in time, which is not good for their game.'

The book is split into sections, but the main focus is to provide instruction on bowling, batting and fielding. As well as Andy's words providing invaluable advice, there are many photographs, providing pictorial detail to aid understanding. One interesting aspect is that three pages are dedicated to Bodyline. The publisher would have wanted the book to cover the topic because of its relevance at the time of publication. Andy recognised that Bodyline had been in county cricket for years; bowled by medium-pacers, it was referred to as leg-theory and was designed to slow scoring down. Andy was not in favour of fast bowlers adopting the tactic and was clear in his thoughts. 'If this particular type of bowling finds favour with a majority of county teams, I am afraid that the game will deteriorate as a spectacular entertainment.'

* * *

Coinciding with Andy's book being published was his appointment as assistant cricket coach at Eton College. It would be the beginning of a nine-year relationship in which Andy would provide coaching to Eton's cricketers. When Andy joined Eton, George Hirst was the coach. The ex-England and Yorkshire cricketer had been in the role since 1920 and finally retired in 1938.

Hirst's greatest asset was his ability to communicate and gain respect. It was something that Andy duplicated when he took over the role. After Andy's death, a quote in *The Tatler* demonstrated how he conducted himself in the role, 'Quite part from being one of the nicest chaps you could meet, it was impossible to be on the wrong foot if you listened to and understood what he told you.'

Arguably Andy's finest achievement at Eton was a thumping victory in the annual match against Harrow in 1941. The match was held at Agar's Plough, one of the playing fields at Eton, instead of the usual home of Lord's. It was the first time since 1918 that the match had been moved, but more than 5,000 spectators attended.

Eton batted first and scored 190 before a rainstorm stopped play and changed the conditions. Harrow were unable to score at anywhere near the same rate and found themselves bowled out for 54 in 31 overs and suffered a 136-run defeat. Although the manner of the win, due to the conditions, may have soured the win a little for Andy it would still have been sweet to get one over his good friend and regular cricketing adversary from their playing days, Patsy Hendren, who was Harrow's coach.

* * *

In the late 1930s, Andy was involved with Ellens Cricket Club, in Rudgwick, West Sussex, which was led by Major Charles Carlos Clarke. Carlos Clarke's family were known to the British royal family, and he owned the grounds at Ellens Green where the club played. Andy provided coaching and was involved in several charity games at Ellens.

In one match in 1937, more than 2,000 spectators watched Ellens play against a team selected by Percy Fender which featured such names as Andy Sandham, Douglas Jardine and D.J. Knight. Andy's role was to umpire and he was joined by Herbert Strudwick.

The game was repeated in 1938 and 1939 with large crowds in both years.

* * *

One of the more random events that Andy took part in was a darts match in April 1938. The event took place at Mitcham Stadium in London, and featured a bunch of sports stars and a team from the Royal Army Service Corps. The stars were an unlikely bunch. There was ex-British heavyweight boxing champion, 'Bombardier' Billy Wells, 1936 world speedway champion Lionel van Praag from Australia, and British tennis champion Dan Maskell, later to become the BBC's voice of tennis. Later in the year, Andy was one of the guests for the Football Association's 75th anniversary match in which England beat a Rest of Europe team 3-0.

* * *

In 1940, the *Nelson Leader* carried a story retelling Andy's experience at The Oval in front of a large Bank Holiday crowd. He had dropped two catches, much to the chagrin of the home supporters, in successive balls when the same batsman sent another ball high in the air towards Andy. 'Ducat positioned himself to take the catch, when a Cockney voice, in dire distress, yelled, "Blimey, he'll miss it; give him a bucket." Fortunately for his peace of mind, Ducat did not need the bucket.'

* * *

Andy spent his last few years at the small country estate of Great Enton at Witley in Surrey. The property was owned by American playwright Robert E. Sherwood. The Pulitzer Prize-winner had wanted a base just outside London and purchased Great Enton in 1932. Each summer was spent at the estate, but as the Second World War began Sherwood moved back to the US and became speechwriter for President Eisenhower. The estate was made up of the main house, cottage, and bungalow in beautiful grounds. The main house boasted eight bed and dressing rooms, four bathrooms, and four reception rooms. The interior was furnished with fine velvets, rosewood, mahogany and oak furniture. Sherwood was a man of refined taste.

Andy and Vera lived on the estate with Joyce Barbour and Richard Bird. David Foot provided an insight into life at Great Enton in *Beyond Bat and Ball*. He painted a picture of the contrast between the bacchanalian, showbiz lifestyle of Joyce and Richard, co-existing with Andy and Vera's much quieter ways.

* * *

At the start of the Second World War, Britain had two main fears about the mainland. The first was one based on vulnerability to invasion. Secondly, there was increasing paranoia that the enemy was already among the population. The concept of the Fifth Column arose in the Spanish Civil War (1936–39) where members of the population were actively working to aid and abet the would-be invaders.

Some quarters of the British government were sceptical of the threat. One member who wasn't was the First Lord of the Admiralty, Winston Churchill. When Churchill became prime minister, on the resignation of Neville Chamberlain, one of the first matters attended to was to formalise a national body to defend the nation.

Secretary of State for War, Anthony Eden, announced in a radio broadcast that a defence force was to be formed and called for volunteers aged between 17 and 65, who were not in military service, to help defend the nation from the advancing German Army. While Britain was calling for its men to serve, German forces were getting closer. France, Belgium and the Netherlands would soon fall, and Britain would be the next target.

The force was originally called the Local Defence Volunteers (LDV) but would soon be renamed to the now instantly recognisable Home Guard. More than 1.5 million volunteers joined up in the first three months which created many logistical problems.

Basic items such as arms and uniform were in short supply or not available at all.

The early days of the Home Guard resembled the chaos depicted in the British TV comedy programme, *Dad's Army*. The sitcom portrayed an inept platoon who regularly used everyday items instead of military issue, especially in training manoeuvres. However, many historians such as S.P. Mackenzie, author of *The Home Guard*, take great pains to explain that these issues were soon sorted out and the Home Guard became an effective part of the domestic war effort in Britain.

It was divided into seven command areas and Andy's home county of Surrey fell into London command and South Eastern command. The house at Great Enton was located close to Godalming, in the south-east of the county, so when Andy answered the call for volunteers, he was assigned to the 5th Surrey Battalion, based in the village of Bramley.

Andy's form of enrolment for the Home Guard has survived and shows that he signed up on 25 January 1941, and that he was residing at Great Enton as this point. The form confirms that Andy joined C Company of the 5th Battalion of Surrey Home Guard and the company commander signed off the application.

Due to its proximity to London, Surrey's skies were regularly lit up by dogfights as British planes intercepted German aircraft. Harriet Hyman Alonso, Robert E. Sherwood's biographer, confirmed that Great Enton suffered bomb damage during the war. The night of 9 April 1941 demonstrated the danger that Andy faced at home and in his role as a member of the Home Guard.

Just after 10:50pm on that evening, a Boulton Paul Defiant night fighter took off from Biggin Hill in Kent and encountered a Heinkel He111 bomber on its way to drop bombs on Birmingham, around 50 minutes later. The British fighter opened fire and made many direct hits, and the Heinkel, irreparably damaged with three of its four-man crew killed, crashed into the woods less than two miles from Great Enton.

Such activity in the night sky would have been reported as part of the Home Guard's night-time patrols looking for enemy sightings. Home Guard training was geared to engaging the enemy, should they land on British soil, with time on the rifle range being part of their training. It would have taken many ex-soldiers, like Andy, back to their time serving in the First World War.

As it had been in the First World War, sport played a large part in maintaining fitness levels. The Home Guard was no exception. In July 1941, the 5th Surrey Battalion played the 5th Sussex Battalion in a cricket match at Lord's. The Sussex team featured three ex-county cricketers: Jack Eaton, Arthur Somerset and John Mathews. Surrey's team had less experience with Andy being the only former county cricketer.

Sussex batted first and scored 242. Andy fielded well while Lt Bob Attwell was the pick of Surrey's bowlers with 3-32. In response, Surrey did not bat well. Despite a small crowd, Andy was given an ovation when he walked out to bat. However, he did not last long and was out stumped for a duck. Surrey collapsed to 92 all out to suffer a 150-run defeat. Despite the cricket being of differing quality, the concept was adopted, and other matches were arranged.

* * *

On the morning of 23 July 1942, Andy left the house at Great Enton to head to Lord's for the Surrey v Sussex Home Guard match. On the way, he was involved in a car accident and arrived late to the match as a consequence. Sussex Home Guard had won the toss and decided to field.

Andy batted at No.5 and scored 17 before the lunch interval. After the resumption, he scored steadily and added another 12. Jack Eaton was bowling for Sussex Home Guard and after a delivery whistled past Andy he turned to Sussex's wicketkeeper and joked, 'That was a fast one.' Eaton returned to his mark and came in to bowl again. An attempted yorker jarred low on Andy's bat, and rebounded in the direction of mid-on. Andy moved away from the crease, rocking back on to his heels before collapsing.

Bob Attwell, Andy's batting partner, rushed to him and removed his false teeth before trying to resuscitate him as best he could. A stretcher was brought out, and he was removed to the dressing room before being taken to the nearest hospital by ambulance. On arrival at the Hospital of St John and St Elizabeth, just over half a mile away, Andy was pronounced dead. Some of the players who witnessed his collapse thought that he was already dead when he hit the ground.

Unsurprisingly, the match was abandoned, and Andy's last innings was halted at 29 not out. In some ways, there are parallels to the death of Australian cricketer Phillip Hughes in 2015. The shock factor for the players and spectators, as well as the fact that it happened on a cricket pitch.

Despite Andy's untimely death happening more than 30 years previously, a grim reminder of that fateful day remained at Lord's. Steven Lynch, international editor for *Wisden Cricketers' Almanack*, said, 'My first job, at the end of June 1975, was in the MCC Club Office, in the bowels of the Lord's pavilion. It was the old boiler room, and the storage area ran underneath the Long Room. We became good at working out whether a wicket had fallen in Tests etc., by the noise through the floor.

'It was probably on my first day that I was being taken around these rooms at the back and was shown the office's rather rudimentary first-aid kit – one of those old small red boxes with a white cross on top.

'Next to it, standing up propped against the wall, was an old stretcher – quite a solid thing with thick wooden struts. The canvas was green and faded, and on the whole, it looked like a cast-off from the army. I made some comment about it, and the lady showing me around – the office manager Miss Jones, who was MCC's first female head of department, I believe – said, "Oh yes, that's the one they brought Mr Ducat in on when he collapsed at the crease in

1942." I'm not sure I twigged at the time that he'd actually died, but I looked it up later – and determined I wasn't going to need the stretcher if I could help it!'

A post-mortem was conducted and was sufficient to not require an inquest. The cause of death, according to the death certificate, was 'syncope coronary heart disease'. It's a chastening thought when you consider how well Andy had looked after his health over the years. The only factor contrary to his healthy lifestyle was that he was a smoker which was normal for men at that time.

Andy's funeral took place four days later at Golders Green Crematorium. It was attended by many of his sporting colleagues, as well as officials from the various sporting teams he had represented in his life. Surrey colleagues Jack Hobbs, Andy Sandham, Herbert Strudwick, Ted Brooks and Bob Gregory were there, as well as Shrimp Leveson-Gower. Sir Pelham Warner represented MCC, while the Football Association, Arsenal, Aston Villa and Fulham all sent representatives to pay their respects. The Rev. Dr Ewart James, from the church that Andy attended in Southend, said, 'Ducat showed us how to play the game. He leaves with a clean record.'

After the service, Andy's ashes were scattered in the cremation grounds. Anna Waldron, deputy general manager at Golders Green Crematorium, was able to locate the records of the service, cremation number 54536, but could not confirm where exactly the ashes had been placed in the grounds. She suspected that it was on the crocus lawn.

According to *Beyond Bat and Ball*, Sir Pelham Warner arranged for Vera and Daphne to be driven back to Great Enton after the service. Warner, writing Andy's obituary in *The Cricketer*, recognised that he was an 'exceptionally well built and fine looking man with a charm of manner which made him universally popular'.

Anyone who had been involved in Andy's life could not help but be affected. Many words were written about how he had enriched peoples' lives. One of the first to comment was the cricket master at Eton who said, 'Andy was idolised by the boys. They regarded him as one of the greatest athletes ever … he will always be remembered for his quiet charm and modesty.' A few days later, an obituary was printed in *The Eton College Chronicle* where they recognised Andy's 'unfailing kindness, unquenchable good-humour, and a shrewd and critical knowledge of the game of cricket'.

Even as far as Arbroath, where the Ducat family had originated, Andy was mourned. In the *Arbroath Guide*, he was celebrated for the 'reflected glory that he brought to the town in the realm of sport'. *The Observer* carried an obituary written by R.C. Robertson-Glasgow and 'Crusoe', as the old cricketer was known, talked of Andy's 'quiet and delightful character' and how 'beautifully balanced in mind and body' he was.

POSTSCRIPT

'Nothing showy, insincere or envious ...'

IN CASE you have got this far and were still unsure, I can provide clarity around the pronunciation of Andy's surname. It was open to interpretation throughout his career and many a sporting spectator had attempted to pronounce the name in praise or admonishment. As a surname, it derives from the gold coin used in Europe in the Middle Ages. The pronunciation of Andy's surname, according to *Illustrated Sporting and Dramatic News* in a 1925 interview, was 'Dewcat, not Duckat.'

Looking back at Andy's sporting life, it's safe to say that his achievements will not be matched. Not because of what he did, but because the multi-discipline international sportsman is a thing of the past, certainly, in the more financially driven sports of football and cricket. In Andy's lifetime, it was possible because sports teams had made less of a financial investment in players. In modern football and cricket contracts have more control over players than ever before.

Sport in Andy's time was far more compartmentalised, so playing football in the English winter and cricket in the summer was much easier to do. Even when Andy took over as manager of Fulham, he was able to negotiate so he could fulfil both roles. Undoubtedly, had Andy been born a hundred years later, then he would have been forced to choose between sports at an early age.

Despite the sporting landscape being amenable to being a dual sportsman, it was still a superb achievement. There were quite a few names throughout Andy's life and after. Names such as English sporting greats Ian Botham and Geoff Hurst have represented England at one sport and played the other professionally, but just 13 have the honour of being England internationals for both sports. Clare Taylor, who kindly provided the foreword because she was the most qualified to speak about the achievement, was the 13th and most probably last dual international for England.

Andy's seven caps across two international careers do not accurately represent his contribution to either sport. There were far fewer international matches when Andy was playing. However, there is an argument to be made that he should have won more caps in both sports.

It was not fair for Andy to win just one cap at cricket. The circumstances in 1921 were such that England's selectors did not know their best team and made poor decisions around players. In 1921, nine players were selected for their only Test. It's an extraordinary number of players who had one chance to establish themselves against an impressive Australian team, then be scrapped and not considered again. Only in 1879 (six) and 1892 (seven) was there such a churn in England's Test selections.

Focusing on Andy's Headingley Test, seven changes were made from the previous match at Lord's. Only Frank Woolley and Johnny Douglas played in all of the first three Tests – Douglas even lost the captaincy after Lord's, such was the chaotic approach to team selection. One can only guess why England's selectors thought that these decisions would provide a more favourable outcome.

Andy's first-class record in 1921 provides a compelling argument that he deserved more than one Test match. His average was 47.02 while accumulating 1,881 runs, including five centuries. His average was better than Hendren's, Jupp's and many others. Andy's fielding ability, which would hold more currency in the current game, does not seem to have figured in the decision to drop him.

Also, the fact that the Ashes had been lost could have been used to give players like Andy and Wally Hardinge two or three Tests to establish themselves.

The counter-argument would have been around technique. His proclivity to playing towards the leg side could have been a contributory factor to his vulnerability to fast bowling. There is much merit to this; Andy never truly found a way to consistently counter speedsters like Ted McDonald.

Andy received far more recognition in the football world, but I would argue that he was hard done by with just six international caps. Andy appears to be a perfect midfielder: resolute in defence, with the ability to open games up with a run or a pass, extreme fitness to cover large areas of the pitch, and an excellent reader of games. Yet he was awarded just six caps, in two blocks ten years apart. The First World War did include that time, but it feels that he was not given enough time to grow into international football. Also, it's arguable that Andy would have peaked as a footballer during this time of enforced absence.

Andy's football form nosedived after the 1920 FA Cup Final. Although there were glimpses of his form, it was not consistent. Perhaps a move to Fulham, and the more physical nature of Second Division football, did not help him. Despite this he was still recognised as a positive force in the game. An article in *Illustrated Sporting and Dramatic News* in 1922 said that 'Andy Ducat is one of those men that enrich the games they play. It would be a very good thing for professional football if more men of his type played the game in the winter.'

Andy's golden period was definitely in his later years at Woolwich Arsenal. Playing in a team constantly struggling against relegation is a threat and an opportunity. The threat is two-fold: not having players of your ability to meet your standards, and being relegated. The opportunity is that your skills are obvious, and you stand out more. However, that only works if your games are seen. Andy's move to Aston Villa would have been an attractive one as he would have players of equal, and greater, ability. However, the broken leg at Hyde Road would delay the opportunity before the outbreak of war changed the landscape completely.

Injuries are accepted as part of a sportsperson's life. For someone who played two sports professionally all year round injuries are inevitable because of the strain put on the body. Andy had one potentially career-ending injury but managed to come back, albeit almost two years later.

Early in his career at Woolwich Arsenal, he suffered an injury and was sent for a non-surgical procedure. In Edwardian England, the concept of a 'manipulative surgeon' was not recognised by the medical profession. Herbert Atkinson Barker was one such practitioner who used manipulation, such as chiropractic and osteopathic techniques, and Andy was sent for a consultation for Barker's rapid-cure techniques. He was back playing football in no time. By the 1920s, when Andy's arm was broken, imaging techniques had improved hugely since his leg injury and the prognosis was always positive.

Andy's supreme fitness, geared around his healthy diet, was a key factor in the longevity of his career. It would have been partly why he was disappointed not to have got another contract extension at Surrey because he was still physically fit. Perhaps Andy's eyesight might have been the only area where that wasn't the case.

Many people, including David Foot, have suggested that Andy's death was a 'fitting one'. I must respectfully disagree. I am left with a feeling of sadness over the manner of Andy's passing. I feel sad for the many fledgling cricketers who did not get the chance of being coached by a knowledgeable and passionate teacher. Also, I feel sadness for Daphne, who did not have her father at her wedding the following year. Most of all, I feel sadness for Vera. Although she was used to Andy being away for long periods, he would eventually return by walking through the front door with a bag of dirty sports kit. Andy left Great Enton on the morning of 23 July 1942, kit bag in hand, and never returned.

I refer to Andy's own words on the subject of loss after the unfortunate death of Harvey Darvill in 1924. Those words would have been equally applicable to Andy's death, 'The loss to the club of a fine player has its serious side, but it is a secondary matter when compared with the family's sense of personal loss, which was crushing in its suddenness.'

One of the continuing themes throughout the book was the transient nature of life. Andy's life spanned Victorian times, when mortality rates were high, two World Wars, when slaughter accounted for millions of deaths, and Andy's own unfortunate demise at the relatively young age of 56. This book was written as a celebration of Andy's life, rather than a reminder of his uniqueness in death, but the spectre of mortality is not far from the narrative.

The final word on Andy Ducat goes to Patsy Hendren. In an article written by the cricketer in 1925, he summed up Andy perfectly: 'Admiration for Mac, as he is known in the cricket world, is by no means confined to frequenters of The Oval. He is one of the most loveable men in the game, and is a model of what a professional player should be.

'Perhaps the best description one could give of him is that he is the personal embodiment of the ideal sort of sportsman one reads on in boys' books – the hero who performs great and gallant deeds for his county and his country, and who represents England at both football and cricket.'

Bibliography

Books

Cricket

Booth, K., *Ernest Hayes: Brass in a Golden Age* (Cardiff: ACS Publications, 2008).

Brooke, R., *A History of the County Cricket Championship* (London: Guinness Publishing, 1991).

Ducat, A., *Cricket* (London: Hutchinson & Co., 1933).

Foot, D., *Beyond Bat and Ball: Eleven Intimate Portraits* (London: Aurum Press, 1995).

Harte, C., & Whimpress, B., *The Penguin History of Australian Cricket* (Camberwell: Viking, 2008).

Hutcheon, E.H., *A History of Queensland Cricket* (Brisbane: Queensland Cricket Association, 1946).

Lemmon, D., *The History of Surrey County Cricket Club* (London: Christopher Helm, 1989).

Mason, R., *Plum Warner's Last Season* (1920) (London: Epworth Press, 1970).

McCrery, N., *Final Wicket: Test and First-Class Cricketers Killed in the Great War* (Barnsley, Pen & Sword, 2015).

Palgrave, L., *The Story of the Oval and the History of Surrey Cricket 1902 to 1948* (Birmingham: Cornish Brothers, 1949).

Ross, G., *A History of County Cricket: Surrey* (London: Arthur Baker Limited, 1971).

Streeton, R., *P.G.H. Fender: A Biography* (London: Faber & Faber, 1981).

Sweetman, S., *Dimming of the Day: The Cricket Season of 1914* (Bedford: ACS Publications, 2015).

Warner, Sir P., *Cricket Between Two Wars* (London: Sporting Handbooks, 1946).

Webber, R., *County Championship Cricket: A History of the Competition from 1873* (London: Phoenix Sports Books, 1957).

Football

Attwood, T., Kelly, A. & Andrews, M., *Woolwich Arsenal: 1893-1915 – The Club That Changed Football* (Corby: Hamilton House, 2012).

Farrelly, J., Abbott, C. & Russell, J., *Aston Villa: The First One Hundred and Fifty Years Vol One* (London: Legends Publishing, 2020).

Goodyear, D. & Matthews, T., *Aston Villa: A Complete Record 1874-1988* (Derby: Breedon Books, 1988).

Lerwill, J., *The Villa Way 1874-1944* (Birmingham: A & JL Solutions, 2018).

McColl, B., *A Record of British Wartime Football* (Self published, 2014).

Morris, P., *Aston Villa: The History of a Great Club 1874-1961* (London: The Sportsman's Book Club, 1962).

Ollier, F., *Arsenal: A Complete Record 1886-1990* (Derby: Breedon Books, 1990).

Slade, M.J. (Ed.), *The History of the English Football League Part One: 1888-1930* (Houston: Strategic Book Publishing and Rights Co., 2013).

Turner, D. & White, A., *Fulham: A Complete Record 1879-1987* (Derby: Breedon Books, 1987).

Wilson, J., *Inverting the Pyramid* (London: Weidenfeld & Nicholson, 2018).

General

Crook, P., *The Surrey Home Guard* (Midhurst: Middleton Press, 2000).

Hyman Alonso, H., *Robert E. Sherwood: The Playwright in Peace and War* (Amherst: University of Massachusetts Press, 2007).

Mackenzie, S.P., *The Home Guard* (Oxford: Oxford University Press, 1995).

Mallinson, A., *Fight to the Finish: The First World War – Month by Month* (London: Bantam Books, 2018).

Tennyson, L., *From Verse to Worse* (Edinburgh: Cassell and Company, 1933).

Newspapers, Journals and Periodicals

United Kingdom: Arbroath Herald and Advertiser for the Montrose Burghs, Athletic News, Belfast News-Letter, Belfast Telegraph, Biggleswade Chronicle and Bedfordshire Gazette, Birmingham Daily Gazette, Birmingham Mail, Buckinghamshire Examiner, Chelmsford Chronicle, Chelsea News and General Advertiser, Cornishman, Coventry Evening Telegraph, Cricket: A Weekly Record of the Game, Cricket and Football Field, Daily Mirror, Daily Standard, Daily Telegraph & Courier (London), Derby Daily Telegraph, Dudley Chronicle, Dundee Courier, Dundee Evening Telegraph, Ealing Gazette and West Middlesex Observer, Eastern Daily Press, Express & Star, Football News (Nottingham), Globe, Illustrated Police News, Illustrated Sporting and Dramatic News, Kentish Independent, Lancashire Evening Post, Leeds Mercury, Lloyd's Weekly News, London Daily News, London Evening Standard, Lowestoft Journal, Manchester Courier and Lancashire General Advertiser, Newcastle Daily Chronicle, Northampton Chronicle and Echo, Nottingham Evening Post, Pearson's Weekly, Portsmouth Evening News, Reynolds News, Sheffield Daily Telegraph, Sheffield Evening Telegraph, Sheffield Independent, Smethwick Telephone, Sports Argus, Southend Standard and Essex Weekly Advertiser, South London Press, Staffordshire Sentinel, Star Green 'Un, Sunday Post, The Cricketer, The Eton College Chronicle, The Guardian, The Observer, The Referee, The Scotsman, The Sporting Life, The Sportsman, The Tatler, The Times, Western Daily Herald, Western Morning News, West London Observer, Westminster Gazette, Woolwich Gazette, Worthing Gazette, Worthing Herald, Yorkshire Post and Leeds Intelligencer.

International: Evening News (Sydney), Hamilton Daily Times, Morning Bulletin (Rockhampton), Referee (NSW), The Brisbane Courier, The Telegraph (Brisbane), Toowoomba Chronicle and Darling Downs Gazette, Truth (Brisbane).

Internet
Ancestry
British Newspaper Archive
Charles Booth's London
CricketArchive
Croydoncommon.com
England Football Online
ESPNcricinfo
Find My Past
Howstat.com
Howzstat Cricket Database
Newspapers.com
Professional Footballers' Association
Wartime Memories Project
Wikipedia
YouTube

Andy Ducat timeline

1886	Born in Brixton
1903	Plays for Southend Athletic
1905	Signs for Woolwich Arsenal
1906	Joins groundstaff at Surrey CCC
1910	Wins three England caps at football and scores winning goal versus Wales
1912	Sold to Aston Villa for £1,200 Breaks leg against Manchester City
1914	Returns to professional sport Marries Vera Barbour
1916	Called up to Royal Garrison Artillery
1918	Daughter Daphne is born
1919	Scores a triple century in a day
1920	Named as a *Wisden* Cricketer of the Year Recalled to England football team Captains Aston Villa to FA Cup win
1921	Transferred to Fulham Wins England cricket cap at Headingley Test match
1922	Opens sports outfitters shop
1924	Breaks arm in cricket nets Retires from playing football to become Fulham manager
1926	Leaves Fulham
1929	Travels to Australia to coach Queensland
1931	Retires from cricket after Surrey contract not extended
1933	Starts coaching at Eton College
1941	Signs up for Surrey Home Guard
1942	Dies at Lord's during cricket match

Statistics

Cricket Statistics

Minor Counties

Year	M	I	NO	Runs	HS	Ave	100	50	Ct	O	M	Runs	W	BB	Ave
1906	6	9	0	364	81	40.44	0	4	1	-	-	-	-	-	-
1907	7	10	0	333	210	33.30	1	1	6	-	-	-	-	-	-

First class

Year	M	I	NO	Runs	HS	Ave	100	50	Ct	O	M	Runs	W	BB	Ave
1906	1	1	0	18	18	18.00	0	0	0	-	-	-	-	-	-
1907	1	2	0	27	19	13.50	0	0	0	-	-	-	-	-	-
1908	11	17	1	487	77*	30.44	0	2	7	15.0	3	57	0	-	-
1909	27	45	4	1080	114	26.34	1	5	17	-	-	-	-	-	-
1910	27	42	1	1239	153	30.22	1	8	12	8.0	1	44	1	1-16	44.00
1911	23	37	2	1081	104	30.89	2	6	5	8.0	0	27	0	-	-
1912	21	33	2	758	137	24.45	2	2	5	1.1	0	9	0	-	-
1914	25	38	6	1370	118	42.81	4	7	7	14.0	3	38	1	1-38	38.00
1919	23	35	3	1695	306*	52.97	4	4	20	24.2	5	88	2	1-10	44.00
1920	23	38	5	1245	203	37.73	3	3	21	142.3	41	302	16	3-12	18.87
1921	27	43	3	1881	290*	47.03	5	5	13	50.0	9	133	1	1-18	133.00
1922	2	44	6	1250	108*	32.89	1	8	3	28.0	4	89	0	-	-
1923	26	42	2	1565	134	39.13	5	6	12	4.0	0	18	0	-	-
1925	8	13	0	564	128	43.38	1	3	7	-	-	-	-	-	-
1926	22	30	3	1245	235	46.11	4	4	6	9.0	3	34	0	-	-
1927	30	45	5	1637	166	40.93	4	11	12	-	-	-	-	-	-
1928	24	33	3	1660	208	55.33	5	9	22	7.1	1	26	0	-	-
1929	34	56	4	1826	171	35.12	4	9	19	5.0	0	19	0	-	-
1930	33	48	6	2067	218	49.21	5	14	14	4.0	1	8	0	-	-
1931	17	27	3	678	125	28.25	1	3	4	10.0	3	11	0	-	-

International

Year	M	I	NO	Runs	HS	Ave	100	50	Ct	O	M	Runs	W	BB	Ave
1921	1	2	0	5	3	2.50	0	0	1	-	-	-	-	-	-

Football Statistics

		League		FA Cup		International	
		Apps	Goals	Apps	Goals	Caps	Goals
1904/05	Woolwich Arsenal	10	1	-	-	-	-
1905/06	Woolwich Arsenal	15	4	2	1	-	-
1906/07	Woolwich Arsenal	4	1	-	-	-	-
1907/08	Woolwich Arsenal	18	1	2	-	-	-
1908/09	Woolwich Arsenal	33	1	4	1	-	-
1909/10	Woolwich Arsenal	29	3	2	-	-	-
	England	-	-	-	-	3	1
1910/11	Woolwich Arsenal	33	3	2	-	-	-
1911/12	Woolwich Arsenal	33	5	1	-	-	-
1912/13	Aston Villa	4	-	-	-	-	-
1914/15	Aston Villa	26	3	2	-	-	-
1919/20	Aston Villa	20	1	6	-	-	-
	England	-	-	-	-	2	-
1920/21	Aston Villa	24	-	5	-	-	-
	England	-	-	-	-	1	-
1921/22	Fulham	25	-	1	-	-	-
1922/23	Fulham	16	-	1	-	-	-
1923/24	Fulham	23	-	3	-	-	-

Index

Abel, Billy 94
Abel, Bobby 94–95, 114–115, 118, 146, 156, 165
Allen, Gubby 175, 206
Allom, Maurice 203, 206
Ancoats Hospital 88–89
Anfield 41, 50–51, 102, 106, 137
Armstrong, Warwick 46, 141, 145
Aston Villa 9, 25, 36–37, 41, 49, 52, 58, 66–68, 73, 75, 82, 85–87, 101, 108–109, 120, 124, 126–127, 136, 151, 228, 236, 240, 244
Attwell, Bob 234–235
Australians 45–46, 78, 83, 114, 143, 216–217
Bache, Joe 41, 52, 87–88
Barber, Tommy 91, 102
Barbour, Horace 90, 107
Barbour, Joyce 183, 220, 232
Bardsley, Warren 78, 83, 145, 209
Barling, Tom 191–194, 200–201, 216–218, 224
Barnato, Woolf 198–199, 217
Barson, Frank 121, 123–124, 127, 129, 138, 140, 182
Belfast 29, 36, 41, 51–52, 245
Bird, Morice 46, 79–80, 84, 92
Bird, Richard 220, 232

Blackburn Rovers 22, 37, 41, 44, 49, 51–52, 55, 57, 66, 77, 111, 126, 136
Blythe, Colin 61, 72, 99, 120
Bolton Wanderers 51, 75, 105, 124, 126
Bradford City 44, 50, 52, 55–57, 67, 74, 76, 87, 101, 171, 173, 175, 182
Bradford Park Avenue 104, 106, 137, 153
Bradman, Don 209, 211, 214, 216
Bramall Lane 67, 70–71, 80, 125
Bramley 233
Brentford 35, 169
Brewery Road School 16
Brisbane 207–209, 211–214, 243, 245
Bristol City 29–30, 50, 52, 55, 57, 68, 138, 169
Brittleton, Tom 75–76
Brixton 15–16
Brooks, Ted 202, 218, 236
Buchan, Charlie 123–124, 181
Buckinghamshire 31, 33, 192, 245
Bullock, Fred 127, 136
Burnley 23, 102, 111, 121–122, 126, 136, 139, 170–171
Burrows, Robert 60
Bury 26, 41, 43, 50, 59, 65, 67, 74, 77, 162

INDEX

Bush, Harry 70–71, 79
Cambridge University 30, 39, 59, 157, 165, 169, 177, 197, 203
Cardiff 33, 53–54, 124, 163, 170, 243
Carr, Arthur 72, 133, 196, 206
Carter, Sammy 145–146
Casuals 184
Chelsea 41, 44, 52, 58, 74, 87, 101, 105, 111–112, 121, 125–126, 137, 140, 178–179, 245
Cheltenham Festival 63, 226
Clapton Orient 67
Coleman, Tim 29–30, 35, 66
Common, Alf 34, 42–43, 65, 73, 76–77
Constantine, Learie 167
Coventry City 151, 169, 176
Craven Cottage 50, 149, 151–154, 160, 168–170, 172, 174, 176, 178, 180, 182–183
Crawford, Jack 38–40, 44–45, 59, 103, 118–120, 143
Crompton House School 18
Crompton, Bob 18–20, 55, 57, 104
Croydon Common 34, 42–43
Crystal Palace 34, 42, 136, 152, 179
Cuffe, Jack 85
Darvill, Harvey 175, 242
Dean, Dixie 10, 134, 182, 184
Derby County 23, 36, 54, 124, 126, 136, 140, 153, 169–170, 174
Dorrell, Arthur 127–128, 139
Douglas, Johnny 72, 142–143, 145–146, 149, 165, 185, 197–198, 201–202, 222, 230, 239
Ducat, Andrew 15, 20, 154
Ducat, Daphne 112, 212, 236, 241
Ducat, Florence 15

Ducat, Vera 91, 96, 107, 112, 212–213, 232, 236, 241
Duleepsinhji, KS 177, 187, 219, 222, 224
Durham 166, 190, 198
Eaton, Jack 234
Edgley, Harold 102, 125, 128
Edward VII 59
Ellens Cricket Club 230
England 11, 13, 28, 35–37, 45–46, 51–57, 67, 69–71, 75–76, 79–80, 87, 91, 104, 108, 110, 117–118, 123–124, 126, 130, 136–137, 139, 141–147, 150, 157, 160–161, 174, 177, 184, 186–187, 191, 193, 200, 207–209, 213–214, 218, 230–231, 239, 241–242, 246
Essex 17–21, 24, 27, 30, 33, 40, 45, 60, 69, 80–81, 95, 132, 142, 155, 157, 164, 166, 185, 187, 190, 192, 197, 202–203, 216–217, 220, 224–225, 228, 245
Eton College 9, 13, 229, 237, 245
Evans, Bobby 42, 55, 75, 192
Everton 23–24, 28, 35, 37, 40–41, 46, 52, 57, 66, 68, 74, 76, 101, 105, 122–124, 136, 138, 182
Exeter City 105
FA Cup 11, 23, 25–26, 28, 30, 36, 42–44, 54, 56, 67, 75, 91, 105, 122–123, 125–128, 136, 138–139, 153, 162, 170, 174–175, 182, 240
FA Selection Committee 67, 75–76
Fairfax, Alan 209, 216
Fender, Percy 93–95, 98, 130–134, 146–149, 155–160, 163–165, 167–168, 178, 190, 192, 194–195, 197–199, 201–203, 205, 216, 221–222, 224, 230, 243

Foot, David 62, 173, 228–229, 232, 241
Footballers' Battalion 9, 109
Freeman, Tich 158, 187, 192
Front Wanderers, The 9, 110–111
Fry, CB 44, 95, 195, 222
Fulham 9, 35, 75, 141, 151–154, 157, 159, 161–163, 169–176, 178–185, 228, 236, 238, 240, 244
Garland-Wells, Monty 200
Geary, Albert 155, 178, 187, 203
Gentlemen of Philadelphia 39
Gilbert, Eddie 213–214
Gilligan, Arthur 117, 195, 211
Gilligan, Harold 117, 211
Glamorgan 33, 163–164, 172, 190, 194, 199, 203, 207, 215
Glasgow Celtic 30
Gloucestershire 40, 47, 60, 63, 69, 71, 78, 99, 155, 157, 164, 178, 185, 189, 194, 199, 206–207, 216, 219, 221, 226
Goatly, Edward 47, 71–72, 85, 95
Golders Green Crematorium 236
Goodison Park 101, 110, 122, 182
Gover, Alf 217
Great Enton 13, 231–234, 236, 241
Gregory, Bob 179, 188, 200, 204–205, 222, 236
Gregory, Jack 143, 145
Gregory, Syd 46, 78
Grimmett, Clarrie 212, 216
Gunasekara, Churchill 118, 232
Gunn, George 79–80, 114, 117
Halse, Harold 87
Hammond, Wally 164, 190, 199, 221
Hampden Park 56
Hampton, Harry 73, 87, 101, 103–104, 106, 109, 111

Hardinge, Wally 28, 36, 41, 57, 112, 144–145, 147, 158, 205, 240
Hardy, Sam 41, 52–53, 55, 57–58, 62, 73, 87–88, 104–105, 121–124, 126–127, 131, 135–136, 138, 140
Harrison, Henry 45, 47, 72, 78, 96, 114–116, 155–156
Harrop, Jimmy 41, 86–87, 121, 123, 127–128, 140
Hawthorns, The 121, 123, 137
Hayes, Ernie 27–28, 32, 44–45, 47, 60, 62, 72, 77–79, 81, 83, 85–86, 93, 96–97, 99, 117, 243
Hayward, Tom 28, 32, 38–39, 48, 61, 69, 71, 79–80, 83, 85, 95, 97–99, 163, 190
Hearne, Jack 40, 70, 97, 117, 133, 135, 143–145, 149–150, 160, 189, 192, 194
Hendren, Patsy 117, 130, 133, 150, 159–160, 164, 168–169, 188–189, 192, 194, 212, 221, 230, 239, 242
Hibbert, Billy 57
Highbury 122, 124
Hillsborough 35, 125, 153
Hirst, George 48, 70, 94, 229–230
Hitch, Bill 32, 61–62, 72, 77, 81, 83, 85, 94–95, 98–99, 116, 119, 141, 148, 155–156, 159, 172
Hobbs, Jack 28, 32, 38–39, 44–45, 48, 60–62, 69, 72, 78–80, 83, 85, 91, 94–99, 112, 114–119, 130–133, 142–143, 145–146, 148, 154–157, 159–160, 162–163, 165–167, 177–179, 181, 185–189, 192–193, 195–196, 198–203, 205–208, 212, 215–216, 218–219, 221–224, 226, 236
Holmes, Percy 130, 178, 208
Holte Hotel 90, 107, 112

INDEX

Home Guard 9, 13, 105, 232–234, 244
Honor Oak 177
Hospital of St John and St Elizabeth 235
Huddersfield Town 11, 127, 136, 139
Hull City 36, 152, 169–170
Hyde Road 36, 43, 88, 241
Iddon, Jack 193, 199, 205, 217
Ireland 36, 51–53, 67, 136
Iremonger, Albert 79, 106
Jardine, Douglas 149, 165–167, 185, 187–189, 191, 198, 202, 222–224, 230
Jeacocke, Alfred 141–142, 156, 165–166, 185, 188–189
Jessop, Gilbert 63, 70–71, 138
Jones, Lot 88, 105, 124
Jupp, Vallance 134, 145–147, 203, 239
Kelleway, Charlie 78, 83, 110, 113–114, 209
Kelso, Phil 21–23, 25–26, 29, 35–36, 151, 161, 169–170, 172
Kent 28, 31–32, 40, 57, 61, 64, 71–73, 84, 98–99, 118–120, 133–134, 147–148, 157–158, 167, 187–188, 192–193, 198–199, 205–206, 218, 233
Kilner, Norman 165, 188
Kirton, Billy 125, 127–128, 138
Knight, DJ 116, 119, 149–150, 230
Lancashire 27–28, 45–46, 59, 61, 71, 84, 97, 119, 130, 134, 147–148, 157–158, 166, 170, 181, 183, 186–187, 191–192, 196, 199, 202, 205, 217–218, 223, 245
Larwood, Harold 188, 191, 206, 214, 216
Latham, George 54
Leicester Fosse 41, 43, 57
Leicestershire 69–70, 72, 84–85, 95, 132–133, 141, 149, 156, 159, 164, 186, 188–189, 194, 196, 208, 217, 223
Leveson-Gower, Shrimp 190, 198, 236
Leyland, Morris 225
Leyton 29, 43, 45, 52, 80, 95, 132, 142, 179–180, 185, 197
Linkson, Oscar 109
Liverpool 25, 29, 35–36, 41, 43, 50, 52, 54–55, 57, 73, 75, 86–87, 102–103, 106, 110, 123, 126, 136–138, 144, 182
Llanelli AFC 170
Lockton, John 148, 159, 177
Lord's 12–13, 46, 86, 98, 117, 134, 143, 147–149, 189, 194, 203, 215, 221, 230, 234–235, 239
Macartney, Charlie 78, 83, 141, 145
MacLaren, Archie 97
Makepeace, Harry 27, 57, 144, 157, 167, 193
Manchester City 23, 26, 36, 43–44, 55, 66–67, 74, 88–89, 105–106, 128, 135, 137
Manchester United 36, 44, 55, 57, 65, 67, 75–76, 87, 89, 104, 106, 109, 121–122, 124, 136, 170, 182
Marshal, Alan 38–40, 48, 60
MCC 70, 99, 189, 195, 201, 209–212, 215, 221, 235–236
McCabe, Stan 216
McDonald, Ted 65–66, 143, 145–146, 186–187, 191, 196, 199, 202, 205, 214, 217, 223, 240
McGibbon, Charlie 58
Mead, Phil 117, 131, 143, 147

Meredith, Billy 24, 55, 124
Middlesbrough 36, 50–51, 65–67, 74–76, 102, 106, 120–121, 124, 175, 182
Middlesex 40, 46–47, 70, 72, 85–86, 96–97, 99, 109, 117–119, 130, 133–135, 144, 147–150, 159, 165–168, 188–190, 194, 199–200, 206–207, 245
Millwall 43, 179
Morrell, George 36, 49
Morse, Elijah 175
New Zealanders 193
Newcastle United 25–26, 28, 35, 41, 50, 56–57, 73, 102, 121, 126, 137
Noble, Monty 46, 209–210
Northamptonshire 28, 44–45, 63, 77, 93, 130, 134, 142–143, 148, 199, 203
Norwich 29
Nottingham Forest 35, 43, 49, 54–55, 66–67, 153, 183
Notts County 24, 26, 40, 49, 52, 66, 75, 101, 104, 106, 138, 152, 182
Old Trafford 46, 88, 97, 110, 121–122, 134, 147–148, 157, 161, 164, 186–187, 196, 202, 217, 223
Oldfield, Bill 209, 216
Oldham Athletic 66, 88, 104, 121, 135, 170
Oxenham, Ron 209
Oxford University 18, 27, 29, 32, 39, 60, 69, 132, 165, 204, 244
Parker, Charlie 185, 199, 219, 221
Parkin, Cecil 145, 157, 164
Peach, Alan 115, 131–132, 134, 160, 164, 199, 203, 221, 227
Pendleton, Jack 123

Pennington, Jesse 55, 57, 108–109, 124, 126
Plumstead 23, 25–26, 30, 36, 41, 43–44, 49–50, 53, 56, 58, 67, 73–76
Ponsford, Bill 216
Port Vale 120, 174, 176, 182
Preston North End 25, 36, 58, 77, 124, 126, 136, 180, 183
Prouse, William 174, 176, 182
Quaife, Willie 110, 192
Queens Park Rangers 122
Queensland Cricket Association 207, 243
Ramsay, George 110–111
Ranjitsinhji 80, 155
Reading 26, 32, 34, 152, 212, 229
Relf, Robert 80
Reynolds, Arthur 103, 153, 170, 176, 245
Rhodes, Wilf 62, 192
Rinder, Frederick 87, 103
RMS *Titanic* 77
Roose, Leigh 23–24, 41, 54–55, 75–76
Rotherham County 124, 162
Royal Garrison Artillery 108, 111
Rushby, Tom 28, 47–48, 59, 69, 79, 85–86, 94–95, 116, 119, 146
Russell, Jack 124, 133, 155, 197, 244
Sandham, Andy 71–72, 114–115, 118, 130, 132–135, 142–143, 147–150, 155–156, 158, 160, 163–164, 166–167, 178, 185–188, 191–196, 199, 202–203, 205–208, 215–217, 219, 221–224, 226, 230, 236
Sands, Percy 27, 29, 73
Santall, Reg 110, 192, 224
Satterthwaite, Charlie 43

INDEX

Scotland 15, 17, 36, 54, 57–58, 110, 125–126, 156, 166, 179
Shaw, Joe 66, 76
Sheffield United 23, 25, 30, 36, 41, 43, 49, 55, 57, 66, 75, 102, 121, 137
Sheffield Wednesday 42, 127
Shepherd, Tom 56, 147, 149–150, 157, 166, 168, 177, 185–186, 188, 190–191, 193, 197, 200–201, 204–206, 215–218, 222–224
Small Heath 23
Smart, Tommy 115, 123, 127, 137, 140
Smith, Razor 46, 48, 59–61, 63–64, 68–69, 72, 80, 83
Somerset 38–39, 47, 62, 72, 93–94, 119, 131–132, 146–147, 155, 163, 165, 177, 188, 190, 192, 194, 198, 205, 207, 218, 221–222, 226, 234
South Africa 83, 157
South Shields 154, 173
Southend Athletic 20–21, 24
Southend United 20, 32, 124, 160, 168
Spiksley, Fred 9, 174–176
Squires, Stan 207, 218, 225
Staffordshire 28, 105, 245
Stamford Bridge 110, 125, 127
Stephenson, Clem 87, 102, 104, 106, 121–122, 127, 140
Stevens, Greville 118, 165–166
Stockport County 180, 183
Stoke City 23–26, 28, 124, 175, 183
Strudwick, Herbert 70, 95, 142, 164, 194, 230, 236
Sunderland 23, 30, 35, 41, 43, 49, 53–55, 57, 65–67, 76, 91, 123–124, 139, 166, 181
Surrey 11–13, 27–33, 37–40, 44–48, 59–64, 69–72, 77–81, 83–87, 90–99, 113–120, 130–135, 141–143, 146–151, 155–160, 163–168, 172–173, 177–179, 185–208, 210, 212, 214–219, 221–228, 231, 233–234, 236, 241, 243–244
Surrey Club and Ground 27, 31, 37, 84
Sussex 4, 13, 40, 61, 63, 80, 84, 93, 98, 115, 117, 132, 134, 147, 156–157, 159, 164, 168, 185, 187, 193, 195, 197, 202, 206, 216, 219, 222–224, 230, 234
Sutcliffe, Herbert 130, 156, 159, 178, 191, 204, 208, 219
Swansea Town 180
Table football game 180
Table Tennis 161–162
Tarrant, Frank 40, 46
Tate, Maurice 186, 195, 222, 224
Taunton 64, 72, 119, 146, 190, 226
Tennyson, Lionel 117, 143–146, 158, 244
The Oval 22, 27, 31–32, 37–38, 44–46, 48, 59–60, 62, 64, 69, 71, 77–78, 80, 83–85, 92, 94–96, 98, 113–115, 117–118, 130–131, 133–134, 142–143, 149, 154–156, 158–159, 164–168, 172–173, 185, 187–188, 190, 192–193, 195, 197–203, 205–207, 214–216, 218, 221, 224, 226, 231, 242–243
Torrance, Jimmy 152–153, 161, 169, 176
Tottenham Hotspur 26, 34, 50, 58, 66, 68, 75, 106, 123–124, 126–127, 135–136, 139, 140, 168, 174
Travers, Barney 152–154
Trent Bridge 45, 60, 71, 79, 95, 114, 132, 141, 156, 195, 202, 216, 222

Trott, Albert 40
Trumper, Victor 46
Tull, Walter 68
Tyldesley, Dick 164, 187, 199, 205, 217
Tyldesley, Ernest 122, 136–137, 139
Villa Park 49, 73, 90, 101–102, 104, 106, 110–111, 121, 123, 128, 135, 139–140
Voce, Bill 202, 206, 216
Wales 36, 42, 53–55, 67, 71, 76, 113, 124–125, 138, 163, 211
Walker, Billy 122, 125, 127, 136–137, 139
Wallace, Charlie 91, 101–102, 126–127
Warner, Pelham 47, 70, 134–135, 143, 195, 236, 243–244
Warren, Ben 36, 67, 78, 83, 209
Warwickshire 39, 45, 59, 68–69, 94–95, 99, 107, 110, 114–115, 131–132, 141–142, 165, 168, 178, 188, 192, 194, 196–197, 199, 202, 204, 215, 219, 223–224
Wass, Tom 60, 79
Watford 25
Wedlock, Billy 51–52, 55, 57

West Bromwich Albion 55, 57, 76, 101, 105, 108, 121, 124, 126, 136–137
West Ham 21, 25–26, 33
West Indians 167
Westcliff Athletic 20
Weston, Tommy 111, 127, 188, 207
White Hart Lane 58, 75, 123, 139
Wilkinson, Cyril 92, 94–96, 115, 131
Wiltshire 28, 31–32
Wisden 9, 60, 70, 118, 130, 235
Woodfull, Bill 216
Woolley, Frank 72, 98, 117–119, 143, 145, 158, 195, 211, 219, 239
Woolwich Arsenal 9, 20–26, 28–30, 34–37, 40, 42, 48–50, 52–53, 55–58, 65–66, 70, 73–74, 76, 82, 88, 91, 240–241, 244
Worcestershire 31–32, 45, 60, 69, 71, 78, 85, 93–94, 134, 215
Wyatt, Bob 168, 188, 197, 215, 224
Yorkshire 31, 38, 40, 46, 48, 61–63, 80, 94, 98–99, 118–119, 130, 132, 134, 149, 156, 158–159, 165, 168, 178, 191, 194, 198, 200, 204, 207, 218, 225, 230, 245